1997

THE

CONSTITUTION

AND LAWS

OF THE

CHURCH OF SCOTLAND

Edited by

JAMES L. WEATHERHEAD

Principal Clerk of the General Assembly
of the Church of Scotland, 1985-96

Published by
THE BOARD OF PRACTICE AND PROCEDURE
at 121 George Street, Edinburgh
1997

A

1997

ISBN 0 86153 246 5

Printed for the Church of Scotland by
PILLANS & WILSON GREENAWAY LTD., EDINBURGH

CONTENTS

PREFACE

Practice and Procedure in The Church of Scotland, edited by the Rev. Dr. James T. Cox, was first published in 1934, and the sixth edition was published in 1976. It owed much to *A Digest of Laws and Decisions relating to The Church of Scotland*, by the Rev. Dr. William Mair, first published in 1887. These books are usually referred to as "Cox" and "Mair", which is the practice followed in referring to them in this book.

In 1986 the Board of Practice and Procedure, after consultation with the Committee on Publications, decided to proceed with the production of a completely new publication, rather than produce yet another revision of Cox, and reported accordingly to the General Assembly in 1987.

Preliminary work was undertaken by a Steering Committee and an Editorial Committee appointed by the Board. An initial plan of the contents was drawn up, and substantial contributions were written by the late Very Rev. Dr. Peter Brodie, the Very Rev. Dr. W. B. R. Macmillan, the Rev. Dr. Finlay Macdondald (now the Principal Clerk), the Rev. A. Gordon McGillivray (then the Depute Clerk), the Rev. A. Ian Dunlop, and Mr. J. G. G. Lees. At this stage also considerable assistance and advice was given by the then Procurator, Mr. G. W. Penrose, now Lord Penrose; the then Solicitor of the Church, Mr. R. A. Paterson; the Very Rev. Prof. John McIntyre; and the Rev. Prof. D. W. D. Shaw.

It became evident however that differences in both style and approach meant that the contributions could not simply be put together to form a uniform volume, and it has been my task as editor to adapt, modify, and re-write them, as well as to incorporate material from my own research and experience. While I must therefore accept responsibility for this book as a whole, and especially for any shortcomings, I gratefully record my indebtedness to all those named above, whose work has enabled me to achieve a degree of accuracy and objectivity which would not otherwise have been possible. Prof. Shaw had contributed an article on *Law and Order in the Church* to the *Liturgical Review* of May, 1972, and this I found particularly valuable in relation to the introductory chapter. In 1995, Mr. McGillivray produced *An Introduction to Practice and Procedure in the Church of Scotland*, and this too has been of considerable assistance (see p. 102).

I am grateful also to colleagues in the Board of Practice and Procedure, members of the staff in the Church Offices, and Presbytery Clerks, with whom, during my years of office as Principal Clerk, I have discussed many legal questions, and from whom I have learned much. I am particularly grateful to the present Procurator, Mr. R. A. Dunlop, not only for his specific contribution on evidence, but also for many useful conversations, and to the present Solicitor,

Mrs. Janette Wilson, also for helpful conversations, and for making relevant material available.

The whole process has taken longer than originally hoped, and when it became clear that the new book would not be available by the time the last copies of Cox had been sold, I gave priority to the production of the loose-leaf book of *Acts of the General Assembly from 1929* which was published in 1994, with the valuable assistance of the Rev. A. Gordon McGillivray. This publication is kept up to date by the issuing of additional material after each General Assembly.

In 1995, *The Law and Practice of the Kirk*, by the Very Rev. Dr. Andrew Herron, was published, partly, he says, to fill the vacuum until this book could be produced; but it is much more than a stop-gap, and will surely continue to have its own distinctive and significant place in the literature on church law.

I have not here reproduced detailed material which is already included in the loose-leaf publication of the *Acts of Assembly*, preferring, with some exceptions, to leave the legislation to speak for itself, and giving references to particular Acts rather that trying to summarise them or offer detailed commentary on them.

This is for two reasons.

First, many Acts have been amended or repealed over the years, and this process will no doubt continue, so that details from them included here could render the book out of date fairly soon, which happened with Cox.

Second, there is a danger that summaries or expositions in a book such as this will impose particular interpretations on pieces of legislation, and may come to be relied on instead of the legislation itself. Nevertheless, I have felt free to offer some comment and explanation in areas where, in my judgement, it is better to do this. I do however advise readers to consult the original legislation, and for this reason I have included the text of much of the Basis and Plan of Union (all of the Basis and some of the Plan), and the text of Act XIX, 1889, among the Appendices.

The present book is therefore a companion to the loose-leaf *Acts of Assembly*.

Although Regulations are not contained in the loose-leaf publication, they are even more liable to change. I have included only a few of these, and for the rest I have simply indicated where up to date copies may be obtained.

Act XIX, 1889, on Forms of Procedure in Trials by Libel and in Causes Generally, has acquired new importance because, after a long period in which there was no Trial by Libel, recent years have seen one or two, and judicial procedures have come to renewed prominence in several cases under the Act anent Congregations in an Unsatisfactory State, with appeals to the Judicial Commission.

There have been attempts, also in recent years, to have civil courts review the procedure or judgements of church courts, and these have all failed, as the civil courts have recognised the independent jurisdiction of church courts. What is surprising is that those who sought such review were apparently ignorant of the constitutional position. Even if that were not so, the constitutional position of the Church is of such intrinsic significance that it must have prominence in a book of this kind.

It is a feature of our times that, with the decline in church membership there has gone a decline in public understanding of the Church and its official standards, and, in particular, a failure to realise how the relationship to formal standards has changed in the past 150 years or so. Secular journalists recently produced a survey about the beliefs of ministers, and presented it in a manner which revealed no knowledge or understanding of Scottish church history, of the outcome of notorious heresy trials, of the existence and significance of the Basis and Plan of Union of 1929 and the several Declaratory Acts referred to therein, or of the Declaratory Articles. The recognition of liberty of opinion was not easily won, and it should not now be allowed to go by default through general ignorance.

There is therefore an emphasis in this book on the nature of the Church's constitution; and a brief account of its history is included. The Church does not live in a vacuum, operating administrative laws like the rules of a private club. It has a legal system, separate from but related to civil law, and a public constitution because it is a public body, with public responsibilities and a public purpose. That public purpose is to bear witness to Christ, to preach the Gospel, and to serve Christ. The constitution and laws of the Church exist, not to inhibit and restrict that purpose, but to facilitate it.

In that spirit, this book is humbly offered to the Church.

Edinburgh, April, 1997   JAMES L. WEATHERHEAD.

EDITORIAL POLICY

Central to the order of the chapters is the phrase in *Article IV* of the *Declaratory Articles*, which states the "matters spiritual" in which the Church has exclusive jurisdiction as "doctrine, worship, government, and discipline." After three introductory chapters, on the legal, historical, and constitutional background to the present position of the Church, chapters on doctrine and worship follow. The subject of government includes chapters on legislation and judicial functions, reflecting the Church's authority to legislate and adjudicate finally, and that of discipline includes a chapter on Trial by Libel. The section on doctrine, worship, government and discipline is followed by a section on church courts, with chapters on the common factors in meetings and procedure preceding chapters on the three courts, and the remaining chapters, may be classified as ministry, congregational matters, and ecumenism, the last being a reminder that the Church of Scotland lives today in an international and interdenominational context, as part of the Holy Catholic or Universal Church.

No arrangement of chapters can avoid the fact that certain matters belong to more than one classification. This has been accommodated both by cross-references, and by some repetition where the coherence of the chapters concerned appeared to require it.

Some Latin phrases have been translated and explained where they occur, but some, such as *ex officio*, are assumed to be still part of common parlance. A glossary of Latin words and phrases has nevertheless been included.

Other terms, of which basic knowledge has been assumed in the text, are included in an appendix of definitions.

Capitalisation is a matter on which fashions change, but the general policy has been to use capitals of the names of church courts and their officials, and of formal titles of subjects or bodies. Church has a capital where it is a noun, except when it means a church building, but lower case is used when it is an adjective, except when it appears in a title such as Church Extension.

References to the General Assembly are so frequent that it has been referred to simply as the Assembly, except where the context appeared to demand the full title. Although in formal documents and legislation "General Assembly" is treated as a plural noun, the more colloquial singular has been used throughout. In this matter, even Cox was not consistent, and Mair used the singular, e.g., as quoted by Cox, "the Assembly is the interpreter of its own laws." The practice adopted here is to avoid convolution and infelicity, and does not imply a desire for change in formal documents and legislation.

To facilitate the use of this book as a work of reference, the headings of sections within chapters are listed at the beginning of each chapter, and in a table of contents at the beginning. Chapter names and numbers are in headers.

In the index, section headings appear in alphabetical order within the index as a whole, and also under the name of the chapter. Other words, phrases, and subjects are included alphabetically.

A list of Acts of Assembly gives these in chronological order, together with an indication of their subject-matter. In the event of an Act being repealed and replaced by a new Act, it should be possible in most cases to find the new Act by looking up the subject in the loose-leaf publication of the *Acts of the General Assembly since 1929*.

The bibliography is a list of books, many of which have not been referred to in the text, but are gratefully acknowledged to have been helpful in its compilation, giving more comprehensive treatment to some of the subjects dealt with.

This book has been produced using Microsoft Word, the Word Processor for MS-DOS, Version 6. The editor is therefore responsible for any typographical errors which may have occurred in spite of the facility provided in the programme for checking spelling. He is grateful to his wife for reading some preliminary text, and to the Principal Clerk for reading the text in its penultimate form and making helpful suggestions.

Thanks are offered also to departments in the Church Offices: to Publicity and Design for scanning much of the material in the appendices, thus avoiding the tedium of copy-typing, to the Computer Centre for technical assistance, and to Miss Chris Brown, Principal Administrative Officer in the Principal Clerk's Office for invaluable assistance; and also to Messrs. Keith Rezin and Jim Campbell who, with others at Pillans and Wilson Greenaway, have contributed their expert knowledge and skill to the final production.

J. L. W.

TABLE OF CONTENTS

XII. PROCEDURE

XIII. GENERAL ASSEMBLY

XIV. PRESBYTERY

XV. KIRK SESSION

XVI. MINISTRY

DOCUMENTATION

Acts of Assembly are referred to by year and number, e.g. "Act IV, 1984." The full text of these (since 1929) is to be found in *Acts of the General Assembly since 1929*, available from the Principal Clerk's Office, 121 George Street, Edinburgh, EH2 4YN (see Preface, p. vi). The most significant parts of Act I, 1929, which is the Basis and Plan of Union, will be found in Appendix B, and Declaratory Acts referred to in the Basis are in Appendix C. Act XIX, 1889 is in Appendix E.

Regulations are referred to by year and number, e.g. "Reg. 2, 1995." These are contained in Part III of the Volume of Reports for the year in question. Copies are held by Presbytery Clerks, as well as by the Principal Clerk, but copies of particular Regulations may usually be obtained from the Departments concerned, in the Church Offices, at the above address. Regulations about loose-leaf and computerised records are printed in Appendix F.

References in the form "1996, Sess. 2" are to the **Minutes of the Assembly**, and the Session during which the matter referred to occurred. These are in the hands of Presbytery Clerks and the Principal Clerk.

Books referred to in the text only by the surnames of their authors and a page number are:

MAIR, The Rev. Dr. William, *A Digest of Laws and Decisions relating to The Church of Scotland*, Fourth Edition, 1912.

COX, The Rev. Dr. James T., *Practice and Procedure in The Church of Scotland*, Sixth Edition, 1976.

HERRON, The Very Rev. Dr. Andrew: *The Law and Practice of the Kirk: a Guide and Commentary*, First Edition, 1995.

I. INTRODUCTION

1. The Need for Law

No large body of people can have an orderly existence as a coherent community without law. The history of Israel in the Old Testament shows how law and structures of authority were required as the tribe developed into a nation. Other great civilisations show a similar development, notably that of Rome, whose Civil Law (*Corpus Iuris Civilis*) influenced not only the Canon Law (*Corpus Iuris Canonici*) of the mediaeval Church but also the civil law of many nations, including Scotland.

Law is a necessary part of the structure of the Church as an institution. It serves to define the institution and its relationships with other institutions, especially the State; and it regulates the way in which its office-bearers and members relate to each other and to the institution as a whole and its constituent parts. Its purpose is to declare the corporate identity of the Church, and to ensure that all things are done decently and in order within it (I Cor. 14:40).

2. Church Legislation

The Church is a community under authority, and it receives the right and power to regulate its own affairs from Christ, who is the King and Head of the Church. In Christian theology, "the powers that be are ordained of God" (Rom. 13:1), and so the State has ultimately the same authority. The laws of Church and State in Scotland today still have some affinity because many of them have roots in the old Civil Law and Canon Law, and indeed in the Bible itself.

There is however a significant difference. In civil law in the UK, all laws have equal status. Civil courts cannot, for example, declare an Act of Parliament to be *ultra vires*, as being contrary to fundamental laws of the constitution (cf. the *Constitution of the United States*), because there are no such fundamental laws. In church law there are laws of different status. The Word of God contained in the Scriptures is the supreme rule of faith and life; then there are the *Declaratory Articles*, of which the first cannot be changed by the Church, and the others can be modified only by special procedure; and there is also legislation which has been passed under the Barrier Act. Each of these, in the order given, is superior to the next, and all are superior to ordinary legislation (see Section 5*d* below).

3. Law and Theology

The relationship between civil law and theology goes back to the Bible, especially Romans 13, where Paul deals with civil government. In that chapter are to be found what Justinian's *Institutes* later stated to be the three basic precepts of the law:

1) "to live honestly" (*honeste vivere*, cf. Vulgate, Rom. 13:13, *honeste ambulemus*),

2) "to injure no-one" (*neminem laedere*). There is no verbal equivalent in the Latin of Rom. 13:10, but the meaning is similar: "Love worketh no ill to his neighbour." Paul goes further in giving love as the motive for the import of the precept.

3) "to render to each his due" (*suum cuique tribuere*, cf. Vulgate, Rom. 13:7, *cui tributum, tributum*) This is reminiscent of Jesus' saying about rendering unto Caesar the things that are Caesar's, and to God the things that are God's, in response to a question about tribute (Mk. 12:17).

Justinian's precepts implicitly recognise that there are limits to what law can enact, or what can be achieved by legal process. The limitations of law in the sphere of morality were well put by Stair (see below, p. 3): "You cannot poind for unkindness." The difference between Justinian and Paul in the second precept shows that law cannot enforce love; it can only prohibit injury.

Nevertheless, jurists have given attention to the motivation, or the spirit of law. Ulpian, before Justinian, had said of justice (*iustitia*, which is the word used for righteousness in the Vulgate) that it was the resolute and continuous will (*constans et perpetua voluntas*) to render to each his due, which is very close to the concept of hungering and thirsting after righteousness (Mt. 5:6).

The Greek word for righteousness in the New Testament (δικαιοσυνη) is the word used for justice by Plato and other ancient Greek philosophers. While law cannot enforce an attitude of mind, a certain attitude of mind, namely a hunger and thirst for justice, is basic to the enactment and judicial application of law.

The relevance of this to church law is obvious.

4. Jurisprudence

There are comparable elements in church law and in civil law. Both are concerned with rules which ought to be obeyed. The Assembly passes Acts, as does Parliament; and laws of evidence in church courts are similar to those in civil courts. Rules of natural justice apply in the Church as anywhere else: for example, such rules as that both sides should be heard, that no-one should be a judge in his or her own cause, and that justice should not only be done but should be manifestly seen to be done. Nevertheless, there are significant differences in the ways law is understood in Church and State, which deserve some consideration.

Ecclesiastical jurisprudence is a matter to which little attention appears to have been paid in the Church of Scotland, and this is not the place for an extensive treatise, but it will be helpful for the understanding of church law to give consideration to some of the principles involved, beginning with a secular Scottish jurist who knew his theology.

5. Fundamentals and Expediency

a) Stair

A distinction between fundamental precepts and expediency is significant for church law, and is also well known to jurists. For example, the Earl of Stair, "The Father of Scots Law", in his *Institutions of the Law of Scotland*, 1681, (Book I, Tit. I) speaks of divine law, or the law of nature, "written by the finger of God upon man's heart." This is a clear reference to Romans 2, 14 & 15; but it was also a basic concept of Greek philosophy and Roman jurisprudence that there was a fundamental law embedded in nature, part of the natural order of things, to be discovered as scientific laws are discovered.

Stair says that this law is also called equity. He continues, "The first principles of equity are these three: 1. That God is to be obeyed by man; 2. That man is a free creature, having power to dispose of himself and all things, in so far as by his obedience to God he is not restrained; 3. That this freedom of man is in his own power."

Within this area of freedom, the power involved is the power to make laws, and these are known as "positive law", that is to say, law which is laid down; but this positive law is subordinate to divine law, or natural law.

Stair goes on to say that "as the natural law is *in aequo*, so the positive law is *in bono* or *utili* [which might be paraphrased as *for the public good, or expediency*] . . . if man had not fallen, there had been no distinction between *bonum* and *aequum*, nor had there been anything more profitable than the full following of the natural law. But man being now depraved, and wanting justice, or that willingness to give every man his right, therefore in this estate it is profitable for him . . . to make up societies of men . . ."

This reference to societies of men is similar to the concept of the "social contract." According to this theory, the basis of law is to be found in a common recognition among groups of people, such as nations, that law is necessary, and consequently a common agreement about a law-making authority. When this theory becomes detached from the recognition of natural law, so that positive law is the only law there is, it leads to despotism, and to such doctrines as, in the UK, the Sovereignty of Parliament. If Parliament recognises no fundamental law to which it is itself subject, and is constrained only by the people at infrequent general elections, sovereignty easily becomes, as Lord Hailsham famously said, an "elective dictatorship", and the "Divine Right of Kings" becomes a divine right of Parliament. It is not insignificant in this context that the Church resolutely opposed the Stuart claims to divine right. In 1689 the Scottish Claim of Right declared that James VII had "forefaulted" the right to the Crown by "altering it from a legal limited monarchy to an arbitrary despotic power."

Stair's "social contract" includes the distinction between *aequm* and *bonum*, which is that between divine law and positive law, between fundamental precepts and expediency, so that there are legal limits to sovereignty.

He reiterates the point by saying, "God seemeth to do with men, as princes do with their ambassadors, to whom they give some express instructions wherein they have no latitude in their negotiations, with power to the rest to do as they shall judge most fit upon the place."

b) Calvin

Calvin, in his *Institutes of the Christian Religion* (Book IV, Ch. X), says, "Let us understand that if in every human society some kind of government is necessary to insure the common peace and maintain concord . . . this ought specially to be observed in churches, which are best sustained by a constitution in all respects well ordered . . . We must always carefully attend to Paul's injunction, that all things be done decently and in order . . . [which] . . . cannot be observed unless order and decency are ensured by the addition of ordinances, as a kind of bonds."

Later, Calvin says that "the whole sum of righteousness, and all the parts of divine worship, and everything necessary to salvation, the Lord has faithfully comprehended, and clearly unfolded in his sacred oracles, so that in them he alone is the only Master to be heard. But as in external discipline and ceremonies, he has not been pleased to prescribe every particular that we ought to observe (he foresaw that this depended on the nature of the times, and that one form would not suit all ages), in them we must have recourse to the general rules which he has given, employing them to test whatever the necessity of the Church may require to be enjoined for order and decency. Lastly, as he has not delivered any express command, because things of this nature are not necessary to salvation, and, for the edification of the Church, should be accommodated to the varying circumstances of each age and nation, it will be proper, as the interest of the Church may require, to change and abrogate the old, as well as to introduce new forms."

There are clear similarities between Stair and Calvin. The distinction between fundamental precepts and expediency is common to them both.

c) Church Law

Paul makes the same distinction when he says, "I speak this by permission, and not of commandment" (Rom. 7:6), and when he says "all things are lawful for me, but all things are not expedient" (Rom. 10:23).

The *Scots Confession*, dealing with "Generall Councellis", says, "Bot the cause of Councellis . . . wes partlie for confutation of heresies. and for giving publick confession of their faith to the posteritie of Goddis written Word, and not by ony opinion or prerogative that they culd not erre, be reason of their general assemblie: And this we judge to have been the chiefe cause of general Councellis. The other wes for gude policie, and ordour to be constitute and observed in the Kirk, quhilk, as in the house of God, is [it] becummis *al things to be done decently and in ordour*. Not that we think that any policie and ordour in ceremonies can be appoynted for al ages, times, and places: For as ceremonies, sik as men have devised, are bot temporall; so may and aucht they to be changed, when they rather foster superstition then that they edifie the Kirk using the same." The two purposes of councils given here clearly correspond to the distinction between fundamentals and expediency.

It is not unreasonable to suppose that Calvin influenced the Scottish reformers, and that their teaching was known to and reflected by Stair. In other words, what we have here is a distinctive element of the Scottish Reformation, to which this Church adheres (*Article I*).

The distinction between fundamentals and expediency is of great importance for an understanding of church law. It is obvious that the authority of the Church cannot extend to denying the truth which is in Christ. There are fundamental doctrines which define and bind the Church, and church law can declare what these are, but it cannot alter them. This basic constitutional law for the Church is derived from the Word of God which is contained in the Bible, and from the fundamental doctrines of the Christian faith derived from Scripture. It is the law of God, which the Church must declare and interpret, and can only declare and interpret. Apart from some very significant declaratory law affirming these things, the area in which church law operates is therefore that of expediency.

d) Levels of Expediency

Once the basic distinction between levels of law is recognised, the way is open to recognise that there can be different levels of law within the area of expediency.

There is a clear distinction in the *Declaratory Articles* (see pp. 16, 18, & 159) between what is fundamental and cannot be changed (*Article I*), and what is expedient and may be altered by the Church (all the other *Articles*). Nevertheless, the other Articles are part of the constitution which can be changed only by special procedure, so that they in turn are to be regarded as superior to ordinary legislation. By similar reasoning, Barrier Act legislation is inferior to the *Declaratory Articles*, but superior to ordinary legislation.

At every level of expedient law, particular laws must be consistent with basic principles. (cf. Calvin, as quoted above: "we must have recourse to the general rules which he has given, employing them to test whatever the necessity of the Church may require to be enjoined for order and decency.") All legislation in the area of expediency must be "agreeable to the Word of God".

While the distinctions between fundamental precepts and expediency, and between different levels of expediency can be clearly stated, and easily understood in theory, questions can arise about whether a particular precept is fundamental or not, or as to whether and to what extent one particular law is superior to another. For example, an Act passed under the Barrier Act because of the nature of its basic substance may also for convenience contain some related administrative provisions which really belong to an inferior level. That is why some amendments of Barrier Act legislation are not considered to require Barrier Act procedure. Questions may also arise about the status of provisions which have become law by consuetude. (see below, p. 9) The short answer is that the Church, which means the Assembly in this context, is the sole judge.

e) Illustration from Civil Law

An illustration from civil law may help to clarify some of the issues.

It is easy to derive, from the basic precept that one should injure no-one, a rule that all traffic going in the same direction must keep to the same side of the road. That is a rule of expediency, derived from a fundamental precept. Although it may not be the only rule which could be so derived, it is certainly "agreeable to" the precept. There is no principle of expediency, far less a fundamental precept, from which it can be deduced that the left side should be chosen, rather than the right. Nevertheless, expediency requires that a choice be made by the legislators.

The same precept about injuring no-one means that dangerous driving should be an offence. However, if every case before the courts involved argument about, for example, whether overtaking on a particular corner was dangerous or not, the time taken over each case would be unacceptably long. Therefore, for this reason among others, double white lines are painted on roads, and a driver who crosses them has committed an offence. It is much easier to answer the question, "Did the driver cross the white lines?" than to decide whether this was dangerous. The rules about white lines are rules of expediency. It is in theory possible that in certain circumstances crossing a white line would not be dangerous, and a conviction in such circumstances might therefore be unjust. In this way, the possibility of injustice is inherent in some laws based on expediency.

In church terms, it could be argued that a basic rule is that a Church must have some form of discipline; but whether this is presbyterian or episcopal is a choice of expediency. The choice for this Church is included in the *Declaratory Articles*, but not in *Article I*. Although the relative merits of these may be hotly debated, the debate is basically in the area of expediency, albeit at a high level, rather than of fundamental precepts, although there are those, on both sides, who maintain that their polity is essential to the Church, and therefore a fundamental principle. Here we encounter the distinction between *esse* and *bene esse* (i.e. between what is essential to the Church, and what is for its well-being), similar to Stair's distinction between *in aequo* and *in bono*.

The rules about road traffic are obviously at a different level from those about church government, but in terms of parliamentary legislation, civil law in the UK recognises no distinction of level or status between road traffic Acts and the 1707 Act to secure presbyterian government (but see Chapter III, p. 17).

If a Church has chosen a presbyterian system, it may also have decided, as a further matter of expediency that twenty-one should be the lower age limit for appointment to the eldership. This could give rise to injustice, as a much younger person might be much more spiritually mature than someone over twenty-one; but the expedient rule means that time-consuming discussions about whether a particular person is too young are avoided. Nevertheless, it is surely clear that the Church cannot regard the age rule as being at the same level as the requirement that a person chosen should be suitable for appointment in terms of life and doctrine.

6. Room for Change

In the area in which the Church legitimately legislates, there is always room for change, as the Church develops within a changing society, as Calvin pointed out. In this context, there is the possibility that a law deduced from a fundamental precept, and judged therefore to be itself fundamental at the time, may nevertheless have to be modified on the basis that there has been a change in methods of reasoning, so that the logic of the original deduction no longer stands, or a change in circumstances, requiring the fundamental precept to be applied in a different way.

It is relevant here to quote what Professor T. F. Torrance says about juridical law: ". . . certain legal concepts, even some which have been accorded a central place in the legal system, were thrown up in the contingencies of socio-politico change clothed in forms conditioned by obsolete cultural patterns. As they have reached us they have been shaped through modes of thought which it was found necessary to use at the time, and were defined in that system in such a way that they were connected to transitory notions. But now those transitory notions have fallen away, so that the legal rules and propositions which helped to define them must be altered; otherwise they can only obscure and distort the basic concepts of the law which they were originally designed to serve." (*Juridical Law and Physical Law*, p. 59)

No church-made law is therefore to be regarded as being like the laws of the Medes and Persians, which could not be changed (Dan. 6:8). Although the fundamental precepts remain, it is a matter of expediency that laws can be changed, and even a matter of principle that they should. (*Ecclesia reformata, semper reformanda*— see p. 19). Law should not be allowed to bind the Church to live in the past. The law is for the Church, not the Church for the law. For this reason, a living Church will always be reviewing its legal system, including traditions which have become law by consuetude (see below, p. 9), in the light of ultimate truth discovered in the Word of God. Divine law, revealed by God, and so available to be discovered by the Church, is the standard by which church-made law is to be judged.

Once the Church has made laws, however, they are binding, regardless of their level or status. It is a matter of good order that every particular law must be adhered to, unless and until the Church is persuaded to amend or repeal it. The freedom in the area of expediency is freedom of the Church to legislate, not freedom of its members to ignore legislation. The Church is able, in other words, to regulate its own life by making rules about what is or is not expedient, in the area of freedom in which all things are lawful in terms of fundamental precepts, and these subsidiary rules have the force of law in the interests of decency and order.

If it appears that an expedient rule may in certain circumstances give rise to occasional injustice, the Church has to decide whether or not to change it. For example, the lower age limit for membership of Kirk Sessions might be changed to eighteen, or it might be abolished altogether, but the Church would have to decide whether the consequences of such change might be less acceptable than the current rule. This consideration would be in the area of expediency, as it involves no fundamental precept.

7. Law and Legalism

Good law properly used is not legalistic, but there are various forms of legalism from which law as such should be distinguished.

Legalism in a theological sense is the belief that obedience to the law is the way of salvation; but, as St. Paul found, we are not under law, but under grace. Church law is not the same thing as "the law" in the biblical sense, although it is related to it, in that offences against biblical law may be the occasions of church discipline and censures; but the proper use of law in the Church does not contradict the statement that we are not under law but under grace as far as salvation is concerned.

Law sets out the ways in which those who are under grace ought to do things "decently and in order." It does not prescribe all the things they ought to do; nor does it proscribe all the things they ought not to do. The fact that there is no law requiring a particular action does not exclude the possibility that such action is a spiritual or moral imperative; nor does the absence of a law against a particular action imply that it is spiritually or morally right. On the other hand, a good deed, against which there is no law, does not require a formal permissive law before it can be done.

It would certainly be a form of legalism to think that knowing the law, always adhering to it, and never breaking it, was the supreme rule for members and office-bearers of the Church. The supreme rule of faith and life is not church law but the Word of God contained in the Scriptures of the Old and New Testaments (*Article I*).

Legalism in the legal sense is bad law, or an abuse of law. The spirit of the law, in legal terms, is to be perceived in the principles on which it is explicitly or implicitly based, and in the purpose it is designed to achieve. A particular piece of legislation may be legalistic if it is enacted in the wrong spirit, or it may become legalistic if it has not been amended to meet changed circumstances. There is however always a presumption that the Assembly acts within its own constitution, and that its laws are agreeable to the Word of God (see also Chapter IV, p. 29).

On the presumption that law has been enacted in the right spirit, legalism is a matter of insisting on the letter of the law, or obeying only the letter of the law, as against the spirit of the law (see also Chapter VIII, p. 61). Having regard to the spirit of the law will not justify disobedience; and in practice it will usually involve a person in doing more than the letter of the law requires, not less.

In short, legalism is a wrong attitude to law, and it should have no place in the faith and life of church members, or in the enactment and application of the law of the Church.

8. Consuetude and Desuetude

Apart from the legislative process whereby the Church enacts, amends, and repeals laws, custom is a significant source of church law. A custom may acquire the force and status of law by consuetude, and a law may be amended by consuetude, or may lose its force and status by desuetude. These terms are used of the effect on law of actual practice over a significant period of time. No specific period is prescribed, and ultimately it would be for the Assembly to decide in any disputed case. This kind of process is recognised by *Article II*, which refers to certain constitutional documents, "as these have been or may hereafter be interpreted or modified by Acts of the General Assembly or by consuetude."

It is clearly, by definition, not possible to find a legislative source for an invariable practice which has become law by consuetude, but legislation is nevertheless required if that practice, having acquired the force of law, is to be changed or discontinued. For example, when the Church decided to accept the eligibility of women for the eldership (1966), and for the ministry (1968), it did not have to repeal any legislative prohibition, although some linguistic amendment was required in some places where the law *assumed* that only men would be eligible; but a specific legislative Act was required in each case to change what had been the invariable practice. Moreover, the Barrier Act procedure was used, because the law by consuetude was regarded as of such a status that its alteration involved a major constitutional change.

On the other hand, when old laws have fallen into desuetude, there is no need for the Assembly to pass legislative Acts repealing them. It would therefore be futile to attempt to win a case in a church court by quoting an obscure old Act which had not been formally repealed, if that Act had not been applied for a very long time.

9. Legal Obligation

The obligation to obey church law rests on the fact that the authority of the Church is derived from Christ, and this is made explicit by the ordination and commissioning vows, and by the signing of the Formula (see pp. 164-165).

The vows contain the question:

> "Do you acknowledge the Presbyterian government of this Church to be agreeable to the Word of God; and do you promise to be subject in the Lord to this Presbytery and to the superior courts of the Church, and to take your due part in the administration of its affairs?"
>
> (Note that the phrase is "agreeable to" the Word of God, not "prescribed by" it. Note also that, since the abolition of Synods, only one court is superior to the Presbytery, namely the Assembly.)

The Formula is:

> "I believe the fundamental doctrines of the Christian faith contained in the Confession of Faith of this Church.
>
> "I acknowledge the Presbyterian government of this Church to be agreeable to the Word of God, and promise that I will submit thereto and concur therewith.
>
> "I promise to observe the order of worship and the administration of all public ordinances as the same are or may be allowed in this Church".
>
> (For the significance of the phrase "contained in", see p. 26)

10. Sanctions

A sanction is something which constrains people to obey the law. The main sanction in church law is conscience, which constrains people to honour the vows they have made. Where this sanction has failed, the Church, through its courts, applies sanctions in the form of censures, as provided for in the laws relating to discipline, the ultimate sanction being excommunication (see Chapters IX & X, and Appendices B & E).

Act IX, 1996, provides a different kind of sanction, in that a vacant congregation with unjustified shortfalls in contributions to central funds may not be allowed to proceed to call a minister until such shortfalls have been met.

Although members of the Church do not make the same explicit vows as office-bearers, they are subject to the law in virtue of their having become members by commitment to Christ, by whose authority the Church legislates.

They make a further commitment when they sign a call to a new minister, and respond to a question at his or her induction. Conscience should likewise constrain them, and they are subject to discipline.

11. Conclusion

The most important conclusion to be drawn from the above considerations is that law is the servant of the Church, not its master. Law is, like the Church itself, subject to the Word of God contained in the Scriptures, and law which declares fundamental doctrine, or which is held to be directly derived from the Word of God, cannot be changed, but that is because of the supremacy of the Word, not the supremacy of the law.

In the area of expediency, where the Church is free to legislate, to make new law, or to amend or repeal existing law, but always in agreement with the Word and the fundamental doctrines, there are laws of differing status. Expedient laws which are superior to ordinary legislation include the *Articles* (other than *Article I*, which is fundamental), Acts passed under the Barrier Act, and probably some laws by consuetude which have been so widely accepted and taken for granted as basic that no-one has thought to incorporate them in formal legislation.

Law however is a flexible instrument for change in the hands of the Church. It is made by the Church for the Church, in the interests of its own efficiency and effectiveness. It is not an impediment to change, and its function is not to bolster up human traditions, even if they have become law by consuetude. Indeed, precisely because the very reason for the existence of this area of expediency is the need to be able to adapt to changing circumstances and modes of thought, there is a continuing obligation to consider change. The Church must not make the commandment of God of none effect by its tradition (Mt. 15:6).

Like the law in the Old Testament, church law is to be regarded as a gift of God, to be used to his glory.

II. HISTORY

1. Catholic

"The Church of Scotland is part of the Holy Catholic or Universal Church" (*Article I*). Its origins are to be found in the New Testament Church, and in the people of God under the Old Covenant.

The Gospel was brought to Scotland by such missionaries as Ninian, who established a Christian settlement at Whithorn in the 5th Century, and Columba with other Scots from Ireland in the 6th Century, whose base was Iona. The Church which came into being was modelled on that organised by Patrick in Ireland, with practices different in some respects from those of the Church of Rome, but the Roman forms were officially adopted at the Synod of Whitby in 664. These were consolidated by the initiatives of Queen Margaret at the end of the 11th Century.

2. Reformed

The authority of the Pope was repudiated in Scotland in 1560, and the Church was reformed. The leading figure in the Scottish Reformation was John Knox who, with others, drew up the *Scots Confession* and the *First Book of Discipline*, dealing with doctrine and government.

3. Presbyterian

The conciliar system (see p. 37) of church government evolved in a period of conflict between presbyterian and episcopal systems, the Stuart Kings favouring episcopacy as a way of controlling the Church through the appointment of bishops.

Under the leadership of Andrew Melville, the Church produced the *Second Book of Discipline* in 1581, and from this emerged the presbyterian system which was ratified by the Scots Parliament in 1592.

In 1612 episcopacy was restored, provoking a strong reaction which took the form of the National Covenant, following which the Glasgow Assembly of 1638 abolished episcopacy and deposed the bishops. During the period of the Civil War in England, several documents were produced, in an attempt to unify the Church in Scotland and in England with a presbyterian polity. Chief of these was the *Westminster Confession of Faith*, which became the Subordinate Standard of the Church of Scotland, but was not adopted in England.

With the restoration of Charles II, episcopacy was once again established, but under William of Orange the Church of Scotland became "by law established" as presbyterian in 1690, and it has remained presbyterian ever since.

In 1707 the presbyterian government of the Church was further secured by an Act which accompanied the Treaty of Union, as an essential part of it. This was designed to protect the Church from interference by a British Parliament with a majority of English members (see Chapter III, p. 17).

4. Secessions and Disruption

When patronage was restored in 1712, this was seen by many as a breach of the 1707 legislation, and it was the main cause of several secessions from the established Church. Divisions within the seceding bodies were partly reconciled by the formation of the United Presbyterian Church in 1847, by which time the Free Church had been formed by the Disruption of 1843.

5. Declaratory Acts

After some experience of heresy trials, and in the light of biblical scholarship and new theological insights, Churches sought to modify the extent to which the *Confession* should be absolutely binding on its office-bearers, in order to permit a certain amount of liberty of opinion. To achieve such modification, the United Presbyterian Church passed a Declaratory Act in 1879, and the Free Church passed a Declaratory Act in 1892 (see Appendix C, p. 175).

6. The Free Church Case

The Free and U.P. Churches united in 1900 to form the United Free Church, but a minority of the Free Church stayed out of the Union and, in an action in the civil courts, obtained ownership of all the former Free Church properties. The Declaratory Acts of 1879 and 1892 were both referred to in the "Free Church Case" (*Bannatyne and Others v. Lord Overtoun and Others*, and *Young and Others v. Macalister and Others*), in which the basis of the judgement of the House of Lords in 1904 was that the Free Church was, in law, a trust which could not competently depart from the *Westminster Confession*, which was part of its "trust deed". On that basis, those who had entered into the

Union of 1900 did not carry the legal identity of the Free Church with them into the United Free Church, and accordingly the whole property of the former Free Church belonged to those who did not enter the Union, who were still, in law, the Free Church.

This created an impossible situation, because the Free Church was far too small to be able to manage the whole property involved, and Parliament intervened by passing *The Churches (Scotland) Act, 1905*, which set up a Commission to divide the property equitably between the Free Church and the United Free Church.

7. Act XIII, 1910 (Church of Scotland)

The Church of Scotland took advantage of the fact that the 1905 Act was going through Parliament by arranging to have a clause inserted granting it power to alter its form of subscription to the *Confession*. In virtue of this it was able, by Act XIII, 1910, to modify its own relationship to the Confession, using the formula: "I hereby subscribe the Confession of Faith, declaring that I accept it as the Confession of this Church, and that I believe the fundamental doctrines of the Christian Faith contained therein."

8. United Free Church Act, 1906

The United Free Church, in 1906, passed an Act anent the Spiritual Independence of the Church, in order to make specific constitutional provision for its right to modify its own constitution and standards.

Whether this would have been sufficient to prevent another property action in the 1929 Union was not put to the test in the courts, because due provision was made for an equitable distribution at that time.

9. The *Declaratory Articles*

When negotiations for the union of the Church of Scotland and the United Free Church were undertaken, the matter of the freedom of the Church was high on the agenda, and the experiences of the several Churches with regard to civil and ecclesiastical legislation on doctrinal matters were taken into account in the drafting of the *Articles Declaratory of the Constitution of the Church of Scotland in Matters Spiritual*, so that the spiritual independence of the Church would be clearly stated in terms which would be recognised by the civil law (see Appendix B, p. 159).

10. The Church of Scotland Act, 1921

The Church of Scotland Act, 1921, (see p. 179) recognised the *Declaratory Articles* as the lawful constitution of the Church.

These *Articles* declared that church government in spiritual matters was derived from the Lord Jesus Christ, and was not subject to civil authority. The Act provided that it would not come into force until the *Articles* had been approved by the Assembly. When this had been done, the Act came into force by Order in Council, on 28th June, 1926, and the way was open for the union of the United Free Church and the Church of Scotland.

11. The 1929 Union

The Union took place in 1929, the united Church being known as "The Church of Scotland". The Basis and Plan of Union (see Appendix B) included specific references, not only to the *Declaratory Articles*, but also to the *Declaratory Acts* of 1879 and 1872, as well as to the *United Free Church Act of 1906* and the *Church of Scotland Act XIII, 1910*.

12. National Church

While, in terms of its own constitution, the Church of Scotland was recognised as the national Church in Scotland, it was no longer properly described as "by law established", because the law had now explicitly recognised that the Church was established by the Lord Jesus Christ. This means that, while the 1707 Act (see Section 3 above, and p. 17) may still be regarded as law protecting the Church from State interference, and is in this sense reinforced by the 1921 Act, it cannot be construed as preventing the Church from modifying its own constitution without reference to the State, in terms of the *Articles*.

13. Church and State

This ultimate settlement of the various conflicts between Church and State is a significant landmark in the history of the Church. Only a few attempts have been made to challenge the Church's authority in the civil courts, and these have all failed.

The relationship with the State is symbolised when the Assembly meets, by the presence of the Monarch in person, or more usually in the person of a Lord High Commissioner, who sits in the throne gallery, outwith the Assembly itself, and is invited to address the Assembly, but not entitled to intervene in its business.

NOTE

This brief history is of the Church *of* Scotland, and not of the Church *in* Scotland. The process whereby the Roman Catholic Church moved from being rejected in 1560 to its present position, and the development of the Scottish Episcopal Church after 1690, could too easily be over-simplified in a brief summary, but these Churches are now, with others, in full membership of ecumenical bodies, along with the Church of Scotland. Information about the constitutional history and legal status of these Churches will be found in *The Laws of Scotland, Stair Memorial Encyclopedia*, Vol 3, Paras. 1610-1667.

III. CONSTITUTION

1. *Declaratory Articles*

The Church of Scotland is the National Church in Scotland. Its basic constitutional document is the *Articles Declaratory of the Constitution of the Church of Scotland in Matters Spiritual* (usually referred to as the *Declaratory Articles*), in the Schedule to the Church of Scotland Act, 1921.

Although the *Basis and Plan of Union, 1929,* names the *United Free Church Act anent Spiritual Independence, 1906,* as well as the *Declaratory Articles*, as leading documents setting forth the general constitution of the Church, the main principles of the former are included in the latter, and it is therefore convenient to concentrate here on the *Declaratory Articles* (see Appendix B, p. 159), as set out in the Schedule to the Church of Scotland Act, 1921 (see Appendix D).

2. Church and State

These *Articles* state, among other things, that the Church receives from Christ, its Divine King and Head, "the right and power subject to no civil authority to legislate, and to adjudicate finally, in all matters of doctrine, worship, government, and discipline in the Church." (*Article IV*)

In accordance with that statement, the 1921 Act does not purport to give the Church its constitution, or to grant it spiritual independence, but declares the *Declaratory Articles* (drawn up by the Church) to be lawful, and to prevail over all (State) statutes or laws then in force affecting the Church. Moreover, the Act provides that it shall come into force by Order in Council "after the *Declaratory Articles* shall have been adopted by an Act of the General Assembly of the Church of Scotland."

3. Spiritual Independence

The fact that the State did not confer independence on the Church, but recognised the divine authority of the Church's claim to be independent, and made even this recognition conditional upon approval by the Church, shows that both the content and the manner of the legislation fully acknowledge the Church's independence of the State.

4. Fundamental Law

This is a matter of great constitutional importance. Since Parliament has recognised that there is an area where its writ does not run, namely the government of the Church of Scotland in matters spiritual, the 1921 Act is a legislative recognition of a limitation on the Sovereignty of Parliament. As such it may arguably be regarded as fundamental law which cannot be amended by ordinary legislation.

The question of fundamental law is however a debatable one. (For a full consideration of the subject, see *The Laws of Scotland, Stair Memorial Encyclopedia*, Vol 5, Paragraphs. 338-358) It has been argued that the Treaty of Union, 1707, contained "entrenched clauses", which were clauses purporting to legislate for all time coming, and were designed to impose certain limitations on the sovereignty of the new Parliament thereby created. Thus the Treaty of Union is to be regarded as the written constitution of the United Kingdom, contrary to the usual claim that there is no written constitution.

The *Protestant Religion and Presbyterian Church Act, 1707,* was incorporated into the Treaty of Union, and similarly entrenched. It was designed to protect the Church of Scotland from interference by the new Parliament, but the re-introduction of patronage, which was one of the major factors of the Disruption, was in breach of this. Since Synods are specifically mentioned in it, a question arose at the time of their abolition as to whether Parliament would have to be asked to amend it, but the Church took the view that the terms of the 1921 Act made this unnecessary.

5. Sovereignty of Parliament

In practice however Parliament has tended to regard itself constitutionally as a continuation of the English Parliament, and consequently to regard the Sovereignty of Parliament as meaning that no Parliament can be absolutely bound by the legislation of previous Parliaments. It has felt free to repeal or amend even some of the entrenched clauses of the Treaty of Union.

If Parliament were, on this latter view, to consider itself able to repeal the 1921 Act without the consent of the Church, and were to do so, the Church would still be bound to regard the *Declaratory Articles* as its constitution. It could not do otherwise, except by modifying the *Articles*, which would require the approval of successive General Assemblies and the consent of two-thirds of the Presbyteries in two successive years, and even that procedure cannot change

Article I. Repeal of the 1921 Act would therefore create a major constitutional conflict.

It is important to remember that conflict between Church and State was a reality from the time of the Reformation, through the Disruption and much else, until the 1921 Act resolved the conflict. This Act is therefore of immense importance to the Church of Scotland.

6. International Courts

While the 1921 Act stands it is clear that Parliament has formally recognised that it has no authority in matters spiritual. It cannot by any treaty have surrendered to any international court an authority which it does not have. Accordingly, no international court can have authority to review decisions of courts of this Church in matters spiritual.

7. The Question of Establishment

Professor Burleigh, in *A Church History of Scotland*, states (p. 404) that it was often asked at the time of the negotiations for the 1929 Union, whether the Church would be an established or a disestablished Church, and answers the question by saying that "it would be neither, . . . in the *Articles* both words are avoided as outmoded. The expression 'The Church as by law established' is not of ecclesiastical provenance. It was a novelty in 1690, and the Church was not happy about it as it seemed to deny its true nature."

If establishment means no more than recognition as a National Church by the State, the Church of Scotland is established; but if establishment means established by the State, it is not established. Nevertheless, the terms of the 1921 Act are not consistent with the view that the Church was thereby disestablished. Accordingly, it is best to understand the Church in terms of what the *Declaratory Articles* actually say, rather than seeking to fit it into outmoded and misleading categories.

8. Contents of the *Declaratory Articles* (see p. 159)

1. ARTICLE I

The status of *Article I* is given in Article VIII, which lays down a procedure whereby the Church may modify or add to the Articles, but only "consistently with the provisions of the first *Article* hereof, adherence to which, as interpreted by the Church, is essential to its continuity and corporate life." In other words, the first *Article* cannot be amended in any way, but the Church has the right to interpret it.

The first *Article* states the essential doctrines of the Church, and its basic nature and functions. It affirms the Church's adherence to the Scottish Reformation, its reception of "the Word of God which is contained in the Scriptures of the Old and New Testaments as its supreme rule of faith and life", and its avowal of "the fundamental doctrines of the Catholic faith founded thereupon."

This *Article* does not make a verbal identification of the words of Scripture with the Word of God, but states that the Word of God is "contained in" the Bible, thus leaving scope for the application of the phrase "as interpreted by the Church," and also for liberty of opinion (see Chapter IV, p. 27).

Similarly, the concept of adherence to the Scottish Reformation is not defined. Given that *ecclesia reformata, semper reformanda* (a reformed Church is always requiring to be reformed) is a Reformation principle, the Church, as an organic body, can evolve and develop, and is indeed obliged to do so, without thereby ceasing to adhere to the Reformation. This also is a matter for interpretation by the Church.

[The Latin phrase was endorsed by the Assembly's decision to "reaffirm the Church's commitment to its continual reform— *ecclesia reformata sed semper reformanda*" (1986, Sess. 5). The use of *sed* (but) suggests that the Church needs to be reformed in spite of having been reformed, and *ergo* (therefore) might have been better, suggesting that commitment to continual reform is intrinsic to a reformed Church, which is also the significance of the comma as used here.]

While *Article I* does not define the "fundamental doctrines", clearly these must include those actually stated in the Article itself, and equally clearly those stated are not a full statement of every fundamental doctrine. Scripture, however, is the primary source of the fundamental doctrines; but it is significant that the *Article* speaks of the "fundamental doctrines of the Catholic faith." If any question should arise as to whether a particular doctrine is fundamental, that is also a matter for interpretation by the Church.

2. ARTICLE II

Article II states that the government of the Church is presbyterian, exercised through Kirk Sessions, Presbyteries, and General Assemblies. It states that the "principal subordinate standard" is the Westminster Confession of Faith, "containing the sum and substance of the Faith of the Reformed Church." Again, the use of the word "containing" is significant, leaving scope for interpretation and liberty of opinion. It refers to other leading documents in the spheres of worship, order, and discipline, but recognises that these may be interpreted or modified by Acts of Assembly or by consuetude.

3. ARTICLE III

Article III states the historical continuity and identity of the Church, and acknowledges that, "as a national Church representative of the Christian Faith of the Scottish people it has a distinctive call and duty to bring the ordinances of religion to the people in every parish of Scotland through a territorial ministry."

The extent to which the Church may still be representative of the Christian faith of the Scottish people depends on how this phrase is interpreted. Even if a majority of citizens do not profess the Christian faith today, it is still part and parcel of the history which has shaped Scotland, and the Church has an important rôle in representing it.

It is basic to the Church's understanding of itself as a national Church that its ministers, office-bearers, and congregations have obligations to the people of the parish who are not members, in addition to the obligations ministers and office-bearers have to congregations. For example, all parishioners are entitled to the services of the parish minister in connection with marriages and funerals.

4. ARTICLE IV

Article IV states that the Church has received from the Lord Jesus Christ "the right and power, subject to no civil authority, to legislate, and to adjudicate finally, in all matters of doctrine, worship, government, and discipline" and thus affirms the independence of the Church.

5. ARTICLE V

Article V deals specifically with the Church's right to determine her own doctrinal standards. It refers to "due regard to liberty of opinion in points which do not enter into the substance of the Faith", without defining "the substance of the Faith", but it is clear that this must be found in Scripture, as interpreted by the Church, and in the Confession interpreted in the light of Scripture; and it must include at least those doctrines stated in the first *Article*.

6. ARTICLE VI

Article VI deals with the status of the civil magistrate and the mutual duties of Church and State. The extent to which civil authorities may recognise their obligations in terms of this *Article* is possibly open to question, in a society which is multi-cultural and multi-faith; but the Church still adheres to this Article, and claims the right to speak to the State in terms of it.

7. ARTICLE VII

Article VII recognises the "obligation to seek and promote union with other Churches in which it finds the Word to be purely preached, the sacraments administered according to Christ's ordinance, and discipline rightly exercised." These criteria come originally from the *Scots Confession*, 1560, in which they are stated to be the "notes of the true

Kirk". A union on these terms is therefore consistent with adherence to the Scottish Reformation, in terms of the first *Article*.

It is significant that neither in the Scots Confession, nor in the 1592 Act of the Scots Parliament, nor in *Article VII*, is "discipline rightly exercised" specifically equated with presbyterian polity. It is impossible to predict how "discipline" may develop in this Church or in other Churches, but it would be wrong to think that no union with another Church whose discipline does not conform to current presbyterian polity can ever be effected in terms of this *Article*. The important question would be whether the polity of another Church sufficiently achieved the purposes of presbyterian discipline, namely the repression of vice and the nourishment of virtue (see Chapter IX, p. 62).

The point at issue in the Free Church case after the 1900 Union (see Chapter II, p. 13) was whether a Church could evolve and change and still remain the same Church, and the implication of the judgement of the House of Lords was that it could not. It is precisely in order to guard against such a mistake in the future that *Article VII* provides for union with other Churches "without loss of its identity."

There is no reason in law why *Article II*, which deals with discipline in the sense of government, should not be modified, as has already happened in connection with the abolition of Synods (but see below under *Article VIII* for the question of what amounts to modification).

8. ARTICLE VIII

The matter of the continuity of the identity of the Church is included also in *Article VIII*, which provides the conditions and procedure for modifying or adding to the *Articles*, with the specific exception of *Article I*, which is essential to the "continuity" of the Church.

A question arises as to the extent to which an amendment amounts to modification, and a possible criterion would be that any proposed alteration which would in normal procedure be treated as a counter-motion would go beyond modification, and would therefore not be competent, whereas the formal procedure for modification would be by way of amendment. It is for the Church to decide, and in the case of proposed modification of any *Article*, the procedure is such that there would be a presumption that any modification approved by three successive Assemblies, and by two-thirds of the Presbyteries in two successive years would be one which the Church had thereby agreed to be competent.

9. ARTICLE IX

Article IX ratifies and confirms the Church's constitution, "subject to the provisions of the foregoing *Articles*." The *Articles* are not therefore the whole constitution, which is set out more fully in the Basis and Plan of

Union, but they affirm the essence of the constitution, including the important matter of its relationship to the State and civil law.

9. Christian, Catholic, Reformed, National, and Free

The 1921 Act has been described as a treaty between Church and State. One result of this is that the National Church is in fact more autonomous than a "free" Church might be, precisely because its freedom is so formally recognised. It is also significant that Section 2 of the 1921 Act states that "Nothing in this Act or in any other Act affecting the Church of Scotland shall prejudice the recognition of any other Church as a Christian Church protected by law in the exercise of its spiritual functions." Thus the independence of the Church of Scotland benefits other Churches by becoming a norm for religious freedom generally, and it should not be seen as a privileged position over against other Churches. If it were nevertheless argued that the Act gives an unfair privilege to the Church of Scotland compared with other Churches, or with other religions, the progressive remedy for such alleged unfairness would be to expand Section 2 of the Act in order to give wider recognition to religious freedom.

References in the *Articles* to the fundamental doctrines of the Catholic faith, the sum and substance of the faith of the Reformed Church, and the fundamental doctrines of the Christian faith, indicate that the Church of Scotland is a Christian Church which is both Catholic and Reformed. It is also both national and free.

10. The Basis and Plan of Union

The Basis and Plan of Union of October 1929 was an Act of the General Assemblies of the Church of Scotland and the United Free Church, meeting together, whereby the union of these two Churches was effected, and many provisions were made for the united Church, the Church of Scotland, thereby constituted.

It was not included in the loose-leaf book of *Acts of the General Assembly from 1929* because that book records Acts of Assembly of the united Church subsequent to the Union. Nevertheless, this is clearly an important document for the Church (see Appendix B, p. 154).

11. The Basis

The Basis (see p. 154) contains the Uniting Act in four main sections and an Appendix.

1. THE UNITING ACT

The first section of the Uniting Act contains a preamble in narrative and declaratory form, with a summary of salient historical events and of the reasons for proceeding to union, and ends with the enactment of the union.

The second section makes declarations about the nature of the Church, and lists certain leading constitutional documents.

The third section provides for previous enactments of both Churches to continue in force, and for a means of dealing with conflicting or materially different legislation and practice.

The fourth section provides that the two General Assemblies together shall have the powers of a General Assembly of the united Church.

2. THE APPENDIX

The Appendix contains the *Declaratory Articles* and the U.F. Act of 1906, and the Preamble, Questions and Formula to be used at Ordinations and Inductions.

12. The Plan

The Plan (see p. 166) has the following main sections:

> CONSTITUTION AND POWERS OF COURTS
> TRAINING OF THE MINISTRY
> PROPERTY AND FINANCE
> RULES AND FORMS OF PROCEDURE
> DISCIPLINE
> CONSTITUTION AND ADMINISTRATIVE REGULATIONS OF ASSEMBLY
>   COMMITTEES
> RELATIONS WITH OTHER CHURCHES

Apart from those on Rules and Forms of Procedure, and on Discipline, these have been almost entirely superseded by subsequent legislation, and are largely of historical interest. A few matters might still turn out to be of contemporary relevance, such as the fact that two Roman Catholic priests were admitted to the ministry of this Church without re-ordination, one in 1735 and one in 1884, and these might be regarded as precedents if the question were to arise again. The full text of the Plan is available in the official records of the Assembly.

1. RULES AND FORMS OF PROCEDURE

The section on Rules and Forms of Procedure contains a sub-section on Election and Appointment of Ministers, which has been entirely superseded by subsequent legislation. A short sub-section on Function, Ordination and Induction of Ministers contains definitions which are still applicable. A third and final sub-section on Sundry Matters, contains matter which is still relevant. For example, although Cox (p. 119) speaks of a Presbytery appointing Assessors to act with a Kirk Session only when there is "an insufficient number of ruling elders to form a quorum", this sub-section provides also for Assessors "in cases of difficulty at the discretion of the Presbytery."

2. DISCIPLINE

The section on Discipline contains sub-sections on Principles, Censures, and the Record Apart, under the heading, "Applicable to all Courts". The rules these contain are still operative. The next main sub-section, on procedure in Kirk Sessions, is still applicable as far as it goes, but is not a complete treatment of the subject. The sub-section on procedure in Presbyteries has been modified and expanded by the terms of Act VII, 1935.

The differences between this part of the Plan and the 1935 Act require further comment, and are dealt with in Chapter XII: Trial by Libel.

IV. DOCTRINE

1. Doctrine and Law

The relationship between doctrine and law has already been referred to (Chapter I), in terms both of civil law and church law.

Law is clearly subordinate to doctrine, in that church law must be consistent with "the supreme rule of faith and life", which is the Word of God (*Article I*). While law cannot compel belief, it can state what beliefs a person must have in order to be eligible for membership of the Church, or for office in it. This function of law was exercised, in respect of office-bearers, both by civil law and by church law from the time of the Reformation until civil law was excluded by the *Declaratory Articles*.

2. The *Westminster Confession*

The *Westminster Confession of Faith* was approved by the Assembly of 1647, and ratified and established by Acts of Parliament in 1649 and 1690, and was thus a doctrinal statement which was enacted by Church and State. It is, according to *Article II*, "the principal subordinate standard" of the Church. That to which it is subordinate is "the Word of God which is contained in the Scriptures of the Old and New Testaments" (*Article I*), "as interpreted by the Church" (*Article VIII*).

When biblical scholarship and new theological insights raised questions about some of the statements in the *Confession*, so that people who had subscribed to it, were moved to interpret parts of the Scriptures in ways which were at variance with it, the subordinate status of the *Confession* tended to be ignored. In such cases, the *Confession* was alleged to be so legally binding that it must prevail, and that allegation in effect involved ceasing to recognise the subordinate status of the *Confession*, and treating it as a standard superior to the Scriptures, imposing particular interpretations on them. Scholarly theologians of the highest intellectual and spiritual integrity were on this basis accused of heresy.

3. Modification of Relationship to *Confession*

That is why steps were taken in the various Churches to modify the formal relationship to the *Westminster Confession* (see Chapter II, p. 13, and Appendix C). The main object of these, as finally stated in the *Declaratory Articles*, was to secure that the Church had the right to determine doctrinal matters, and to affirm "liberty of opinion in points which do not enter into the substance of the Faith."

While it has not been seriously suggested that liberty of opinion is itself a fundamental doctrine, it is historically and constitutionally a major characteristic of the Church.

4. Key Words: "contained in"

Both in relation to the Scriptures and in relation to the *Westminster Confession*, the *Declaratory Articles* use the phrase "contained in". This is quite explicitly to recognise that the Scriptures are not *per se* the Word of God, but that the Word of God is contained in them, and that the fundamental doctrines are not the whole of the *Westminster Confession*, but are contained it in. The constitutional history of the Church leading to the *Declaratory Articles* is evidence of the importance of this understanding.

It was a matter of deliberate policy that the doctrines stated in *Article I* were few in number, and that only those which were clearly fundamental and essential to a Christian Church were included. Being evidently cardinal doctrines, they are of the utmost importance, but it was realised that the addition of other doctrines at this point, or even rigid definitions of the doctrines stated, could lead to legal difficulties in relation to civil law, and inhibit the right of the Church from time to time to modify doctrinal standards.

5. Broad Church

A member or office-bearer of the Church is free to believe that all the words in the Bible are together literally the Word of God, but that is not required of all members and office-bearers. Likewise a member or office-bearer is free to believe that all the doctrines in the *Confession* are fundamental, but again that is not required. The constitutional possibility of different beliefs is what allows the Church to be described as a "broad" Church.

When, by Act V, 1986, the Assembly decided no longer to affirm certain specified parts of the *Westminster Confession*, relating to the Pope and the Roman Catholic Church, it concluded, "This Church therefore dissociates itself from the above statements and does not require its office-bearers to believe them." The effect of this was to state that, whatever doctrines contained in the *Confession* are fundamental, these are not, and therefore office-bearers may exercise liberty of opinion in respect of them. The effect was not to exclude office-bearers who did believe them.

6. Conscientious Objections

Questions are sometimes raised about conscientious objections to such obedience as the law requires. In no case is individual conscience a valid reason for disobedience. In the case of the re-marriage of divorced persons, the law makes provision for ministers who have conscientious objections (Act XXVI, 1959), but since this is part of the law, no question of disobeying the law on grounds of conscience arises in respect of it.

7. Law and Scripture

Since the Assembly is bound to act in terms of its own constitution, and must be presumed to have done so in passing any legislation, there is a further presumption that legislation passed by the Assembly does not contradict the receiving of the Word of God contained in the Scriptures as the Church's supreme rule of faith and life, as interpreted by the Church.

As the norm is that any law enacted by the Assembly is consistent with the Church's interpretation of Scripture, an individual with a conscientious objection based on a different interpretation of Scripture is in fact opposing individual conscience to the collective conscience of the Church. It is a misrepresentation of the position to claim that, because Scripture is superior to law, the law can be disobeyed with impunity on the basis of individual interpretation of Scripture.

8. Liberty of Opinion

It is true that the law recognises liberty of opinion in points which do not enter into the substance of the faith, and it is also true that most of the law of the Church does not enter into the substance of the faith. This means that there is liberty to believe that the law is wrong, but not liberty to disobey it. Anyone who believes that the law is contrary to Scripture, is entitled to hold that opinion, and is also entitled to express it, and to seek to persuade the Church to change the law.

In the Preface to the *Scots Confession* it is stated by the authors that "if any man will note in our Confession any chapter or sentence contrary to God's Holy Word, that it would please him of his gentleness and for Christian charity's sake to inform us of it in writing; and we, upon our honour, do promise him that by God's grace we shall give him satisfaction from the mouth of God, that is, from Holy Scripture, or else we shall alter whatever he can prove to be wrong." That is the spirit in which any challenge to the law should be raised and dealt with.

9. Changing the Law

If an office-bearer simply chooses to disobey the law as it stands, and becomes the subject of disciplinary action, the principle that a court should not change the law in the course of a case applies, so the case must proceed under the law as it stands. In 1976, in issuing a case, the Assembly affirmed its "confessional belief, shared with the Universal Church and particularly with all branches of the Reformed faith, that re-baptism is in violation of the doctrine of one baptism, whether of infants or of believers, and of the article that baptism is to be administered but once to any person." (1976, Sess. 7)

That statement comes very close to stating that the doctrine of one baptism is fundamental and of the substance of the faith, and might be so construed.

A "test case" cannot be a method of changing the law, and is more likely to produce a re-affirmation of it, which will make any subsequent attempt to change it more difficult. It would also be a cumbersome way of seeking an interpretation of the law, although the case just referred to certainly did that.

The proper way to seek a change in the law, or clarification of its meaning, is to persuade a Presbytery to approach the Assembly by Overture, or, failing that, to petition the Assembly.

If all attempts to have the law changed have failed, an office-bearer who believes the law is wrong must either obey that law in accordance with ordination or commissioning vows, or withdraw from office, or refuse to obey in the clear knowledge that disciplinary action will follow (see Chapter IX, p. 63, for further reference to the 1976 case on "second baptism").

Additional Note on Conscience

In general it is of course morally and spiritually right to follow the leading of one's conscience, but nevertheless the dictates of conscience may be based on inadequate knowledge or understanding. Account must be taken also of the root meaning of the Latin (*con + scientia*) from which it is derived, namely "knowledge shared with others." The closing words of the Book of Judges ("In those days there was no king in Israel: every man did that which was right in his own eyes.") might be paraphrased as, "If there were no law in the Church, everyone might follow his or her own conscience."

There are situations in which people feel bound by conscience to break the law, and while their conscientious views may be respected as such, they do not render them immune from the legal consequences.

See also Chapter XX of the *Westminster Confession.*

V. WORSHIP

1. Liturgical Freedom

There is no prescribed liturgy in the Church of Scotland, and ministers enjoy considerable freedom in matters of worship. *Article II* states that the Church's system and principles of worship are in accordance with *The Directory for the Public Worship of God,* 1645, as that "has been or may hereafter be modified by Acts of the General Assembly or by consuetude."

While the *Directory* is deliberately not prescriptive in liturgical matters, it is careful "to hold forth such things as are of divine institution in every ordinance," and continues, "and other things we have endeavoured to set forth according to the rules of Christian prudence, agreeable to the general rules of the word of God; our meaning therein being only, that the general heads, the sense and scope of the prayers, and other parts of publick worship, being known to all, there may be a consent of all the churches in those things that contain the substance of the service and worship of God."

The freedom this allows to ministers is that "each one, by meditation, by taking heed to himself, and the flock of God committed to him, and by wise observing the ways of divine providence, may be careful to furnish his heart and tongue with further or other materials of prayer and exhortation, as shall be needful upon all occasions."

Since the *Directory* is concerned more with principles than with mandatory law, its full consideration is outwith the scope of this volume. Much in it that is apparently mandatory has been modified by consuetude.

Nevertheless, the main principles set out are those on whose basis our forms of worship have grown and developed. It is still worthy of study and attention by all who have responsibility for the conduct of worship, and by all who seek to understand the traditions of worship in this Church.

2. Common Order

Successive books of *Common Order* have been "authorised" by the Assembly, especially since the 1929 Union, although the first was in 1564. In accordance with the principles of the *Directory,* they are not regulative, although they contain valuable material, worthy of use, with or without modification, in a Church which is both catholic and reformed.

3. Innovations

Act VII, 1866, provides that, the supervision of worship being a function of Presbyteries, they are to enjoin the discontinuance, or prohibit the introduction of any novel practice in worship which is inconsistent with the laws and usages of the Church, or a cause of division in a congregation, or unfit from any cause to be used in the worship of God. If an injunction is made under this Act, an appeal does not sist it, and it must be obeyed until final judgement is given.

4. Prescribed Material

In services of licensing, ordination and induction of ministers, ordination and admission of elders, and commissioning of deacons, the prescribed Preamble and Questions must be used and the Formula must be signed. These may be modified only by the Assembly, which has recently agreed to the use of some verbal alterations in the interests of inclusive language. (Reports, 1991, p. 8) The basic Preamble and Questions, together with the Formula, for the ordination of ministers, are contained in the Plan of Union, 1929 (see pp. 163-165), those for elders in Act X, 1932. The substance of these, with appropriate modification of the narrative part of the Preamble, and of the Questions, is used in other services, of which details may be found in the *Ordinal and Service Book* (3rd Edition, 1962), with the provisos that the Questions for Readers were subsequently revised by Act XVII, 1992, and introduction to a terminable appointment has been replaced by induction to terminable tenure, by Act IV, 1984.

5. Conduct of Worship

Act II, 1986, provides that the minister is responsible for the conduct of worship. If the minister is present, and therefore accepting personal responsibility, there is considerable scope for involving other people, or groups, in all or part of the service. If the minister is absent, only those categories of qualified people listed in the Act are authorised to conduct worship.

6. Benediction

Only an ordained minister should close a service of worship with a benediction, which is a blessing, ending with such words as, "be with *you* all." Others should close the service with a prayer, which may be in the same words as a benediction, but ending with the words, "be with *us* all." This is because *The Directory for the Publick Worship of God* states, "let the minister dismiss the congregation with a solemn blessing", and *The Form of Presbyterial Church Government* lists among the duties of a pastor, "to bless the people from God." Blessing is therefore a ministerial function.

An apparent exception is the singing by the congregation of the Aaronic Blessing (Num. 6:24-26) at a baptism, but this is not an individual act. It is rather the Church itself doing something which is normally done for it by a minister, and it is not substituted for the blessing at the close of the service.

Blessing is also a ministerial duty. It appears to have become fashionable for meetings, and even sometimes acts of worship, to be concluded by all present saying "The Grace" (a modification of II Cor. 13:14) together. This may be acceptable at informal meetings, or acts of worship conducted by a person who is not ordained, or even, like the Aaronic Blessing, in the course of a service, but it is not a benediction, and if a minister is conducting a service of worship and neglects to give a benediction in proper form at the close, the people are deprived of the blessing from God to which they are entitled.

The authorities quoted above are, in *Article II*, stated to be standards with which this Church's principles of worship are in accordance, "as these have been or may hereafter be interpreted or modified by Acts of the General Assembly or by consuetude." There has been no interpreting or modifying Act in this matter, and the fashion referred to has certainly not been in existence for long enough to amount to consuetude.

It may also be observed that, while it is obvious that prayer may be offered for people who are not present, a benediction is a blessing on those who have been engaged together in worship, and it is therefore inappropriate, after such a phrase as "be with you all", to add words which purport to include others, for example, "and all whom you love."

7. Administration of the Sacraments

There are only two sacraments in the Church of Scotland, and in Reformed Churches generally: Baptism, and the Lord's Supper, or Holy Communion.

Act XVII, 1963, sets out the terms and conditions on which infants may be baptised.

Act IV, 1975, gives the categories of persons authorised to administer the sacraments, which include ministers of other denominations, on certain conditions.

The above two Acts are self-explanatory, but the basic rule is that only an ordained minister may administer. Although the Kirk Session decides when the Sacrament of the Lord's Supper, or Holy Communion, will take place, the administration of the sacrament is a ministerial act. The Kirk Session need not be constituted for the sacrament, and while it is one of the traditional rôles of the elders to assist the minister in the distribution of the elements, the minister may invite others to do so.

Administration of the sacraments in private is provided for by Acts XXIII, 1955, and XXI, 1956.

8. Admission Vows

Several forms of the vows of church membership have been authorised by the Assembly. These, as approved by the Assembly in 1935, and in 1968, are to be found in successive editions of the books of *Common Order*. While the reference in Cox to the 1935 form is given as "1935, xiii", which suggests that it is Act XIII, 1935, it is in fact a reference to Session 13 of the 1935 Assembly, at which a form of vows submitted by a committee was approved by deliverance. The 1968 form was also approved by deliverance on the report of a committee. The latest form is in Act XII, 1996.

While none of these is prescriptive, so that any of them may be modified in use, or other forms may be used, the law requires that they should amount to a public profession of faith. Such profession implicitly involves commitment to the Church, and it is good practice to make this commitment explicit. While it would be invidious to have such a rigid form that questions of the validity of a person's membership could be raised if it were not exactly adhered to, it is important that all members make substantially the same commitment, whatever form of words is used.

9. Confirmation

The term "confirmation" does not appear in legislation, and there is no "sacrament of confirmation" in the Church of Scotland. The sacrament of baptism, being complete in itself, requires no subsequent confirmation.

Calvin, having dealt robustly with the notion of confirmation as a sacrament purporting to complete baptism, "which cannot even be named without injury to baptism," was prepared to use the term for profession of faith, and envisaged a boy of ten years of age presenting himself to the Church for this purpose. "Thus, while the whole Church looked on and witnessed, he would profess the one true sincere faith with which the body of the faithful, with one accord, worship one God." Stating that this was confirmation in the ancient practice of the Church, and that it was accompanied by laying on of hands, to give "more reverence and dignity" to the act, he continued, "This laying on of hands, which is done simply by way of benediction, I commend, and would like to see restored to its pure use in the present day." (*Institutes*, Book IV, Chapter XIX)

The Anglican *Book of Common Prayer* requires godparents at the baptism of an infant to be told that "this infant must also faithfully promise by you that are his sureties (until he come of age to take it upon himself) that he will renounce the devil and all his works, and constantly believe God's holy Word, and obediently keep his commandments." Questions are then put to the godparents, as if to the child, and are answered by them, speaking as if they were the child. It is easy to see how, in such circumstances, later confirmation is confirmation by the baptised person of the vows taken in his or her name.

At the baptism of an infant in this Church however, parents take vows confessing their own faith, and promising to bring the child up in that faith. They do not vicariously promise anything "in the name of the child", so there can be no question of these vows being later confirmed by the baptised person.

In 1966 a report on the doctrine and practice of confirmation, submitted to the Assembly by the Panel on Doctrine (1966 Reports, p. 233), suggested that the part of the service which can be called confirmation is when, by prayer, the Holy Spirit, with all his gifts and strengthening power is invoked upon those who have professed their faith. This report was received as fulfilling the remit given to the Panel, but not formally approved; and if its view of confirmation is accepted, care must be taken not to use it in such a way as to imply that the gift of the Spirit was not given in baptism.

The fact is that no explicit statement of the meaning of the word has been approved, but the Assembly has on more than one occasion passed a deliverance referring to an order of service for "Confirmation and Admission to the Lord's Supper."

All that may be said with certainty therefore, as far as the legal position is concerned, is that the Assembly has implicitly accepted Calvin's view that the word may be used of a service of public profession of faith and admission to the Lord's Table.

There remains a substantial difference between admission to full membership of the Church by a decision of a Kirk Session, and admission by a sacrament of confirmation administered by a bishop, involving not only different concepts of confirmation, but also different theologies of infant baptism.

10. Baptism

As in the case of admission vows, there are different forms of the questions put to parents ("one or both" — Act XVII, 1963) or guardians at the baptism of their infant children. They involve the confession of their own faith, and their promise to bring the child up in that faith and in the life of the Church. Practice has varied as to whether the questions, or some of them, are put before or after a child has been baptised. The point of the difference is that, if the questions come first, baptism appears to be conditional on their being properly answered, whereas, if they come afterwards, they are seen as implications of the baptism. In *Common Order*, 1994, the profession of faith by parents or guardians comes before the baptism, and the others after it. A question to the congregation is also included.

Adult baptism is normally combined with admission and confirmation, and vows are taken by the person being baptised.

There·are no godparents in the Church of Scotland, since the concept of godparents is at variance with the law and practice of this Church, as will be evident from what is said above about confirmation. If others appear with the parents, they take no vows, except to the extent to which they share in responding to a question put to the congregation.

After a baptism, the minister should provide a signed certificate of baptism, the general practice being to write this on the back of the birth certificate of the person baptised. Details must also be entered in the baptismal register.

Certified extracts from the baptismal register may be issued by a·minister in a form approved by the Assembly in 1977, as follows:

NOTICE OF BAPTISM

I hereby certify from the records of .... that .... was baptised according to the use of the Church of Scotland, on the .... day of .... in the year of our Lord, 19..(or 20).

Signature:...................., Parish Minister.

11. Marriage

The civil law of marriage is contained in the Marriage Scotland Act, 1977. The basic provision is that on no account must a minister conduct a marriage service unless he or she has received a Marriage Schedule issued by the Registrar. This is a legal requirement, and failure to comply with it could result in a fine, or imprisonment, or both. While the minister should be familiar with the conditions under which such a schedule may be issued, it is better to advise those proposing to be married to find these out for themselves from the Registrar, and to comply exactly with what the Registrar requires.

a) Banns

Banns as a preliminary to marriage in Scotland are no longer required in terms of the 1977 Act, but persons residing in Scotland and proposing to be married in England may still require to have banns called in Scotland. In that event, the English law requires that they be called according to the law or custom of Scotland. Although the calling of banns was regulated by church legislation, which was repealed by the Church, the repealing Act made provision for this special case (Act III, 1978). The banns should be called at the principal service of worship, in the following form:

There is a purpose of marriage between [full name of man] (Bachelor/Widower/Divorced), residing at ...., in the Registration District of ...., and [full name of woman] (Spinster/Widow/Divorced), residing at ...., in the Registration District of ...., of which proclamation is here by made for the first (and only) time (or second and last time).

The banns are called only once if the parties are well known to the minister, and he or she has reason to believe that there is no impediment to their marriage.

When the banns have been duly called, a certificate should be issued in the following form:

> At .... the .... day of ...., 19.. (or 20..)
> It is hereby certified that [full name of man], residing at ...., and [full name of woman], residing at ...., have been duly proclaimed in order to marriage in the Church of .... according to the custom of the Church of Scotland, and that no objections have been offered.
> Signed .... Minister, or Session Clerk.

b) Marriage Services

The 1977 Act, recognising the right of the Church to regulate its own forms of worship, prescribes that the form of ceremony used by a minister must be "recognised" by the Church "as sufficient for the solemnisation of marriages." As there was then no law of the Church recognising any form, the Assembly passed Act I, 1977, setting out the basic minimum for a marriage service. This act also provides that only an ordained minister may solemnise a marriage, so that provisions in the civil law for other persons to do so do not apply to marriage in this Church.

It is not now necessary to include in a marriage service an injunction to the parties that if they know of any impediment to their marriage they should confess it, nor is it necessary to invite anyone present who knows of any impediment to declare it.

While ministers are obliged to solemnise marriages of parishioners (*Article III*), and the civil law permits them to solemnise marriages anywhere, they are entitled to decline to do so in places they consider to be unsuitable in view of the nature of Christian marriage. If it comes to the notice of a Presbytery that a minister is conducting marriages in what it considers to be unsuitable places, it is entitled to instruct him or her to desist from that practice. As marriage is an act of worship, no such instruction would be sisted by an appeal (see above under Innovations, p. 30).

c) Divorced Persons

Act XXVI, 1959, provides that, while ministers are permitted to re-marry divorced persons, on certain conditions, they are not obliged to if they have conscientious objections. As the Act makes clear, such re-marriage should not be agreed to as a matter of course, and the conditions should be carefully adhered to.

d) Foreigners

In the case of a marriage involving a foreigner, who in this case might be a citizen of another country or a person domiciled in another country, the minister should not only consult the Registar about the legal requirements for the marriage, but should seek legal advice, or information from the Consulate of the country concerned, as to whether or not a marriage in Scotland will be recognised in the country of citizenship or domicile, and advise the parties accordingly. The fact that a marriage will not be recognised in another country is not a legal impediment to its being solemnised in Scotland, and so would not justify a minister in declining to officiate.

12. Funerals

While burial or cremation is necessary after a death, a funeral service is not a legal requirement, and indeed *The Directory for the Public Worship of God* states that a dead body should be interred "without any ceremony"; but this is one of the things modified by consuetude, and it is now almost an invariable practice to have a funeral service.

A funeral service is normally conducted by a minister, but this is not legally necessary. There are no restrictions on who may conduct such a service. Nevertheless, a parish minister should not decline to conduct the funeral service of a parishioner, even if such parishioner had no connection with the Church, for this is one of the ordinances of religion (*Article III*). For pastoral reasons, a minister should not decline to conduct a funeral service for a still-born child, if this is requested.

VI. GOVERNMENT

1. Church Courts

The distinctive thing about the presbyterian system is that the Church's authority, received from Christ, is vested in church courts and not in individuals. It is a conciliar system, in which legislative, judicial, and administrative decisions, and supervisory actions, are taken corporately.

The supreme court is the General Assembly which legislates for the whole Church, and is the final court of appeal, although in some matters it is the court of first instance. Next is now the Presbytery, since the abolition of Synods in 1992. The lowest court is the Kirk Session of each congregation of the Church.

While, in secular terms, courts are judicial bodies, church courts are referred to as courts even when they are not acting judicially. When they are so acting, they are courts of the land, and have a concurrent jurisdiction with the civil and criminal courts. It has been judicially stated in the Court of Session that that court has no more right to interfere in proceedings before church courts than it has to interfere in proceedings before criminal courts (*Lockhart v. Presbytery of Deer*, 1851). It is worth noting that this was the situation long before the Church of Scotland Act, 1921.

In terms of territorial ecclesiastical jurisdiction, the Assembly covers the whole of Scotland, Presbyteries operate within their own bounds, and Kirk Sessions within their own parishes. In a sense it is therefore an anomaly that there are Presbyteries and Kirk Sessions furth of Scotland, namely the Presbyteries of England, Europe, and Jerusalem, with their congregations, but without territorial parishes. There are historical reasons for this, and they represent an empirical exception to the otherwise logical system.

For purposes of church law and administration the Presbytery of England is treated in most respects in the same way as a Presbytery in Scotland, and has the same responsibilities. The Presbytery of Europe is specially provided for in Act III, 1996, and the Presbytery of Jerusalem in Act VIII, 1979.

Congregations in other parts of the world are the responsibility of the Board of World Mission.

There are also Kirk Sessions in some units of the Armed Forces (Act VIII, 1952).

2. Membership

Membership of all courts has been confined to men and women who have taken ordination vows as ministers or elders; and recently deacons, who have taken similar vows at their commissioning, were added to membership of Presbyteries and the Assembly. They have all signed the Formula. Thus authority in the Church is exercised by those who have made a specific commitment to its doctrinal standards and to presbyterian church government (see Chapter I. p. 10).

3. Laity

Strictly speaking it is not correct to speak of "lay" participation in presbyterian government, not only because all who participate have been ordained or commissioned, but also because the distinction between clergy and laity does not properly apply to presbyterian polity. "Lay" is derived from the Greek λαος (*laos*), which, in the context of the Church, means the whole people of God, within which, in presbyterian polity, some are authorised, by ordination or commissioning, to perform particular functions. It is therefore not correct to speak of ministers as "clergy" as distinct from "laity". All are part of the *laos*.

It has to be conceded that the term "lay" is often loosely used of those who are not ministers, in the same way as it has come to be used in relation to other professions, e.g. of those who are not doctors, or not lawyers. This imprecise colloquial usage can be misleading in an ecumenical context when, for example, it is suggested that a committee be formed with equal numbers of "lay" and "ordained". Elders are ordained, but the mistaken belief that the eldership is a "lay" body is often encountered in other denominations.

4. Democracy

It is also incorrect to speak of this polity as "democratic", if that term is understood by comparison with political representative democracy. Members of courts are not all elected by the members of the Church. It is true that parish ministers are elected by congregations, but other ministers who are members of courts have not been so elected. In some congregations elders are elected, but in most they are selected by the Kirk Sessions, and in all cases the Kirk Sessions make the final decision as to whether a person should be ordained to the eldership. Whereas in representative democracy authority is conferred on the governing body by those who elect it, authority in the Church is conferred by Christ.

While the right of a congregation to elect and call a minister may properly be called a democratic one, that is only part of the process of appointing a minister. The right to induct a minister belongs solely to the Presbytery, to whose jurisdiction all ministers are subject once they have been elected, called, and inducted.

Ministerial membership of Presbytery is *ex officio*. Each Kirk Session appoints one elder to the Presbytery, but the Presbytery itself may appoint additional elders. The deacons who are members of Presbytery are all *ex officiis*.

Presbyteries appoint a quota of commissioners to the Assembly, and in the case of elders not all commissioners have to be members of Presbytery. Thus the members of Assembly are not directly elected by the members of the Church, and are not appointed to represent them, although in fact the Assembly, being composed of commissioners appointed by and representing Presbyteries, is broadly representative of the whole Church (see Chapter VIII, pp. 55 & 56).

The rationale of this system is that the authority of church courts comes from Christ (*Article IV*), and it is not "government of the people by the people for the people."

When this system is called democratic, what is meant is that government is not entirely in the hands of ordained ministers, but involves the participation of "elders of the people"; and in Kirk Sessions and other courts lords and commoners may sit side by side, with equal status, regardless of civil rank or position.

Cox states that the Church of Scotland is "essentially theocratic and thoroughly democratic" (p. 2), but it is difficult to justify the second part of that statement. It would be more accurate to say that this Church is essentially theocratic and thoroughly conciliar, with democratic elements.

5. Superior and Inferior Courts

In the structure of church courts, courts are superior or inferior to each other. Thus, in relation to the Assembly, Presbyteries and Kirk Sessions are inferior courts, Kirk Sessions being also inferior to Presbyteries. Superior courts have jurisdiction over inferior courts, with only a few statutory or "common law" exceptions. The presumption is always that the superior court has jurisdiction, and if that is challenged the onus of proof is on the challenger.

6. Commissions

The Assembly can delegate powers to commissions, such as the Commission of Assembly and the Judicial Commission, which have been given authority to make final judgements in certain well defined cases. Also, the Assembly, after hearing a case, has frequently appointed a special Commission with powers to issue that case after further investigation (see also p. 43, and Acts referred to there).

7. Financial Boards

In some congregations there is another body to which the generic term "financial court" has sometimes been applied, although the preferred term is "financial board", because they are not church courts, even although one of them is named the Deacons' Court (see Chapter XVII, pp. 130-131).

8. Committees

Courts can appoint standing and special committees with remits to carry out work on behalf of the courts. Since the Assembly meets only once each year, it has many committees over which it exercises control by requiring reports from them every year. In practice, the bulk of the agenda for each Assembly is devoted to supervising committees in this way, legislative and judicial functions occupying less time.

In a few instances, such as the determination of the minimum stipend each year by the Committee on the Maintenance of the Ministry, the Assembly has delegated power of decision to a committee.

The relationship of Assembly committees to inferior courts is sometimes a delicate one, and Presbyteries are properly jealous of their status as courts, over against committees; but committees appointed by the Assembly are acting by authority of that superior court while fulfilling the remits given to them.

In readjustment procedure, the Assembly has explicitly given authority to the Committee on Parish Re-appraisal, in matters coming before Presbyteries, but there is provision for bringing disputed matters to the Assembly for resolution (see Chapter XX, p. 145).

9. Records

All church courts are responsible for maintaining their official records, and for keeping them safely. Any record more than fifty years old, unless still in use, should be sent or delivered to the Principal Clerk, for onward transmission to the Scottish Record Office. This is to ensure that records will be properly preserved and made available for research and other purposes. In some areas agreement has been reached with the Record Office for church records to be held in local authority archives, but even when such an agreement is in force they should go first to the Principal Clerk so that the Record Office may catalogue them and carry out any necessary repairs before passing them on to the local archive.

An inventory of all church records held in the Record Office or local archives is available in the Principal Clerk's Office.

Records may be inspected at the Record Office, or local archive, and may be borrowed for purposes of legitimate research. Requests should be submitted in the first instance to the Principal Clerk, and in the case of requests to borrow congregational records they must be accompanied by extract minutes giving the approval of the Kirk Session and the Presbytery.

Because the church courts are courts of the land, their records are public records, and therefore *extra commercium*, which means that they belong inalienably to the Church. If records have fallen into other hands, the Church has the legal right to recover them. In practice, if someone is in possession of records, having bought them without realising that the seller had no title to sell, the Record Office will sometimes make an *ex gratia* payment to such a person when they are duly returned.

10. Quorum

In church courts the quorum is small. In the Assembly it is thirty-one, of whom at least sixteen must be ministers. It is currently the same in the Commission of Assembly, but this may be modified (see p. 89). In Presbyteries, regardless of their size, it is three, of whom at least two must be ministers. In Kirk Sessions, again regardless of size, it is three, of whom one must be the minister, or Interim Moderator, or other duly authorised minister.

The small quorum enables the courts to function effectively, for example when formal and uncontroversial business is to be undertaken by a Presbytery at a meeting *pro re nata*. As long as there is a quorum, decisions are legally valid, whether those present are many or few.

The quorum of the Judicial Commission is sixteen, but there must be twenty-four members present at the beginning of a hearing.

The quorum of the Property Commission is seven.

There is no provision of a quorum for other commissions, or for committees, or for congregational meetings.

For the quorum of a financial board, see pp. 134-5.

When a count shows that there is no quorum, the meeting must be closed, but all business transacted before then is valid.

VII. JUDICIAL FUNCTIONS

1. Courts

The Assembly, as the supreme court of the Church, is both a court of first instance and an appeal court. Its judgements are final, as are those of Commissions to whom this power has been delegated by the Assembly. The Presbytery is also both a court of first instance and an appeal court. Its judgements are subject to review by the Assembly, or by Commissions as above. The Kirk Session is a court of first instance only. Its judgements are subject to review by the Presbytery of the bounds.

2. Commissions

Provision is made for the Commission of Assembly (Act V, 1981, as amended by Act V, 1994, and see also p. 89), the Judicial Commission (Act II, 1988), the Property Commission (Act XIII, 1992), and other Commissions appointed from time to time, to hear appeals on behalf of the Assembly, it having delegated its own powers to such Commissions. The Commission of Assembly may also act as a court of first instance. Except where express provision has been made to the contrary, procedure in such Commissions is as in the Assembly itself.

3. Committee on Bills and Overtures

When the papers in a case for the Assembly are lodged with the Clerks, they submit them in the first instance to the Committee on Commissions (the Clerks, Procurator, and Solicitor), known for this purpose as the Committee on Bills and Overtures, which decides whether the case should be transmitted to the Assembly, or whether it is so manifestly incompetent that it should not be transmitted, or whether it should be transmitted under reservation of competence; and it reports accordingly on the first day of the Assembly.

If the decision is not to transmit, the parties are entitled to appear at the bar when the report is presented, and put the case for transmission. At this stage, only the question of competence is before the Assembly. If the papers have not been printed, the report should give sufficient indication of their substance to enable the Assembly to consider the competence of the case.

If the decision is to transmit under reservation of competence, the question of competence is not discussed when the report is presented, but is raised at the time appointed for hearing the case.

4. Parties at the Bar

In judicial proceedings, parties are at the bar, which means that if they are members of the court hearing the case they are not permitted to act as such during that case, even if they are not literally at the bar as representatives of the appellants or respondents, or petitioners, but they are not normally required to leave. In an appeal court this includes all members of the court who are also members of the court against whose judgement the appeal is taken. The same is true of review initiated by petition. This is an application of the rule of natural justice that no-one should be a judge in his or her own cause.

A member of a court, who is also a member of a committee appointed by that court, is not for that reason at the bar in judicial proceedings, even if actions by that committee are germane to the case. A committee, being an arm of the court, has as such no interest apart from the interest of the court appointing it, so that members of a committee are not judges in their own cause when acting as members of the court. When so acting, they are not bound to support the actions of the committee concerned.

5. Procedure in Judicial Cases

a) Counsel or Solicitors

Parties in cases before Presbyteries or the Assembly (or the Commission of Assembly, or the Judicial Commission) may be represented by counsel or solicitors, unless such court determines otherwise (but the permission is not qualified in the case of the Judicial Commission: Act II, 1988). They are not entitled to such representation before Kirk Sessions, except with the special permission of such court. When they are so represented they are not permitted to speak themselves, unless called as witnesses (see Plan of Union, section on Discipline, p 171).

b) Citation

Parties in a case should be duly cited, and if witnesses are to be called, they should also be duly cited. Cox (pp. 335-337) states that the Church has not prescribed any forms for this purpose, and goes on to suggest some, whose wording might now be regarded as outmoded. The essentials are that a citation may be delivered personally by an officer of the court duly appointed by the court and with written authorisation, or it may be sent by registered letter or recorded delivery, in which case there must be, on the outside of the envelope, a notice to the effect that the contents are a citation to the court concerned, and that if it cannot be delivered it is to be returned immediately to the Clerk of the court.

Other forms of citation are *apud acta*, which means citing a person in the presence of the court, and edictal citation, which is by public notice.

If parties fail to appear they may be dealt with as contumacious. If witnesses fail to appear after three citations, application may be made to a civil court for a warrant ordaining them to appear.

The citation itself must state that it is issued by authority of the court, and cite the person named to attend the court on a specified date and at a specified time, to bear true witness in the case in question which must also be specified.

c) Contentious Cases

In contentious cases, only those members of a court who have heard all the pleadings are entitled to vote, and their decision as to how to vote must be based only on the pleadings. A member of the court who has arrived late, or who has left during the proceedings and returned before their conclusion, is nevertheless entitled to participate, but not to vote, and is therefore precluded from moving a motion.

In the Assembly, corresponding members (except those representing committees, unless their committees' remits relate to the case) are entitled to participate in cases as in other business, but delegates from other Churches, whose status is in other respects the same as that of corresponding members, are not entitled to take any part in cases.

6. Petition

Petition is a formal method of approaching a court requesting it to take some action. It is a document which sets out briefly the reasons for seeking the action, and concludes with a crave, which specifies the action requested. A petition should be lodged with the Clerk of the court being petitioned, in accordance with the standing orders of that court, certifying where appropriate that intimation has been given to interested parties. The standing orders of the Assembly should be followed, where applicable, in petitions to inferior courts which do not have their own standing orders.

a) Members of Court as Petitioners

Petitioners who are members of the court being petitioned are at the bar of that court. For this reason among others, this kind of petition should not be confused with the kind of petition to which signatures are sought in large numbers. In one case, members of a Kirk Session, who wanted the Session to take a particular action in a controversial situation, prepared a petition and gathered signatures from members of the congregation. They also signed the petition themselves, the result of which was that they were all at the bar of the Session when the petition was taken, and had thus disenfranchised themselves. In that case the Session was gracious enough to allow them to withdraw their signatures at the last minute, so that they could take part in the discussion; but it would have been better if the elders concerned had not signed in the first place.

b) Legitimate Petitioners

Anyone who can show a legitimate interest in the action requested is entitled to petition a church court. It is not necessary for the petitioner to be a member of the Church, and the petitioner can be an individual or a corporate body. The Assembly has received petitions from the Free Presbyterian Church, and from the Grand Orange Lodge.

Petition is the correct course for a Presbytery seeking action by the Assembly on some matter concerning its own responsibilities and jurisdiction, or within its bounds.

If a Presbytery is seeking some change in the law or policy of the Church, the proper course is to proceed by overture rather than petition, although a petition would not be out of order. Normally a Presbytery will choose overture, because then its commissioners will not be at the bar of the Assembly.

c) Proper Form

The proper form of a petition is:

> Unto the Venerable [for inferior courts, Reverend] the General Assembly of the Church of Scotland —
> The Petition of [name(s) of person(s) or body]
> Humbly sheweth —
> [Succinct statement of facts and reasons, preferably in numbered paragraphs]

May it therefore please your Venerable [Reverend] Court to [state action desired, in precise terms], or to do otherwise as to your Venerable [Reverend] Court may seem good. And your petitioner(s) will ever pray.

Individual petitioners sign at the end. In the case of a corporate body, the signature and designation of an office-bearer (or of more than one), who will present the petition, should be appended. The concluding words express an attitude of deference and of waiting.

Procedure for lodging petitions is set out in the Standing Orders of the Assembly, and this should be followed, so far as applicable, in petitions to inferior courts, unless these have their own standing orders.

d) Intimation to other Parties

An important proviso is that petitioners must give timeous intimation to any parties having an interest in the substance of the petition, so that they may apply to be heard at the bar and, if so advised, lodge answers. If such intimation has not been given, the court may decline to receive the petition, or sist procedure until timeous intimation has been given.

e) Procedure

The first question in hearing a petition is whether or not it should be read. Normally it is in print and may be taken as read. This question is a formality, in that it would be unreasonable not to hear at least enough of the substance to enable a decision to be made.

The next question is whether or not the petition should be received, and this is the point at which the question of competence may be discussed, even if the petition has not been transmitted under reservation of competence. This must not involve a discussion of the merits, which may take place only if the petition is received. However, a court is not bound to receive a petition even if it is technically or formally competent, if in the opinion of the court the substance is trivial, offensive, or otherwise inappropriate. Entitlement to present a petition does not include a right to have a petition received. The court is master of its own agenda, and may simply consider that the best interests of the Church would not be served if a particular petition were received.

When a petition has been received, parties are heard, the court may ask questions, and then parties are removed and motions called for. Motions must relate to the crave, e.g., that the crave be granted, or granted to a limited extent, or not granted.

After debate and voting, parties are recalled and judgement is intimated.

7. Reference

When an inferior court is unable to reach a decision on any matter, including a judgement in judicial proceedings, it may refer this to the immediately superior court for decision. A reference would also be appropriate, for example, if a Presbytery were considering a matter of principle in which the whole Church had an interest. It is a formal way of seeking a decision from a higher authority. In some disciplinary matters a Kirk Session is required to refer a case to the Presbytery (see Plan of Union, section on Discipline, summarising part of the *Form of Process, 1707*, p. 171; but see also Chapter XI, p. 64).

When a reference is stated in the superior court, the members of the inferior court are not at the bar, but, in a reference from a Presbytery to the Assembly, for example, a member of Presbytery who is not a commissioner may speak to the reference from the bar.

The first question in the superior court, after the reference has been stated, is whether or not to sustain it. This is not exactly the same as receiving a petition, because that question is one of competence and comes before parties have been heard. What is involved with regard to a reference is not so much a question of competence as of whether the superior court thinks the matter is appropriate for its consideration, which it decides after the reference has been stated.

Nevertheless, the question of competence can be raised in connection with a reference, as happened in a case referred to in Herron (p. 274), in which the matter referred to the Assembly was one on which the Presbytery had finality of judgement (1966. Sess. 11). Dr. Herron's view, which he expressed at the time, against that of the Procurator which the Assembly accepted, is that, while finality of judgement excludes the possibility of appeal, it should not be regarded as preventing a Presbytery, of its own free will, from seeking the help of higher authority. There is much to be said for Dr. Herron's view, and if the matter should arise again it should be remembered that the Assembly is not bound by its own precedents.

If the reference is sustained, the normal process of debate and motions follows until a conclusion is reached.

If the reference is not sustained, the matter goes back to the inferior court for decision.

A reference in terms of Act IV, 1984, is different (see below, p. 52).

8. Review

The Assembly's powers of judicial review extend not only to judgements of Presbyteries in judicial cases, but also to any decision of a Presbytery.

A Presbytery may review a judgement or decision of a Kirk Session; but a judgement or decision resulting from such review may then be taken for review to the Assembly.

"An appeal on part of a case or on a point of procedure does not sist procedure, so that it is not necessary to take such appeals, as they may be included when an appeal is taken on the merits against a judgement which issues a case in a lower court, but if they are taken they will be heard only when an appeal on the merits as above is taken" (Act VII, 1996).

9. No Review of Own Judgements

No court may review its own judicial judgements, but other decisions may be reviewed by the court which made them. Some Presbyteries have a provision in their standing orders to the effect that a decision may not be reviewed until a certain time has elapsed, such as six months. This is a wise administrative rule, to prevent the same subject being debated again and again. Normally a decision should be reviewed, whether or not there is such a six-month or other rule, only if there is a substantial element of *res noviter* (which is an abbreviation of *res noviter veniens ad notitiam,* i.e. new matter coming to the notice of the court). It is for the court itself to decide whether or not to re-open a matter on this basis. If it resolves not to do so, that decision may be taken for review to a superior court; or if it decides to re-open the matter, and reaches a new decision which is either the same as or different from the original decision, the new decision may be taken for review to a superior court.

10. Basis of Review

In judicial cases, review will be on the basis of law, and of evidence recorded at the initial hearing. The appeal court has to judge whether the law was properly stated, interpreted, or applied, whether the evidence was sufficient to justify the judgement, or, in the case of an appeal against a censure, whether this censure was appropriate to the offence.

a) Not a Re-trial

The hearing of an appeal is not a re-trial of the case. "In an appeal, no document shall be read or shall appear among the papers of the court (printed or written) unless it was before the court of first instance, or was offered to it and rejected, and has thence come up regularly; and no person shall be allowed at the bar unless he was at the bar of the court of first instance, or applied to be so and was refused, and has thence come up regularly, or unless he is a member of the next inferior court, complaining in the regular manner" (Act XIX, 1889, see Appendix E). This restriction on documents clearly does not apply to the appeal itself, or to the relevant minutes, or record apart, of the proceedings leading to the judgement appealed against.

b) Evidence

The appeal court does not normally hear evidence again, and does not normally examine the original witnesses. In theory it is entitled to read a transcript or hear a recording of the original evidence, and is entitled to see all the documents in the original case, but there are practical limits to the amount of documentation which can be produced for all members of the court, and to the amount of time a court can spend on a case.

While provision is made in Act II, 1988, for the Judicial Commission to cite witnesses, where it "deems it necessary to hear evidence", and while this provision might be held to apply to appeals before the Assembly, this would nevertheless be an extraordinary procedure, and should be invoked only to clarify an ambiguous point in the original evidence, not to introduce completely new evidence.

If the appeal court is persuaded that new evidence exists, which was not available to the inferior court, or that the inferior court ignored evidence which was available to it, and that the nature of such new evidence is *prima facie* (at first sight, i.e. before full examination) such that it might substantially have affected the original judgement, it should send the case back to be tried again in the inferior court, with an instruction to hear such evidence.

c) Non-judicial Decisions

Review of decisions other than judgements in judicial cases may be on the basis of broader questions of policy and expediency, relating for example to the wisdom of uniting two congregations.

The value of using judicial review procedures even for non-judicial matters is that these procedures provide standards by which a fair hearing is given to both sides in any contentious matter, so that an impartial judgement may be reached.

11. Appeal — Dissent and Complaint

The process of judicial review is normally initiated by an appeal by a party who was at the bar of the court, or by a dissent and complaint by a member of the court. As the procedure for dissent and complaint is the same as for appeal, reference here to procedure for one may be taken as including the other.

An appeal is taken at the time of the judgement being intimated, or of the decision being reached, by the use of the words, "I protest for leave to appeal" (or "I dissent and protest for leave to complain"), followed by "I crave extracts." The 1994 Assembly decided that the practice of "taking instruments" should be discontinued.

The protest for leave is for leave to submit the actual appeal, with reasons, in writing within ten days. A court cannot refuse to allow an appeal.

a) Nomenclature

While Cox states that the use of the proper nomenclature (appeal, or dissent and complaint) is so important that either writing is incompetent and null for a person who ought to have used the other, the cases he quotes in support of this contention are more than a century old, and it may be presumed that a rigid application of this dictum would now be regarded as unduly legalistic, since the only difference between the two writings is that of nomenclature. It is a reasonable expectation that the court would, at the time of oral intimation, draw attention to any such mistaken nomenclature, so that the written document could be submitted in proper form; and it is also reasonable to assume that the Clerk of a court, on receiving a document in the wrong terms, would draw attention to this and give opportunity for the necessary correction.

b) Proper Times

If an appeal is not taken at the time when a judgement or decision is intimated, that judgement or decision becomes final, and subsequent appeal is incompetent. Herron (p. 266) points out that the Presbytery of Glasgow allows this before the end of the meeting at which the judgement was made, i.e. not necessarily immediately after the judgement. This appears to be, as he says, reasonable; and it is certainly within the competence of a Presbytery. However, this provision will not apply in Presbyteries which have not included it in their standing orders. Since an appeal may be withdrawn at any time, the safest course is to appeal at once, thereby allowing time in which to think about whether to proceed with that course.

The written document must be submitted to the Clerk of the court appealed against within ten days after, but not including, the day of the judgement or decision. The time limit cannot be extended, and if the written document is not submitted in time the appeal falls, and the judgement or decision becomes final. The reason for this is that it must be clearly known when a judgement has become final, so that it can be implemented without delay.

c) Sisting

An appeal sists the execution of the judgement or decision, but there may be, albeit rarely, circumstances in which such sisting would be unreasonable. For example, if a minister has been duly elected and called to a charge, and someone appears at the Presbytery meeting immediately prior to the induction, to object to the life or doctrine of the minister, the Presbytery must consider this objection (see Chapter XVI, p. 115). If the Presbytery decides that the objection cannot be sustained and the induction should proceed, the objector, not being a party, cannot appeal. However, if a member of the Presbytery, who was the only one to oppose the decision to proceed with the induction, dissents and complains, rigid application of the rule about sisting would mean that the induction could not proceed. The Presbytery could take the view that the dissent and complaint was so unreasonable that it should proceed to the induction in spite of it.

If, in such or similar circumstances, a Presbytery decides to implement a judgement in the face of a dissent and complaint, it may do so, but the dissent and complaint will still have to be heard by the Assembly (or the Commission of Assembly) and, if it is sustained, the consequences for the minister, the congregation, and the Presbytery, will be very serious. It could conceivably be held that the induction was null and void, but that would mean, for instance, that stipend had been illegally paid and would have to be returned. It would be better for the Assembly, if sustaining the dissent and complaint, to hold that the induction was nevertheless valid, but to instruct the Presbytery to proceed to a Trial by Libel (see Chapter X).

If the Presbytery is convinced that the dissent and complaint has no substance, it may consider that the risk of such serious consequences is minimal, and that the consequences of not proceeding to an induction would be unacceptable.

Accordingly, it may be said that a Presbytery is not absolutely bound to sist execution of a judgement in the face of an appeal, but it should certainly be extremely cautious in departing from the normal rule about sisting (see Notes on Act XIX, 1889, p. 181).

d) Procedure

In the Assembly, the documentation printed for members will be the written appeal, which should state reasons for appealing, which can be amplified by the appellant at the bar, and all the relevant extract minutes of the Presbytery. The respondent may also lodge written answers to the points made in the written appeal.

Parties are called, and identify themselves at the bar, and are then heard in the following order:

1. Appellant
2. Respondent
3. Appellant
4. Respondent, and if new matter is raised
5. The Appellant

Members of the court may then ask questions of the parties at the bar. These are purely to elicit relevant information, or for clarification. They should not be argumentative, nor should they call for opinions from the parties.

Parties are then removed, and motions called for. A court may insist that the parties should withdraw physically at this point, but it is normal in the Assembly for them to remain, without taking any further part in the proceedings.

Motions must be framed in such a way as to dispose of the judgement of the inferior court, i.e. to sustain the appeal and uphold the judgement of the inferior court, or to dismiss it and recall the judgement. They may go on to add a modification, usually introduced by "to the extent of. . ." They may include instructions to the parties.

If the appeal court believes that further investigation is required, it may appoint a commission with powers to issue the case, or it may continue the case and appoint a commission to investigate and report. The latter option has not been much used, because the normal rule is that, when a case is continued, the court adjourns to meet at a particular place and time, and only those who were present at the original hearing may participate in the case when the court re-convenes at that place and time. Nevertheless, it has been known for the Assembly to appoint a commission to report to the next Assembly. In such a case, all the papers before the Assembly should be re-issued to the next Assembly.

After debate and voting, parties are recalled and judgement is intimated.

12. Review by Petition

Judicial review may be initiated by a petition only if the petitioner was either unable to appeal or was obstructed in an attempt to do so. Since an appeal must be taken at the time of the judgement or decision, a party who is present and fails to appeal at that time, or who, after being duly cited to appear is nevertheless absent, cannot subsequently petition.

If a party attempts to appeal at the right time, but is ruled out of order, or if the court refuses to receive the appeal, petition would be the only way of seeking review, and it would in the first instance proceed on the basis of alleging that the attempt to appeal was obstructed.

It is highly unlikely that a superior court would receive a petition from a member of an inferior court seeking review of a decision made by that court in his or her absence, even if not cited as a party, since that petitioner, being a member of the inferior court, should have been present.

In the unlikely event of a person, not being a member of the court, and not having been cited to the bar, being able to show a legitimate interest in a decision or action, petition would be the only way of seeking review, and the petition should set forth the basis of claiming a legitimate interest. A possible basis for such a petition would be that the petitioner should have been cited to the bar and was not.

Petition to the Presbytery is the only way of seeking review of a decision of a congregational meeting.

When petition is appropriate for initiating review of a judgement, although there is no prescribed time after the judgement by which it should be initiated, the standing orders of the appeal court will usually prescribe a time by which it should be lodged before its next meeting, and it should in practice be lodged as soon as possible, with the Clerk of the superior court, and intimated at the same time to the inferior court.

While there appears to be no law to the effect that the lodging of a petition sists the decision in question, the inferior court, on receiving intimation, would be well advised to act on the assumption that the implementation of the decision is sisted, unless there are very strong grounds for implementing it before the petition can be disposed of.

Persons seeking review by petition of non-judicial decisions should consider whether the petition should in the first instance be directed to craving the court concerned to review its own decision.

In a petition for review, the normal procedure for petitions is followed.

13. Review by Reference

Another review procedure is provided for readjustment cases, in the form of reference. The normal use of reference is that an inferior court, being unable to reach a decision, refers the matter to a superior court. The readjustment form of reference is different, in that it comes into force when the Committee on Parish Re-appraisal has declined to concur in the decision of a Presbytery. Since the Committee is not a court of the Church, neither it nor the Presbytery can take the matter to the Assembly by appeal, and therefore the legislation provides for this to be done by reference.

There is provision for parties who would otherwise have had the right to appeal against the Presbytery's decision to be heard at the bar when the reference is stated. If the parties are actually in agreement with the Presbytery, and are in disagreement with the Committee's decision not to concur, they would not in fact have appealed against the Presbytery's decision, but in law they would still have had the right to do so, and it is this legal right which entitles them to appear at the bar in such circumstances. In short, parties representing congregations in such cases always have the right to appear at the Assembly.

In a readjustment reference in the Assembly there is an exception to the normal rule about parties being at the bar in contentious cases. The rules for ordinary reference apply, namely that no member of the Assembly is at the bar. The reason for this exception is that members of the Committee on Parish Reappraisal are not at the bar, and it would be unfair therefore to place members of the Presbytery at the bar in a case which is by definition contentious as between the Committee and the Presbytery.

14. *Nobile Officium*

A power peculiar to the Assembly in judicial matters, as far as the Church is concerned, though it belongs to supreme civil courts also, is the *nobile officium*. Cox states (p. 114) that it is a power "which would seem naturally and necessarily to belong to a supreme court, to determine and order such things as are necessary to be done in a pending case and for which there is no legal provision. It cannot overrule law, but only supply the want of it when necessary."

15. Protestations

At the closing session of the Assembly, protestations are called for. A protestation is made by a respondent in a case in which the other party has failed to prosecute an appeal or complaint, and is a way of recording that the decision of the inferior court has therefore become final.

VIII. LEGISLATION

1. Legislature

The General Assembly is the Church's legislature. When acting within the terms of the *Declaratory Articles*, as interpreted by the Assembly itself, its legislation is not subject to review by any other body, ecclesiastical or civil.

2. Limitations

There are however certain limitations on the power of the Assembly, which prevent us from speaking of the "sovereignty" of the Assembly. Because it must act within the terms of the Church's constitution, as set out in the *Declaratory Articles*, it is not sovereign in the same way as Parliament is considered to be in the civil sphere (see Chapter III, p. 17).

The major limitation on the power of the Assembly is that it cannot amend *Article I,* although it has the right to interpret it.

A further limitation is that a special procedure is required for the amendment of any of the other *Articles.* An Overture to amend any of these requires to be approved by the Assembly, then by two-thirds of the Presbyteries, again by the Assembly and again by two-thirds of the Presbyteries, and finally by the Assembly for a third time, so that the process takes two years and is clearly a deliberate decision. *Article VIII* prescribes this procedure. The only Act passed by this procedure is Act V, 1992, abolishing Synods.

These limitations have not however been imposed on the Church by any external authority. They were passed by the Assembly with the consent of a majority of Presbyteries under the Barrier Act (see below).

The Barrier Act itself provides another limitation on the power of the Assembly to legislate, although it is not, strictly speaking, part of the constitution of the Church. In theory it could be repealed, but only by following the procedure it prescribes.

There are other less formal limitations. The Assembly is internally limited by its own nature. That is to say, all the members of the Assembly have taken vows at ordination or commissioning, and are therefore prevented by conscience from acting in ways contrary to these vows, even if such actions were legally possible. This limitation is recognised in the formal constituting of the Assembly with prayer.

There is also an external limitation in that the Assembly has no means ultimately of enforcing a legislative Act of such an unpopular nature that it would not be respected. There is a sense in which Synods had become an example of this. They had so outlived their usefulness that they were very poorly attended, despite a formal obligation on all members to attend. That obligation could not reasonably be enforced, and this situation contributed to the Assembly's decision to abolish Synods. One reason for the enactment of the Barrier Act was to reduce the likelihood of unenforceable legislation.

Despite the various limitations, the legislative powers of the Assembly are large; and there is no possibility of independent judicial review of legislation, since the Assembly is also the supreme judicature.

There is however an important qualification, namely that the powers of the Assembly must be exercised within its own constitution, and although the interpretation of that constitution is a matter on which the Church is sole judge, a question could conceivably arise as to whether a particular interpretation was in fact more than an interpretation. In such a case it is still possible that a civil court would consider itself competent to intervene.

3. The Barrier Act (see Appendix A)

The Barrier Act of 1697 provides that certain kinds of legislation cannot be enacted without the prior approval of a majority of Presbyteries. The reasons given in the Act itself for this provision are "that it will mightily conduce to the exact obedience of the Acts of Assemblies"; and "for preventing any sudden alteration or innovation, or other prejudice to the Church." This gives formal recognition to the fact that it would be bad practice to enact legislation which was liable to be ignored and disobeyed. Its purpose is not to prevent alteration and innovation as such, but to ensure that "General Assemblies be very deliberate in making of the same."

It should also be noted that the Act, in referring to the "whole Church" having previous knowledge of proposed changes, and such changes being made only "if the more general opinion of the Church" had agreed to them, regards

Presbyteries as representing the whole Church and its more general opinion. While Presbyteries may seek the views of Kirk Sessions, these have no formal place in Barrier Act procedure, and the Act provides no warrant for any kind of referendum of members of the Church.

a) Application of Barrier Act

Barrier Act procedure applies to proposed Acts on doctrine, worship, discipline and government of the Church which are to be "binding Rules and Constitutions to the Church." Any proposed Act which, in the opinion of the Assembly, falls into any of these categories must be approved as an Overture by the Assembly and then sent down to Presbyteries. Other proposed Acts may be sent down to Presbyteries, at the discretion of the Assembly.

In deciding whether or not a proposed Act requires Barrier Act procedure, the Assembly will of course be governed by the terms of the Act. In the event of any doubt about whether these terms apply, the Assembly must decide. Cox (p. 16) quotes Mair as saying, "the Assembly is the interpreter of its own laws."

In one recent case, the Assembly set up a new body, the Assembly Council. At the next Assembly it was successfully argued that this should have been done by Barrier Act procedure, and an appropriate Overture was accordingly sent down to Presbyteries. The majority approved, and the Assembly Council was reinstated the following year, after a year of suspended animation, by Act VI, 1980. The constitution of the Assembly Council was radically changed in 1996, and the 1980 Act was repealed without Barrier Act procedure.

The above case illustrates that one Assembly is not bound by the decisions of a previous Assembly on the matter of the application of the Barrier Act. Accordingly, the fact that an Act was enacted by Barrier Act procedure does not mean that it may be amended or repealed only by the same procedure. [As one Procurator put it, informally, the fact that you used a sledgehammer to crack a nut last time does not mean that you must use it again this time!]

This may be further illustrated by reference to legislation anent the Presbytery of Europe. Act V, 1978, passed by Barrier Act procedure, had three Schedules attached to it, and specifically provided that these could be amended without reference to Presbyteries under the Barrier Act. There appeared to be a clear implication that the Act itself could not be so amended. Nevertheless, Act III, 1996, which is a substantial revision of the 1978 Act, and includes a section repealing that Act, was not sent down under the Barrier Act.

If an Overture fails to obtain the approval of a majority of Presbyteries, it falls, and may not be sent down again in the same form by the next Assembly. If it obtains such approval the next Assembly may enact it, but need not do so. Thus the Presbyteries have a collective power of veto, but not a power to require the Assembly to enact legislation.

b) Returns from Presbyteries

The decisions of the Presbyteries are reported to the Assembly by the Committee for Classifying Returns to Overtures. The report gives the numbers of Presbyteries approving and disapproving, and also the total number of members of Presbyteries approving and disapproving. It is the first of these figures which is legally determinative, each Presbytery counting as one, regardless of its size; but the second figure may be taken into account when the Assembly is deciding whether or not to convert the Overture into an Act.

Presbyteries are required to make returns, but in the event of any not doing so the majority required is of the whole number of Presbyteries, not just those who have made returns.

In making returns, Presbyteries are permitted to send comments, the formal term for this being that such returns are transmitted *"cum nota"*. If an approving Presbytery makes a comment which makes its approval conditional on amendment of the substance of the Overture, or which manifestly contradicts the formal approval, it must be counted as disapproving.

No Overture which has the approval of a majority of Presbyteries may be amended by the Assembly before enactment, unless the amendment is such that it does not alter the substance of the Overture. Thus a purely verbal amendment for the purpose of greater clarity is acceptable.

c) Interim Act

When an Overture is approved for sending down to Presbyteries it may be passed as an Interim Act, which will be as binding as any other Act, but only until the next Assembly. It would obviously be unwise to take this course in a controversial matter which might not receive the necessary approval from Presbyteries, because a change in the law for one year only would not be conducive to good order.

When an Overture has received the necessary approval, but the Assembly is of a mind to amend its substance in some respect, a possible course of action is to amend the Overture, and send the amended Overture to Presbyteries, meanwhile making it also an Interim Act. This has not been done recently, but there are precedents for it in earlier legislation.

4. Acts and Regulations

Legislative Acts of Assembly are laws which are to have continuing effect, until amended or repealed. They are numbered and printed separately each year, and are referred to by number and year, e.g. "Act V, 1984." Regulations differ from Acts only in the nature of their contents. They control administrative arrangements, whereas Acts deal with more fundamental matters. For example, it is an Act which determines the membership of the Assembly, but Regulations lay down the procedure for nominating the Moderator. Anything which is passed by Barrier Act procedure is always an Act.

5. Repeals

A legislative Act is required to repeal a law which is still in force. It is good practice to specify what is being repealed. A phrase such as "all previous legislation inconsistent with this Act is hereby repealed" is sometimes found, but it creates difficulties in identifying what has been repealed, especially if the Act with that clause in it is itself subsequently repealed. It is clear that an Act which has been specifically repealed is not reinstated when the Act repealing it is repealed, and presumably the same would be true of unspecified repeals, if they could be identified.

A legal curiosity occurred in Act XXIV, 1961, which, making some constitutional changes in the rules about membership of Presbyteries, purported to repeal Act I, 1929, "in so far as it is inconsistent with the provisions of this Act" — Act I, 1929 being the Basis and Plan of Union. Act XXIV, 1961, was itself subsequently repealed. A similar provision appears in Act XXVIII, 1966, anent the admission of women to the eldership.

A general repeal of this kind is however implied even if not stated, in that a later Act will prevail over an earlier one which is inconsistent with it. So, for example, in the case of membership of Presbyteries, there is no doubt that the current legislation prevails over the terms of Act I, 1929, with which it is inconsistent (but see below, p. 60 for exceptions with regard to the *Declaratory Articles*, legislation passed under Barrier Act procedure, and law which has come into force by consuetude).

6. Declaratory Acts

The chief use of declaratory legislation is to declare doctrinal standards (e.g. Appendix C), but there have been times when it has been expedient to clarify or consolidate practice by declaratory legislation. A declaratory Act of the latter kind may affirm or repudiate consuetude. It does not make new law, but declares what the law already is.

The law may be declared in ways other than the passing of declaratory Acts. In a case in 1976, the Assembly, by deliverance, made a doctrinal statement about baptism; and, in responding to an overture in 1988, it passed a deliverance affirming the eligibility of an Interim Moderator or *locum tenens* in a vacancy (see p. 115) to be appointed to the vacant charge. Such deliverances are to be regarded as authoritative interpretations of the law, but it may be suggested that it would be better practice to make such interpretations by declaratory legislation.

7. Permissive Law

Law may also be permissive, in that it clarifies some area of doubt about what may be done, rather than prescribing what must be done. An example of this is the affirmation referred to above, that an Interim Moderator or a *locum tenens* in a vacant congregation is not *ipso facto* debarred from receiving a call to be minister of that congregation.

8. Conditional Law

Another type of legislation might be described as conditional. That is to say, the rules state in effect that if a person wants to do something, there is a proper procedure which must be followed. For example, the rules for entering the ministry apply only to those who are seeking to become ministers and to those who supervise the process; and the procedure for taking an appeal against a judgement of a court applies only to those who want to appeal, and to those who must then deal with the appeal.

9. Deliverances

When the Assembly orders a particular action at a particular time, it does not normally pass an Act or Regulation, but passes a deliverance instructing that action. Each year, in the deliverances passed on the Reports of various committees there are usually several instructions to Presbyteries to take particular actions, and sometimes these are accompanied by a further instruction to report their actions to the secretary of the committee concerned, so that a report may be made by that committee to the next Assembly. Likewise, the Assembly may instruct committees to act and to report.

Occasionally the Assembly has passed deliverances which are general instructions, such as a ban on using church funds to provide alcohol. It would be better practice to pass such instructions as legislative Acts, but the fact that this has not been done does not affect the validity of the instructions.

While all instructions are to be obeyed, there is a form of emphatic instruction, namely an injunction. If a court or individual fails to do what is enjoined, such failure may be taken as contumacy, which is a serious offence and may lead to disciplinary procedure.

10. Obedience

Acts, Regulations, Instructions, and Injunctions are all to be obeyed, but the Assembly may choose to urge or invite inferior courts to take actions, and in these cases obedience is not required, but the matter must be considered.

11. Interpretation

The interpretation of church law begins with the actual and literal meaning of the words used. In good law, the words used embody and express the spirit of the law. Plain meaning cannot however be ignored, and questions of interpretation arise only if the words used are ambiguous, in which case the spirit of the law is a criterion of construction. For example, if a section of an Act is found to be ambiguous, it should be interpreted in terms of the perceived purpose of the Act as a whole.

There is a general rule that reference to things said in the debate when an Act was passed is not in order for purposes of interpretation, because those who voted for the actual wording may have done so for reasons other than some of the statements made in its support, and unscripted speeches and spontaneous responses to questions will not normally have the same precision of language as a draft Act or proposed deliverance.

Nevertheless, if the wording of part of an Act is considered to be ambiguous, and the spirit of the law is not manifest from the text of the whole Act, it is not unreasonable to look to the printed text of the report submitted to the Assembly by the committee which sponsored the legislation. For example, the operative section of Act XXV, 1968, is, "Women shall be eligible for ordination to the Holy Ministry on the same terms and conditions as are at present applicable to men." It is not unreasonable to infer from the report that the purpose of this was to implement the doctrinal statement that, in virtue of their baptism, men and women, as members of the Church, have equal rights and status.

The general presumption mentioned above (p. 58) that a later Act will prevail over an earlier one with which its terms are inconsistent, even if it does not specifically repeal that Act or any part of it, is subject to the fact that there are different kinds of law in the Church. It is clear, for example, that any Act must be construed in a manner consistent with the *Declaratory Articles*, and cannot prevail over them. Also, an Act passed under the Barrier Act should prevail, for purposes of interpretation, over Acts not so passed. This latter criterion should certainly be applied by inferior courts, but in the Assembly it is subject to the proviso that the Assembly may decide that an Act passed under the Barrier Act does not require Barrier Act procedure for its amendment or repeal.

It can also be argued that certain rights which exist by consuetude are superior to ordinary legislation, so that a subsequent Act cannot be construed in a manner inconsistent with them. For example, the general provision in Act IV, 1984, Section 4(e), that the Presbytery has an ultimate right to impose readjustment should not be construed to include the right to create a union which has the effect of imposing the minister of one congregation on a vacant one, against the will of the vacant one, because that would contravene what is regarded as a very important tradition which has become law by consuetude, namely that a congregation has a right of call. The general provision, lacking in specification at this point, is not sufficient to set aside this right. [This opinion has not been tested in any case coming to the Assembly. Since any attempt by a Presbytery to impose a minister in this way would almost certainly lead to an appeal, the fact that no such case has come to the Assembly suggests that Presbyteries have acted on the assumption that the right of call prevails in the interpretation of ordinary legislation.]

The importance of the right of call is indicated by the fact that Barrier Act procedure has been judged to be necessary in order to set it aside in particular circumstances, as in specific provisions in Acts IV and V, 1984, and Act IX, 1996. It is only when permission to call has been granted, in terms of these Acts, either in the form of a free call to a vacant congregation, or following some form of readjustment, that the right of call, as opposed to having a minister imposed, comes into operation.

The final authority for the interpretation of legislation is the Assembly, but an inferior court may proceed, subject to appeal, on the basis of its own interpretation. Interpretation is a matter for the court, not for a ruling by its Moderator. The Clerk of a court may express an opinion, but that is not a ruling. The Principal Clerk of the Assembly may, if asked, give guidance in the form of an opinion, but not a ruling.

12. The Spirit of the Law

The general spirit of church law could be stated as "the repression of vice and the nourishment of virtue" (*The Scots Confession*, see Chapter IX), together with doing all things decently and in order; and the spirit in which it should be applied is normally pastoral. It is a matter of shepherding the flock in the ways of righteousness.

For example, the law (Act XVII, 1963) provides a norm to the effect that one parent at least should be a member of the Church before a child is baptised, but it also provides for a baptism in anticipation of parents being shepherded in. Thus, when this law is properly applied, people are not turned away, but shown the way in and encouraged to take it. The spirit of the law points to the way in which the letter should be applied.

There is also a sense in which going beyond what the letter of the law requires involves going beyond what even the spirit of the law requires. Consider the law that a minister is responsible to the Presbytery, not to the Kirk Session, for everything to do with the conduct of worship. The spirit of that law is that the minister, not only as a person educated for leadership in theology and liturgy, but also as a person ordained by a Presbytery as a minister of Word and Sacraments, must be free to conduct worship in accordance with conviction and conscience, which is part of the nourishment of virtue. If a minister nevertheless chooses to consult the Kirk Session about matters of worship, that is not against the law, and it might be considered a very wise thing; but the Kirk Session has no right to expect such consultation, and there is no ground for disciplinary action against the minister on the basis of lack of consultation. However, the law does provide that, in matters of worship, the minister is not to introduce innovations which are causes of division in the congregation, and the Presbytery is bound to take action if this is done (see Chapter V, p. 30).

IX. DISCIPLINE

1. Two Meanings

There are two senses in which the term "discipline" is used in the Church. The first refers to the government, structure and organisation of the Church, and it includes the second, which refers to the ways in which the Church deals with offenders.

The first usage was the earlier one, as used by the Reformers. *The Scots Confession* of 1560 spoke of "ecclesiastical discipline uprightlie ministered, as Goddis Worde prescribes, whereby vice is repressed and vertew nurished", the repression of vice and the nourishment of virtue, being set side by side as the purpose of institutional church structures. This was amplified in *The First Book of Discipline*, and *The Second Book of Discipline*. They are concerned with such things as doctrine, policy, appointment of ministers and provision for them, schools and universities, and duties of civil magistrates, as well as with procedures for dealing with offenders.

The *Declaratory Articles* speak of "doctrine, worship, government, and discipline" as being the areas in which the Church has exclusive jurisdiction, and it is clear that "discipline" is used there in the narrower sense of dealing with offences and imposing censures, distinguished from government.

The whole of the present volume is about discipline in the broader sense; but this chapter is about discipline in the narrower sense.

2. Disciplinary Functions of Courts

Discipline is the exclusive prerogative of church courts, and of commissions to which the Assembly has delegated powers. No other body can exercise discipline.

3. Kirk Sessions

In earlier times, much of the business of Kirk Sessions was disciplinary. Parishioners were brought before the Kirk Session, tried, and punished for various offences, such as those mentioned in the headings of two chapters in the *Form of Process* of 1707: "Concerning Swearers, Cursers, Profaners of the Lord's Day, Drunkards, and other Scandals of that Nature", and "Concerning the Sin of Fornication, Adultery, and Scandalous Carriage tending thereto."

Some sins were considered to be so serious that the Kirk Session had to refer cases about them to the Presbytery, and these included "incest . . . trilapses in fornication, murder, atheism, idolatry, witchcraft, charming, and heresy and error vented and made public by any in the congregation, schism and separation from the public ordinances."

Kirk Sessions have long since ceased to deal with these things by judicial process, and any sinful actions coming to the notice of a Kirk Session are normally referred to the minister, to be dealt with pastorally. Accordingly, the disciplinary procedures in Kirk Sessions are largely of historical interest, and there is no need to detail them here.

4. Removal from Roll or Office

The removal of names from the Communion Roll is a matter of pastoral supervision rather than of discipline. The procedure for this is set out in Act VI, 1938, as amended by several subsequent Acts, and should be carefully followed. Removal from the Roll does not involve excommunication, or any other censure.

Act IX, 1933 provides for removing an elder from office in a congregation (i.e. removal from membership of the Kirk Session, not deposition from the office of elder) for non-attendance. If a Kirk Session wants to remove an elder from office for any other reason, the procedure will depend on the nature of the reason, which will determine the manner of removal.

In a case such as one of neglect of duties other than attendance at meetings, for example, removal from membership of the Kirk Session *simpliciter* (by itself) would probably suffice. In such a case the Kirk Session should be careful to give adequate notice of its intention, and the reasons for it, to the elder concerned, citing him or her to appear, and affording every opportunity of stating a defence. Such removal from membership of a Kirk Session would not amount to suspension or deposition from the office of the eldership, and so it would not affect the elder's ordained status. Such an elder, on transferring to membership of another congregation, would be legally eligible for admission to the Kirk Session of that congregation

In a case involving immorality or defective doctrine, suspension from office, or, in more serious cases, deposition from office, would be appropriate. Certain very serious cases require to be taken to the Presbytery by reference, and in other cases this option is open to a Kirk Session.

In 1976, the case of an elder who had undergone "second baptism" was referred by a Kirk Session to the Presbytery, whose decision was that the elder had failed to fulfil his ordination vows and could not continue in membership of the Kirk Session. The Synod sustained an appeal against this judgement, and the Presbytery appealed to the Assembly. In sustaining this appeal and recalling the decision of the Synod, the Assembly *inter alia* instructed the Presbytery along with the minister and Kirk Session to confer with the elder "with a view to persuading him solemnly and sincerely to repent of his error; otherwise to apprise him of his ineligibility to continue as a member of the Kirk Session." In such a case, ineligibility to be a member of one Kirk Session clearly implied ineligibility to be a member of any Kirk Session.

The options before a Kirk Session in such a case are:

1) to accept a solemn and sincere repentance and take no further action;
2) to accept the elder's resignation;
3) to suspend the elder from office until such time as he does repent; or
4) to depose the elder from office.

In the event of a Kirk Session wanting to take up a serious case of discipline, it should refer to the Presbytery Clerk for guidance about procedure.

5. Presbyteries

Presbyteries still occasionally find it necessary to embark on formal disciplinary proceedings involving ministers, probationers, and licentiates, the procedure being that of Trial by Libel (see next Chapter).

(See also pp. 171-174)

X. TRIAL BY LIBEL

A. PROCEDURE

B. EVIDENCE

A. PROCEDURE

1. Definition

Trial by Libel is the process by which a Presbytery proceeds when a minister or probationer is accused of a censurable offence. *The Form of Process* states that "nothing ought to be admitted by any Church judicatory as the ground of a process for censure, but what hath been declared censurable by the Word of God, or some act or universal custom of this National Church." This is still the case. The libel is a statement of the alleged offence.

It should be noted that, at the time of the relevant legislation, there was no legal difference between a probationer and a licentiate, and this process applies to licentiates even if they are not probationers according to current definitions. It may be presumed that the process would apply also to deacons.

2. Fama

A Trial by Libel follows a *"fama"*, which is defined by Cox (Glossary, p. 827) as a "scandalous report". It is an allegation of censurable conduct. In the normal case, the initiative is taken by the person alleging the conduct in question, who reports it formally to the Presbytery, and the Presbytery acts in response to that. However, the Presbytery must do so carefully (Act VII, 1935, Section 1).

A *fama clamosa* is an allegation which is so public or notorious that the Presbytery is bound to take action in the interests of the Church, even if no formal report has been received.

3. The 1935 Act

The procedure is set out in detail in Act VII, 1935, and should be carefully followed. It is not proposed to summarise or paraphrase that Act here, but rather to draw attention to certain important considerations in connection with it.

The Act is one of those which states that "all prior Acts of Assembly in so far as any of the provisions thereof are inconsistent with this Act are hereby repealed." This means *inter alia* that parts of the *Form of Process* (XI, 1707) which was the foundation document in matters of discipline, no longer apply.

Furthermore, the possibility that the *Form of Process* has been modified by consuetude is recognised in the *Declaratory Articles* (*Article II*), and Cox (p. 12) states that "the changes produced by the lapse of time in the manners and customs of the people and the moral standards of life, which are to some extent dependent thereon, have largely rendered out of date the *Form of Process*."

Cox (p. 321) nevertheless quotes the *Form of Process* as saying, "If the accused confess and the matter confessed be of a scandalous nature, such as the sin of uncleanness, or some other gross scandal (whatever be the nature of his penitence, though all be convinced of it), the Presbytery is *instanter* to depose him *ab officio*" (instantly to depose him from office). It may safely be stated that, in view of what has been said above with regard to consuetude and changes produced by the lapse of time, a Presbytery is not now absolutely required to impose this instant censure.

The position may best be stated by saying that the Church's disciplinary procedures are derived from, but no longer literally prescribed by, the *Form of Process*. Act VII, 1935, is however undoubtedly prescriptive, but it should be read and interpreted in relation to certain provisions in the Plan of Union, 1929, in its section on Discipline (see Appendix B, pp. 171-174).

4. The Plan of Union

The Plan states that "it is the right of the courts of the Church to adjudicate in all matters of discipline, and the court should not be both prosecutor and judge." It also states that "the difficulties occasioned by the numerical size ought to be recognised, and such procedures adopted as will ensure that findings on matters of probation will be reached only by those who have heard the whole of the case." It goes on to provide that there shall be a Committee on Cases which, in a Trial by Libel, shall prepare the libel and prosecute the case. It also requires a Presbytery to commit the hearing of evidence to a committee of its own number, or to a panel of, say, three or five of its own number and two Assessors, appointed from a Committee of Assessors.

The 1935 Act however requires the Presbytery to prepare the libel, and gives it the options of prosecuting the case itself or of inviting the Committee on Law, Property Cases and Discipline to do so, if that committee shall so decide; but that committee is no longer in existence, so that option has fallen. It also gives the Presbytery the option of committing the conduct of the Trial to a committee of its own number, with or without Assessors from the Board of Assessors, whose place in this respect has now been taken by the Board of Practice and Procedure (see below, p. 70).

It is clear that the provisions of the 1935 Act must prevail against those of the Plan, but an important question of principle is raised as to the extent to which the 1935 Act may be seen to have departed from the provision that the court should not be both prosecutor and judge, for this provision is one of the basic precepts of natural justice.

It can be argued that church procedures are inquisitorial rather than adversarial, meaning that the nature of the case is not that the court is adjudicating on a contest between prosecution and defence as adversaries, but is conducting its own inquiry into the matter. Apart from the fact that "inquisitorial" has unfortunate associations in a church context, it must be recognised that, while the point might be valid in relation to the Preliminary Inquiry required by the Act, the Act provides for the appointment of "prosecutors" by the Presbytery, and speaks also of the accused having the right to appoint agents or counsel "for his defence."

The Act requires the Presbytery to appoint "suitable persons" to act as prosecutors in the case, specifying that they should be members of the Presbytery. Moreover, the Act clearly regards the prosecutors as "parties" in the case.

In these circumstances it would be of the utmost importance to ensure that the prosecutors, being parties, should be at the bar, and should take no other part in the case. Although the Act does not specifically state this, the use of the term "parties" implies it. It would be in order for any of those who conducted the Preliminary Inquiry to be appointed as prosecutors.

Although again the Act does not specifically require it, there must a presumption that, if the Presbytery remits the Trial to a committee, no person involved in the Preliminary Inquiry should be appointed to this committee.

The safest course would be for a Presbytery to exercise the options of having both the Preliminary Inquiry and the Trial conducted by committees, ensuring that no member of the first was a member of the second; and further to ensure that, when the second committee submits its report to the Presbytery, the prosecutors are still at the bar.

5. The 1889 Act

Another relevant Act which is still in force is Act XIX, 1889, as amended by III, 1981, "on Forms of Procedure in Trial by Libel and in Causes [cases] generally", whose purpose was "to simplify certain forms and procedure now in use." As this Act is not printed in the loose-leaf book of *Acts of the General Assembly from 1929*, it is included as an appendix to this volume (Appendix E).

The older form of libel had to begin with a "major premise, setting forth the kind, criminality, and punishableness of the offence." One of the provisions of the 1889 Act was that this major premise could be omitted, and would be implied if it were omitted. So now "it shall be sufficient that a libel sets forth facts which constitute a censurable offence." Several styles for a libel were appended to this Act, but Act VII, 1935, offers only one style, with a note referring to the 1889 styles.

6. The Libel

The style in the Schedule to the 1935 Act includes the words, "specify clearly and shortly the offence charged." In order that the charge may be relevant, the libel must set forth:

1) the time of the offence,
2) the place of the offence, and
3) the particular facts inferring guilt.

The time of the offence may not be capable of precise specification, in which case a latitude of time is permissible. For example, a witness may be able to relate an event only to a particular month, in which case the specification of time would be expressed as being between the first and last days of that month. Similarly, if there has been a course of conduct over a period of time, it is appropriate to libel the conduct complained of as taking place "on several occasions" between two dates.

The libel should not specify the evidence to be led, but merely the facts which are supported by the evidence and which are necessary to constitute the offence.

The importance of having the libel in proper form is emphasised by the provision that a libel framed by a Presbytery must be submitted to the Procurator for revision before it is served. Essentially the Procurator will be looking for three things:

1) that, *prima facie* at least, the evidence is sufficient to warrant the charges made,

2) that the draft libel meets the requirements as to specification of time and place, and

3) that the libel sets forth facts sufficient to constitute a censurable offence.

The point of qualifying the Procurator's rôle by the words "*prima facie*" above is that, in certain kinds of cases relevancy may be the main point of dispute. Granted that heresy is a censurable offence, the facts set out in support of the charge may not be in dispute, but the question as to whether they amount to heresy may be hotly disputed. This is a question which must be decided by the Presbytery.

7. Censurable Offences

Mair (pp. 414 & 415) lists a number of offences which had been found relevant in the past (in addition to "the faults which are most commonly to be seen in libels", which would appear to have included intoxication, libidinous practices, and heresy). These include neglect of ministerial duties, poaching, inefficiency, and preaching sermons material parts of which were copies of printed sermons. How many of these would today be regarded as sufficiently censurable as to warrant Trial by Libel is a moot point.

In deciding whether or not an action or statement is censurable, the Presbytery is not making new law, but interpreting the Word of God or an Act or universal custom of the Church (*The Form of Process* — see p. 67 above). A decision that an action or statement is censurable therefore means that it has always been censurable, and has not just become so at the time the decision is made.

If a Presbytery is in any doubt about whether an action is censurable, it can approach the Assembly by Reference to have the matter clarified, or it can enjoin the person not to act in such a way, or to desist from so acting. If an injunction is issued, the person concerned must then either obey it or appeal against it, so that the General Assembly will decide. If the Assembly decides a Reference to the effect that the action is censurable, or if there is no appeal against an injunction, or if the Assembly upholds the injunction on appeal, subsequent disobedience will be contumacy, which is undoubtedly a censurable offence.

In another kind of case, as when adultery is alleged, the alleged offence is obviously a censurable one, and the Presbytery in such a case has to decide whether or not the facts set out in the libel can be proved. At the hearing, the Presbytery will require evidence sufficient to prove such facts. Vague allegations of censurable behaviour which do not specify anything which can be proved are therefore insufficient in a libel.

8. Alterations to a Libel

Cox states (p. 324) that "libellers may be allowed to amend vague charges in a libel, by giving a particular condescendence of the special offences, or to present a new libel, the first having been discharged. An additional libel based on matters unknown when the first was served is competent." He quotes no authority for these statements, and the 1935 Act provides no procedure for such actions. It provides for deletions, but not for additions (Section 22).

Accordingly, the best advice is that a Presbytery should be very careful not to include vague charges in a libel, so that the question of amendment should not arise.

9. New or additional Libel

If a Presbytery dismisses a libel, it may nevertheless "find sufficient grounds otherwise" for suspending the minister (Section 21). Dismissing a libel in terms of the Act will occur before the matter has gone to proof, and does not mean that the minister has been tried and acquitted. Accordingly, the Presbytery is not thereby prevented from proceeding *de novo* to a new libel.

If an additional libel, based on matters unknown when the first was served, is proposed, procedure in the first should be sisted until the additional libel has been framed, revised, and served, in accordance with the provisions of the Act.

10. Assessors

With regard to references in the 1935 Act to the Board of Assessors, it should be noted that, when the General Assembly of 1980 agreed to discontinue this Board, on the recommendation of the General Administration Committee (now the Board of Practice and Procedure), the recommendation was accompanied by the statement, "If and when Assessors are required, the Committee has power to make appointments." The justification for this statement is to be found in Section 31 of the 1935 Act, together with the remit of the Board of Practice and Procedure, "to attend to the general interests of the Church in matters which are not covered by the remit of any other committee." In the analogous case of Act I, 1988 (anent Congregations in an Unsatisfactory State) specific reference is made to the appointment of Assessors by the Board.

The main function of Assessors is to give legal advice and procedural guidance to Presbyteries. In matters of evidence and procedure, where the Church has not made rules of its own, it follows the practice of civil courts so far as applicable. Since there is no requirement for any office-bearer of a Presbytery to be legally qualified, and since trials by libel have been infrequent, it is very probable that a Presbytery undertaking such a trial will have no member who is legally qualified, and no member with any experience of conducting such a trial. Beyond the duty of revising the libel, the Procurator cannot be called upon to assist, because he must be in a position to give impartial advice to the Assembly if there is an appeal.

A note by the Procurator (R. A. Dunlop, Q.C.) of the salient points relating to evidence and the conduct of trials, as applicable to Trial by Libel, will be found in Part B of this Chapter (pp. 74-77). This is not intended as a substitute for taking legal advice.

If a Presbytery has a qualified lawyer in its membership, with experience of court work, it may appoint such a person to give legal advice, or a lawyer who is not a member of the Presbytery may be employed to do so. The latter may turn out to be expensive, and a request for an Assessor or Assessors is the preferred alternative.

11. Committee on Law, etc.

There is also reference in the 1935 Act to the Committee on Law, Property Cases, and Discipline. When that committee was discharged in 1979, its main functions with regard to property were transferred to the General Trustees, but no provision was made for the transfer of functions in connection with the 1935 Act, presumably because they were considered to have lapsed. The remit of the Board of Practice and Procedure would seem to cover this matter also, but, while the Board, through its Committee on Legal Questions, is able, but not bound, "to afford all help in its power in cases of Trial by Libel" if asked by a Presbytery to do so, it may be regarded as highly unlikely that it would agree to exercise the option of itself undertaking the conduct of a case.

12. Standard of Proof

It should be presumed, in the absence at the time of writing of any specific ruling from the Assembly, that the procedure to be followed is that of civil courts as distinct from criminal courts, and accordingly the standard of proof required is "balance of probability" rather than "beyond reasonable doubt." Justification for this view may be found in the fact that balance of probability is the standard in civil actions even in relation to allegations of crime in such actions, so that, even if a censurable offence appeared to amount to an ecclesiastical "crime", the civil standard of proof would still apply in church courts. It may also be noted that in divorce actions in civil courts the standard of proof for an allegation of adultery has, since 1976, been balance of probability.

The amount and weight of evidence necessary to satisfy a court according to this standard of proof may be greater according to the seriousness of the allegations and the circumstances of the case, but such considerations would not justify a departure from that standard of proof.

The presumption here set out about standard of proof may in due course be replaced by a specific ruling from the Assembly.

13. Record of Evidence and Inventory of Process

The 1935 Act requires (Section 13) that "the whole evidence shall be taken down in shorthand and recorded in full." As the General Assembly has now departed from making a verbatim record of its proceedings by shorthand, in favour of electronic recording, that may be taken as a precedent for the view that a Presbytery will fulfil this requirement by recording the whole evidence electronically.

One important provision of the 1889 Act, not contained in the 1935 one, but still in force, is that there must be an Inventory of Process, in which the Clerk shall enter and number all the documents.

14. Censures

The censures which may be applied if a libel is found proven, or if the accused person confesses, are admonition, rebuke, suspension (either for a specific period, or *sine die*), deposition, and excommunication.

Admonition is administered by the Moderator, at a meeting of the court, and consists in addressing the offender, stating the offence, and exhorting him or her to greater rectitude.

Rebuke, which is always accompanied by admonition, is a severer form of censure involving reproof.

Suspension from office debars from the privileges and duties of office. Suspension for a specific period may be removed at the end of that period, on cause shown, by the court which imposed it, and may include removal of a parish minister from his or her charge. Suspension *sine die* (without specifying a date on which it may be ended) continues until the court finds cause to remove it, and always involves removal from a charge.

Suspension as a censure is to be distinguished from suspension during the investigation of a charge, which is not a censure. Suspension of this kind is usually in the best interests of the accused. (See Act XIX, 1931, for expenses involved.)

Deposition is removal from office, involving loss of status. Status can be restored only by the General Assembly, on petition.

Excommunication is the most serious censure, administered only as a last resort.

15. Demission to avoid Trial

It sometimes happens that an accused minister seeks to demit his or her charge, or to demit status, in order to avoid being tried by libel. Demission, however, is not a unilateral act, and requires the consent of the Presbytery (see Chapter XVI, p. 118). An offer to demit should not be taken as tantamount to a confession of guilt, because a person who claims to be innocent may choose, for a reason other than guilt, to opt out of the process of trial by which innocence might be established.

The responsibility of the Presbytery to appoint people to confer with anyone offering to demit is particularly onerous if the offer is made in the face of a Trial by Libel. The Presbytery has the right to refuse to accept a demission and proceed to trial, or, if the offer does amount to a confession, it may treat it as such and apply the appropriate censure.

A serious difficulty about allowing demission before a Trial by Libel has begun is that there will not necessarily be any official record of the circumstances of the demission, because nothing has been proved at that stage. A minister who demits a charge may immediately apply for another one, and a congregation may call such a minister without knowing the real reason for his or her demission.

A minister who demits status may later petition for restoration, and it will be difficult for the Assembly to consider such a petition fairly even if the person concerned admits having been about to be tried by libel, but claims that there was no substance in the charges, and they were never proved. It will be too late at that stage to consider whether the charges were justified or not. Presbyteries should therefore be very cautious about accepting such demissions, and about the way in which they are minuted if they are accepted.

16. Civil Proceedings

The Church cannot administer a censure simply on the basis of proceedings in a civil court (including a criminal court), but must conduct its own trial.

B. EVIDENCE

(By R. A. Dunlop, Q.C.)

The law of evidence is complex, and legal advice should be obtained in advance of any Trial by Libel on the scope of the evidence to be led, and on the means best suited to presenting it to the court. The following brief comments are broad outlines only of some of the general considerations which may arise.

1. Burden of Proof

In any Trial by Libel the burden of proof lies on the prosecution. The conduct of the trial will follow the normal practice in the civil courts of evidence being led by one party and then, if so advised, by the other.

2. Witnesses

Each witness, after taking the oath or affirmation, is examined in chief by the person conducting the prosecution or the defence, according as the witness is for the prosecution or for the defence. Upon the conclusion of evidence in chief, the person conducting the case for the other side is entitled to cross-examine the witness, and thereafter re-examination on new matter brought out in cross-examination may take place by the person who took the evidence in chief. After re-examination the cross-examiner may put further questions with the leave of the court. The court may on the motion of either party exceptionally recall a witness for the purpose of removing ambiguity or palpable error in the evidence already given, or as to matters which could not have been foreseen.

As a general rule leading questions should not be put either in examination in chief or re-examination, although in the absence of objection they may be resorted to for routine and uncontroversial evidence. In cross-examination leading questions may be put.

Witnesses to fact may refer to their papers to refresh their memory on details, but they must have some recollection of the matter spoken to, and the writing must have been made by them at or about the time of the event in question.

The evidence should be relevant to the issues which are to be determined in the trial, and any attempt to elicit irrelevant evidence may be the subject of timeous objection. Evidence on behalf of the prosecutor of facts outwith the scope of the libel is inadmissible if objected to. In cases of doubt, evidence may be admitted reserving questions of competence and relevance for later decision after argument.

As a general rule, all persons capable of giving evidence are competent and compellable witnesses. The following particular cases should be noted:

a) Children

There is no hard and fast rule regarding the competency of child witnesses. The test in every case is whether the child sufficiently understands the difference between truth and falsehood, and the need to tell the truth, and is capable of giving coherent evidence. The court should satisfy itself on these matters before hearing the child's evidence. The oath is not normally administered to children under fourteen years of age, and never to those under twelve, but rather they are cautioned to tell the truth. Although a child may be a competent witness, applying these tests, nevertheless the weight to be attached to such evidence may be diminished on account of the child's age.

b) Prosecutor

The prosecutor should not give evidence against the accused. Any person who is aware of having important evidence relevant to the issues in question has a duty to decline to act as prosecutor.

c) Presbytery Member

A member of Presbytery may be examined as a witness notwithstanding that he or she is also a member of the court sitting in judgement, providing the party proposing to examine states to the Presbytery the particular matter on which the examination is proposed and the Presbytery gives permission (Cox, p. 331). Cox quotes precedents of 1747, 1850, and 1858, for this, but the Assembly is not absolutely bound by its own precedents. Natural justice would suggest that a person should not be the judge of his or her own credibility as a witness. Accordingly, a Presbytery should be extremely cautious about giving the permission mentioned; and certainly, when committing the Trial to a committee of its own number, it should not appoint to that committee any of its members who is liable to be called as a witness.

3. Privilege

Certain witnesses possess a privilege against answering certain questions, that is to say that the law recognises their right not to answer such questions. The privilege belongs to such witness and may be waived by them. No other party has the right to object to a witness waiving privilege, although there may be objection where privilege is wrongly claimed and upheld. The privilege is against answering the question. The rule does not prevent the question being asked in the first place. As a witness may be unaware that he or she has a privilege, the court may in appropriate circumstances draw the attention of the witness to the fact that a privilege exists. The following particular cases may be noted:

a) A witness is not bound to answer any question the answer to which may reasonably be held to expose, or tend to expose, him or her, to a criminal charge of any description.

b) In any proceedings instituted in consequence of adultery, no witness is bound to answer any question tending to show that he or she has been guilty of adultery, provided he or she has not in the same case given evidence in disproof of his or her adultery.

c) There is no rule which protects communications between persons in a confidential relationship, such as an accused and his or her minister, doctor or other similar confidant, although the courts have shown a desire to respect the aversion of such persons to giving evidence regarding such communications. It might be argued that there is a general discretion to uphold such confidences unless the interests of justice dictate otherwise.

d) Although admitting of certain exceptions, communications between a legal adviser and a client are privileged, unless the client has adduced the legal adviser as a witness or waives privilege.

e) Subject to certain limits, communications between husband and wife, made during the subsistence of the marriage, are privileged. Either spouse may invoke the privilege. The privilege does not apply where the conduct of the spouses towards each other is the subject of the inquiry.

4. Evidence

Evidence may be oral, real or documentary.

a) Oral

Oral evidence is the verbal testimony of a witness in court and is likely to be the primary source of evidence in any Trial by Libel. There is now no objection to hearsay evidence (that is, evidence of what others have stated), provided that direct oral evidence by the person to whom the statement is attributed would have been admissible. Nevertheless, hearsay evidence may not carry the same weight as the direct testimony of the person making the statement and if that direct testimony is available it may be preferable that it should be led. Witnesses may be examined as to the making by them of prior statements insofar as they tend to reflect either favourably or unfavourably on their credibility.

b) Real

Real evidence commonly involves the production of some material object, the condition of which may enable inferences to be drawn which are relevant to the issues in question, although it may also have no special significance beyond the fact that it features in the case. Where the actual appearance of a particular object is a material element in any inquiry, it should be produced.

c) Documentary

Documentary evidence involves any writing and includes drawings, plans, maps and photographs. Some documents are probative, that is to say self-proving, and any fact supported by their terms may be held to be established on production of the document in question. For example, entries in the Register of Births Deaths and Marriages are evidence of the facts recorded in them and sufficient evidence of the facts of birth, death and marriage respectively. Proof of such entries is by extract certificate. Other evidence would be required however to link any particular person to the person named in the certificate. Where available, principal documents should be produced, although parties may agree that copies should be treated as principals. Facts which are accepted by both parties may be recorded as such in a Joint Minute of Admissions, which can be tendered in evidence without the necessity of any further proof.

5. Basis of Determination

In considering the issues submitted for its determination, the court should proceed only upon the basis of the admissible evidence led before it. The admissibility of evidence is to be distinguished from the weight of evidence, that is to say the degree of reliance which the court can place upon the evidence. The court may accept or reject the evidence of any witness either in whole or in part. It may do so on an assessment of the credibility or reliability or both of the witness. The degree of reliance which the court may place on a particular piece of evidence may be increased by the fact of its being corroborated. However, if satisfied that any fact has been established by evidence, the court may find that fact proved by that evidence, notwithstanding that the evidence is not corroborated.

XI. MEETINGS

1. Calling

Church meetings of any kind must be properly called. Those entitled to attend should know where and when the meeting will take place, and what its purpose is. Relevant provisions will be found in the chapters on the various courts and in Chapter XVII: Congregation. For commission and committee meetings, the normal practice is to send written notice, with a copy of the proposed agenda.

2. Opening and Closing

All meetings of church courts, commissions, committees, financial boards, congregations, etc., should be opened and closed with prayer.

The opening prayer, which may be supplemented by other devotional acts, is essential to the proper conduct of all church business under God, for those present are there to seek the will of God on the items of business before them.

The closing "prayer" is now nearly always the benediction, if a minister is in the chair. The person in the chair, if not a minister, may either use a suitable prayer or invite a minister present to close the meeting. Strictly speaking the benediction is not a prayer (see Chapter V, p. 31). However, the benediction is recognised as meeting the requirement to close a meeting with prayer.

3. Minutes

a) Contents

Minutes should contain an accurate record of the date, time and place of each meeting, and who was in the chair. A list of those present, and of apologies, should be in the minute itself or in a separate sederunt book.

The minutes should also contain a complete but succinct record of the business transacted.

b) Recording of Decisions

All decisions should be recorded, including the exact terms of motions duly moved and seconded, and whether or not they were approved. It is not necessary to record unseconded motions, nor is it necessary to record details of the debate on any duly seconded motion.

Since a Moderator's ruling on a point of order has the same standing as a decision of the court, it should be recorded, and it would usually be helpful to include a brief statement of the grounds on which the ruling was made.

c) Other Material

It is nevertheless not improper for minutes to contain matter which is not strictly necessary, and a court may feel that the inclusion of such matter will be conducive to understanding the decisions which have been recorded. For example, an old Kirk Session minute showed that the meeting had been held in the churchyard, without recording the reason. It took considerable research to discover that it had been a time of plague, and meeting in the open air was an attempt to avoid passing on infection.

It should be borne in mind that minutes may be referred to in subsequent proceedings in a higher court, and it may be relevant to know that a certain course of action was taken in full awareness of an alternative course contained in a motion which was not seconded, or to be able to show from the minutes why the lower court made the decision under review. Also, explanatory material may be useful to historians in the future.

d) Formal Communications

Minutes should include reference to instructions or recommendations received from a superior court, and extract minutes and correspondence sent formally to a court through its Clerk should likewise be recorded, together with a statement of any related decisions. The text of extract minutes from superior courts or from committees acting on the authority of such courts should be recorded in full, but in the case of letters a brief summary or mention of the subject will usually be sufficient.

e) Approval of Minutes

Ideally minutes should be read over and approved at the conclusion of a meeting, but it is normally unreasonable to expect a Clerk to be able to produce an instant minute, especially at the end of a long meeting. They are normally prepared by the Clerk after the meeting, and read at the next meeting, or printed and circulated before the next meeting, at which they may be taken as read and approved. At this stage they may be amended, in order to make them an accurate record. Accuracy is the only point at issue when the minutes are submitted for approval. It would be improper to amend the minutes in such a way as to change a decision made at the meeting of which they are the record.

When a minute is amended, the amendment should immediately be made in the principal copy in the hands of the Clerk, and initialled by the Clerk and the Moderator. The next minute should record any such amendment.

When a minute has been approved, it must be signed by the Moderator and by the Clerk, even if either was not present at the meeting concerned (Act XV, 1931).

f) Committee Minutes

Committees appointed by a court are required to keep minutes, but when a committee itself appoints a sub-committee, that sub-committee is not required to keep minutes. It will report to the parent committee, whose minutes should then include a record of such report.

4. Meetings in Private

The Kirk Session is a "closed" court, which means that its regular meetings are always in private; but it can, at its discretion, invite others to be present for all or part of a meeting.

Other courts, being "open", meet regularly in public, but may take certain items of business in private. This means that all who are not members of the court ought to leave, but in Presbyteries it is common, and acceptable, that if a journalist is present, he or she is permitted to remain on the understanding that none of the private business will be reported. In practice, most business taken in private is not of sufficient public interest to be reported anyway. The Presbytery always has the option of applying the rule strictly.

Act VII, 1935, prescribes that in all cases of Trial by Libel a Record Apart should be kept, and this has the clear implication that such proceedings are in private. Act I, 1988, (Congregations in an Unsatisfactory State), prescribes that "all procedure in Presbytery under this Act shall be taken in private." Act II, 1988, states, "The Judicial Commission shall decide at any stage of the proceedings whether these shall be taken in private." There is no doubt that journalists should be excluded from private meetings under these Acts. However, if Assessors have been appointed to assist a Presbytery in any such case, they should be permitted to be present.

If the Assembly were to decide to meet in private, the public galleries would have to be cleared, and even the Lord High Commissioner would be required to leave the throne gallery. Although there is no specific ruling, and Standing Orders say that corresponding members are entitled to attend all sessions, they also could reasonably be asked to leave, since their presence in the Assembly is essentially for administrative purposes. Delegates and Visitors should also be asked to leave. In short, only commissioners and members *ex officiis* should remain. Journalists should leave, and electronic recording devices and feeds to the Press Room or anywhere else should be switched off, with the single exception of that required for the verbatim record. Not surprisingly, the Assembly hardly ever meets in private.

5. Record Apart

When a court meets in private on a matter of discipline where moral delinquency is alleged, the proceedings should be recorded in a Record Apart, and not in the ordinary minutes. The rules for this are in the section on Discipline in the Plan of Union, 1929 (see p. 172).

6. Extracts

If there is any item on the agenda about which an extract minute may be required before the minutes can be approved at the following meeting, the minute of that item should be read over and approved immediately. This will be necessary, for example, in the case of decisions made in connection with the translation of a minister, and in judicial matters which may be the subject of appeal. Nevertheless, decisions of a court take effect immediately; they are not sisted until the time when the minute is approved.

Cox (p. 79) states, "A Clerk should be very cautious about giving extracts without the authority of the court." Herron (p. 253) states that the Clerk alone can give valid extracts, "but he can do so only with the consent of the court." Cox's caution has become Herron's absolute rule, but in any event it is the wise course.

Once a decision has been made, and the minute of that decision approved, there is no doubt that it has the authority of the court, from which authority to issue an extract minute may be inferred, but certainly the Clerk should be very cautious indeed about issuing an extract before the minute has been approved.

If a Clerk is asked for an extract minute, or believes that it will be in the best interests of the Church to communicate a decision, before approval of the relevant minute, the cautious course is to communicate the decision by letter, and seek authority from the next meeting of the court to confirm that letter by issuing an extract minute, after the approval of the minute.

In judicial cases, when a judgement has been made and intimated to parties, it is the normal custom for the Clerk to send extract minutes of that judgement to the parties, even if not specifically instructed to do so. Consuetude allows the Clerk to infer an instruction in such circumstances, as it is written confirmation of the judgement already intimated to the parties.

D

XII. PROCEDURE

1. Standing Orders

Procedure for the General Assembly is set out mainly in the Standing Orders, but special procedures are provided in some Acts of Assembly, especially in relation to judicial matters. Inferior courts may adopt their own standing orders, which must of course be consistent with the law of the Church, and in the absence of such standing orders they are guided by those of the Assembly, where applicable.

The procedure for courts applies also to financial boards, congregational meetings, and committees appointed by courts, where relevant.

2. Moderator's Ruling

Each court is presided over by a Moderator, whose function is to conduct the business in an orderly way. The Moderator has the right to rule on points of order, that is to say on matters of procedure and the interpretation of standing orders.

The Moderator's right to rule does not extend to deciding questions of competence in judicial proceedings, nor does it include the right to interpret the law of the Church. These are matters for the court itself to decide.

In all courts the ruling of the Moderator is equivalent to a decision of the court, and may therefore be the subject of a dissent, or a dissent and complaint or appeal in the inferior courts. In the Assembly it is competent to ask for a dissent from the Moderator's ruling to be recorded.

In financial boards, congregational meetings, and committees, the person in the chair has the same right to rule on points of order as does the Moderator of a court.

3. Clerk's Advice

Each court also has a Clerk, to whom the Moderator and the court are entitled to turn for advice on matters of procedure and interpretation, and of law generally.

Indeed, a Clerk is expected to intervene if it appears that the court is about to adopt an improper procedure.

In the Assembly the advice of the Procurator is also available, especially on matters of civil law, and on procedure in cases, in which, so far as it has not made laws or established precedents of its own, the practice of the Church is generally on the lines of the law and practice of civil government.

These office-bearers do not give "rulings", but rather opinions, which may or may not be adopted by the Moderator or the court. If an improper procedure is followed, with or without the advice of the Clerk, the whole court is responsible for the impropriety.

4. Motions

Decisions in church courts may be made by acclamation or by obvious consensus, but even in such cases of obvious agreement a form of words should be put as a motion to the meeting and recorded in the minutes. Where there is no agreement, decisions are made by voting on motions, which must be proposed and seconded.

Amendments and counter-motions are best understood as different categories of motion. An amendment is a motion to make deletions, alterations or additions to another motion, including a counter-motion or another amendment, without substantially changing or contradicting its main object. A counter-motion is a motion to make a substantial change to another motion.

a) Amendments

Usually, but not always, the form of an amendment is to modify the wording of the original motion, while a counter-motion proposes completely different wording; but it is the effect rather than the form which finally determines the category. For example, a motion to modify the wording of another motion by deleting the word "not" from its main clause would normally be treated as a counter-motion. The question of the category into which any motion falls is determined by the Moderator.

Amendments are best disposed of as soon as possible, and certainly before other amendments are moved, although an amendment of an amendment must be taken before the original amendment is disposed of. Voting is "For" or "Against" the amendment, not "For the amendment" or "For the original motion". This is because, if a vote "For the original motion" were carried, that motion would then have been approved and further amendments or counter-motions would be incompetent.

When all amendments have been disposed of, and if there are no counter-motions, a final vote is taken "For" or "Against" the motion, or the motion as amended. If there are counter-motions, a vote is taken among all the motions, namely the original motion, as amended or not, and the counter motions, each member having one vote. The motion with fewest votes is discarded, and the process is repeated until only one motion is left, and then there is a vote "For" or "Against" that surviving motion.

b) Counter-motions

The distinction between an amendment and a counter-motion, and the fact that amendments are disposed of before counter-motions, are important, because such procedure ensures that the details of proposals are decided before the final vote is taken. It is wrong to expect a decision "in principle" to be taken first, because those who are in favour of something in principle might not agree to a particular method of implementing that principle.

c) No Direct Negative

There is no such thing as a "direct negative" in church procedure. If anyone has spoken against a motion, it should be put to the vote, and must be put to the vote if so requested. Since the final vote is always "For" or "Against", there is no need for any further motion to give members the chance to vote against any motion. It is however in order to move a counter-motion in such terms as almost amount to a direct negative, such as a motion "to depart from the matter".

d) Notice of Motion

There are requirements about notice of motion in some specified cases in the Standing Orders of the Assembly; and Presbyteries may make similar provisions. Anything else can be moved without notice as a counter-motion or amendment to a proposed deliverance or to any section of it, with the obvious proviso that it must bear some relationship to what it proposes to change or amend. In some Presbyteries there is provision for notice of motion to be given well in advance of a meeting, and for the motion to be taken as a separate item on the order of business.

5. Voting
a) Majority

Decisions are normally made by a simple majority of persons voting, and this is the rule in the absence of express provision to the contrary. A procedural decision to suspend Standing Orders in the Assembly requires a two-thirds majority, and Presbyteries may have similar provisions.

b) Entitlement to Vote

At any church meeting, the practice of the courts of the Church should be followed, namely that only those present with the right to vote are entitled to do so. There is no provision for proxy votes, or for any form of referendum or plebiscite. The reason for this is that those present are the only ones who are part of a meeting which has been constituted with prayer, and the only ones who hear any argument or debate on the matter to be decided.

Act XXII, 1932, expressly provides that a vote in the matter of union shall be taken at a congregational meeting, and that a vote by plebiscite shall not be valid. This is the only legislative provision on the question of a plebiscite; but it cannot be inferred that a plebiscite would be possible on a matter other than union. The practice of the courts of the Church should be regarded as determinative.

There is nothing to prevent a Kirk Session or financial board from circulating members of a congregation with some form of questionnaire, to discover their views on any matter, but views thus discovered are not binding on the Kirk Session or financial board. Ideally, such a questionnaire will be accompanied by impartial explanatory material.

c) Procedure

Voting is normally open, members standing in their places to be counted. In the Assembly there is provision for vote by papers if required. In this method of voting, those voting stand in their places and hand numbered papers to the tellers to be counted. In the case of congregational meetings to elect ministers, there is provision for a secret ballot, which is optional, except in the case of linked charges and deferred unions and linkings, when it is compulsory (Act V, 1984).

d) Tied Votes

In the event of a tied vote, the Moderator has a casting vote. Reference is sometimes made to the convention that a casting vote should be cast for the *status quo*, but there is no authority for applying that convention in church procedures.

When the votes for and against a motion are tied, the outcome, if the Moderator does not exercise a casting vote, is that the motion has not been carried. That will normally mean that the *status quo* will prevail, even if the motion were reaffirming the *status quo*. Failure to carry a motion reaffirming a previous decision does not overturn that previous decision. In most situations, a casting vote for the *status quo* would therefore have the same effect as not exercising a casting vote.

The situation may be different if the vote is on an amendment which may be at least closer to the *status quo* than the motion.

If the tied vote is between a motion and a counter-motion, both of which involve departing from the *status quo*, the convention could not apply, although one might be closer to the *status quo* than the other. If the Moderator declines to use a casting vote in such a situation, it would be necessary to declare that neither motion has carried. Accordingly, the *status quo* would prevail in such a situation only if the casting vote were not exercised.

The Moderator is a member of the court, and, having no deliberative vote, is entitled to exercise the casting vote in accordance with conviction. That conviction may be the Moderator's personal conviction about the merits of the matter being voted on, or it may be the Moderator's conviction that it would not be in the best interests of the Church to have a motion carried by a majority of one, despite his or her own personal conviction.

Committees follow the practice of the courts appointing them in this matter, so a convener has a casting vote, but no deliberative vote. There are two exceptions: Act V, 1984, provides that the convener of a Vacancy Committee has a deliberative vote and a casting vote (but not if he or she is the Interim Moderator); and the Preses (chairman) has a deliberative and a casting vote in a Committee of Management. However, like the Moderator of a Kirk Session, and the person in the chair in a financial board, a convener of a committee is entitled to introduce and commend items of business from the chair. It would be unreasonable to suggest that he or she should not use a casting vote in support of an item so introduced, but again the question whether a majority of one would be in the best interests of the Church is relevant. (It is possible that a person with a deliberative vote and a casting vote could, on such a basis, use a casting vote differently from his or her deliberative vote.)

In short, it is not reasonable to expect Moderators and others in the chair to apply a rule-of-thumb about the *status quo*, against what might be their better judgement. The best interests of the Church is a preferable criterion.

6. Dissents

When a decision has been reached, any member may ask for his or her dissent to be recorded, and it is in order, though not required, for a member to give reasons for the dissent, which will also be recorded, but they should be stated with great brevity. Both the dissent and the reasons must be given at the time of the decision to which they relate. It is in order for others present at the time to adhere to a dissent.

7. Procedural Irregularities

The general rule about alleged procedural irregularities is that anyone who wants to claim that procedure is irregular should do so at the time, otherwise everything will be presumed to have been done regularly.

If however the allegation is that some major and essential step in a process laid down in legislation has been omitted, such as when an omission in the procedure for calling a minister is drawn to the attention of a Presbytery, it cannot simply be ignored, but the simplest way of correcting the error should be sought. For example, when a Presbytery was on the point of sustaining a call to a minister, it was alleged and admitted that the Interim Moderator and the vacancy committee had omitted the required consultation with the Presbytery's advisory committee. The remedy was not to declare the whole proceedings null and void, but require an immediate meeting, in the expectation that the advisory committee would be able to give retrospective approval to the matters on which its advice should have been sought. That would sufficiently answer in the negative the question as to whether the irregularity had prejudiced the result of the whole process.

Accordingly, if any allegation of irregularity is so serious that the general presumption about unchallenged procedures does not apply, the questions to be considered are whether and to what extent anyone has suffered prejudice as a result, and how best to rectify any error.

8. Verbal Precision

While the procedure for making decisions is the same for all church courts, it may be less formal in the smaller Presbyteries and in Kirk Sessions, than in the Assembly. Nevertheless, any decision reached by consensus or acclamation should always be recorded in a precise form of words agreed by the court. In any contentious matter which may be taken to a superior court, it is particularly important that the minute of the inferior court is unambiguous about the terms of the decision concerned.

Care should be taken in the wording of motions (including amendments and counter-motions). Time spent on framing motions beforehand, or on adjusting motions moved without prior notice in the course of a debate, may avoid much more time being spent on questions of interpretation afterwards. Care should be taken about including words like "wholeheartedly". If a motion "wholeheartedly" welcoming something were passed by 201 votes to 200, the welcome could hardly be called wholehearted; and a motion such as "This court is not divided" would be rendered meaningless if carried by a small majority!

XIII. GENERAL ASSEMBLY

1. Powers of the Assembly

The Assembly is the supreme legislative and judicial body of the Church, and it also has the final say in all matters of administration.

In secular constitutional law generally, stress is laid on the principle of "separation of powers," by which is meant that the legislature, the judiciary, and the executive should be independent of each other. Thus, in the United Kingdom, the law courts are independent of Parliament, and civil servants are not eligible to be Members of Parliament, which is why Members of Parliament "resign" by applying for an office of profit under the Crown. There are exceptions, in that the House of Lords is, in some cases, the final court of appeal; and members of the cabinet, being in charge of departments of the civil service, are members of the executive as well as of the legislature.

In the Church, there is no such separation of powers. The legislature is also the final court of appeal, and paid officials of its administration are eligible to be members of the Assembly on the same basis as any others, although they may be said to hold offices of profit under the Church.

2. Delegated Powers

There is at the time of writing an Overture under the Barrier Act which, if enacted by the 1997 Assembly, would have the effect of transferring most of the judicial functions of the Assembly to the Commission of Assembly, and of substantially reducing the membership of the Commission. It has received the consent of a majority of Presbyteries, but this does not guarantee that it will be enacted by the Assembly.

The Overture contains an important provision to the effect that, while decisions of the Commission will not be subject to review by the Assembly, the Commission itself may decide to refer a case to the Assembly if, in its opinion, an important principle is involved.

This would in some ways be analogous to the fact that by convention the House of Lords acts in appeals through a small body of legally qualified lawyers, most of whom are specially appointed as Lords of Appeal in Ordinary. There is however no provision that the members of the Commission of Assembly should be legally qualified.

If such powers are given to the Commission, this will not involve any change in judicial procedures. It will simply be a case of reading "Commission of Assembly" for "Assembly" at the relevant points, bearing in mind that powers exercised by the Commission will be powers of the Assembly which have been delegated to it, so that it would always be possible for the Assembly to repeal the delegating legislation and revert to exercising these powers itself.

The Assembly has already delegated judicial powers to the Judicial Commission, and to the Property Commission, although it is likely that the Property Commission will no longer be necessary if powers are given as proposed to the Commission of Assembly.

3. Moderator

a) Choice

The opening session of the Assembly is constituted by the Moderator of the previous Assembly, who puts the name of the Moderator Designate to the Assembly for election. The nominee is chosen in the previous October by a committee specially appointed for the purpose. The composition of the committee has varied over the years, but currently it includes representatives appointed by Presbyteries, one from each. Any member of Presbytery is entitled to suggest suitable persons to the Presbytery representative, but that representative is free to make his or her own decision, and is not to be mandated by the Presbytery.

There is a convention, but not a rule, that a person should not seek nomination, and that those intending to make nominations should not indulge in canvassing before the meeting. There is also a convention that, after a vote has been taken in the committee, and a choice made, the committee should agree to make the decision unanimous, which simply means that, although some may have preferred other nominees, all are agreed that the person chosen is worthy of appointment.

b) Duties

It is often said that, strictly speaking, the only duty of the Moderator is to preside over the Assembly but, however true that may have been in the past, consuetude decreed otherwise, and the Assembly of 1962 made appropriate regulations, which were revised in 1980, as follows:

REVISED REGULATIONS GOVERNING THE DUTIES OF THE MODERATOR OF THE GENERAL ASSEMBLY

The Office, Function and Duties of the Moderator of the General Assembly shall be:—

1. To preside over the General Assembly and to perform those duties as stated in the Standing Orders.
2. To visit Presbyteries according to the scheme of visitation sanctioned by the General Assembly.
3. To perform such duties as may be directed by the General Assembly, and to represent the Church of Scotland on historic and national occasions, as they may arise.
4. To be mindful of the views of the General Assembly and of its Committees and Departments, and, when asked to express an opinion on any matter of national or public importance, so far as possible, to consult with the Conveners of such Committees and Departments, but, notwithstanding such consultation, to accept instructions only from the General Assembly.
5. To undertake such other duties as he may choose during his term of office.

4. Officials

The Principal Clerk, the Depute Clerk, the Procurator, and the Law Agent (Solicitor of the Church) are all appointed by the Assembly, on the nomination of the Board of Practice and Procedure. On taking up office, they are required in the Assembly to take the oath, *de fideli*, which is an abbreviation of *de fideli administratione officii*, literally, "concerning the faithful administration of the office." The form of the oath is: "I swear that I will be faithful to the duties of.........", naming the office concerned. (This oath must also be taken by the Clerks of all church courts.)

The Principal Clerk must be a minister. The Depute Clerk need not be a minister, but normally is. The Depute Clerk has no preferential claim to the Principal Clerkship.

The Procurator should be a Q.C., and the Law Agent a solicitor.

The Assembly also appoints a London Agent, and an Assembly Officer.

The Precentor is appointed by the Board of Practice and Procedure, and is not an *ex officio* member.

a) Clerks

The Principal Clerk is responsible to the Assembly for all the duties of Clerk, but may allocate some of these to the Depute Clerk. He is *ex officio* the

Secretary of the Board of Practice and Procedure, and the Moderator's Secretary, and is a full-time employee in the Church Offices. The Depute Clerk is *ex officio* Assistant Secretary of the Board, and a part-time employee. As well as the duties specifically allocated, any other duty of the Clerk may fall to the Depute Clerk in the absence of the Principal Clerk.

The duties of Clerk are to make all necessary arrangements for the Assembly each year, including the issuing of all necessary papers before and during the Assembly, namely: the Volume of Reports; the Order of Proceedings, which includes the Roll of Commissioners, the Standing Orders, Supplementary Reports, Overtures from Presbyteries, and documentation for Cases; and Daily Papers, which may also include Supplementary Reports, Overtures, and documents for Cases, and also contain the Minutes, and Notices of Motion. He also cites parties in Cases.

The Clerk, having received returns from Presbyteries, issues to Presbyteries notice of the number of commissioners they are entitled to appoint, receives the lists of such appointments from Presbyteries, and prepares the Roll of Commissioners.

After the Assembly, the Clerk issues all necessary extract minutes; sends to Presbyteries a note of remits from the Assembly, including Overtures under the Barrier Act; and in due course receives the returns to Overtures and, as Convener of the Committee for Classifying Returns to Overtures, prepares the Report of that committee for inclusion in the Volume of Reports.

The Clerk also prepares and publishes a booklet containing the Supplementary Reports, a list of all the Deliverances approved by the Assembly, and a list of the Legislative Acts, Overtures sent down under the Barrier Act, and Regulations approved by the Assembly.

The Clerks are appointed as a committee to revise the Minutes. These, in their revised form, are printed and published in a final edition of the Volume of Reports, which also includes all the material in the original volume, together with the Roll of Commissioners, Standing Orders, Supplementary Reports, Deliverances, Acts, Overtures under the Barrier Act, Cases with Deliverances, and a list of members of Assembly Committees and representatives on other bodies.

The Clerk is the custodier of records, not only of the Assembly itself, but of all church records duly lodged with him for transmission to the Scottish Record Office.

When the Clerk signs any document over the official designation, "Principal Clerk", or in formal documents "*Cl. Eccl. Scot.*" (abbreviated Latin for "Clerk of [General Assembly of] the Church of Scotland"), that document is presumed to have the full authority of the court. Care should therefore be taken that ordinary correspondence does not purport to come from the Assembly itself. It is better to use headed notepaper with the name and designation printed at the top, and only the signature at the end. However, the difference between an official communication and a communication from an official will usually be evident from the contents.

Other *ex officio* duties which belong to the Principal Clerk are those of Clerk to the Commission of Assembly, the Judicial Commission, and the Property Commission, and those of Secretary to the Nomination Committee, and the Committee to Nominate the Moderator.

In the Assembly, the Clerk may be called on to give advice and guidance on matters of procedure and church law, and during the year gives similar advice and guidance, being frequently consulted, for example, by Presbytery Clerks, and by persons wishing to bring matters to the Assembly by appeal or petition. It is important to note that such advice and guidance is in the form of opinions, and not rulings.

b) Procurator

The duties of the Procurator, whose appointment is part-time, are to attend meetings of the Assembly and the Commission of Assembly, to revise Libels, to conduct litigation in civil courts on behalf of the Church, and to give advice to inferior courts, but requests for such advice should first be submitted to the Principal Clerk for transmission, where relevant, to the Procurator. Normally the Procurator's advice will be on matters of civil law as it affects the Church, but he may also be asked to advise on church law.

The Procurator is also an *ex officio* member of the Board of Practice and Procedure, but is not expected to attend meetings except when his advice is likely to be required.

See Act XXII, 1931, for arrangements when this office is vacant.

c) Solicitor

The duties of the Law Agent are in fact incorporated in the office of Solicitor of the Church of Scotland, which is a full-time appointment. The Solicitor is in charge of the Law Department, which is responsible for the legal work of the Church in matters of civil law, especially in respect of property generally, in the work of the General Trustees, and in briefing the Procurator in litigation. The Solicitor may be approached for advice, for example on questions of contracts of service, by courts and committees, and by financial boards.

The Solicitor is an *ex officio* member of the Board of Practice and Procedure.

d) London Agent

The Assembly also appoints a London Agent, whose main function is to scrutinise legislation passing through Parliament and to advise the Church, through the Solicitor, of any matters affecting its interests. He gives advice on procedures when the Church is seeking parliamentary action. He is also available to advise Government Departments or Members of Parliament on questions affecting the Church.

e) Assembly Officer

The Assembly appoints an Assembly Officer, who is responsible, under the Principal Clerk, for the practical arrangements at the Assembly Hall for meetings of the Assembly, such as cleaning, arranging the furnishings, stewarding, and making the necessary provision for the Assembly Communion Service. He also attends to the needs of the Moderator.

f) Precentor

The Precentor leads the Assembly praise, which is always sung unaccompanied, and was for long entirely restricted to Metrical Psalms and Paraphrases, but recently Hymns have been sung during the Sunday Evening Session, but not at its constitution. He is available to advise the Moderator, who chooses the praise, about suitable tunes.

5. Membership

Members of the Assembly are commissioned each year by Presbyteries, and are called commissioners. Act X, 1994, deals with the appointment of commissioners. The basis on which the quota of commissioners is calculated need not be reflected in the appointments made. For example, retired ministers are not taken into account in the calculation, but this does not prevent the Presbytery from appointing retired ministers within the total number, provided that they are members of Presbytery. It is required that the number of ministers and the number of elders should be equal, deacons being additional to these categories.

Act XXIV, 1969, permits Presbyteries to appoint former Moderators of the General Assembly as commissioners in addition to the quota, and an "equalising elder" must be appointed in respect of each of these. Presumably, in the event of an elder becoming Moderator, an equalising minister would be appointed in subsequent years, as the rule that the number of ministers and elders should be equal would prevail over the literal terms of this Act. The implication of the Act is that it applies to the appointment of former Moderators every year.

Presbyteries normally operate a rota which ensures that each minister is commissioned once in every four years (with the exception of retired ministers, whose frequency of appointment will depend on the number of them in the Presbytery), and a similar rota by which Kirk Sessions are invited to submit names of elders to be appointed, but this is not a legal requirement, and Presbyteries may appoint commissioners on any basis they choose. Most Presbyteries appoint their Clerks every year, and some, if they have Conveners of Assembly Committees in their membership, appoint these in every year of their tenure of such office.

Acts XVIII, 1956; XIX, 1956, as amended by II, 1980; and I, 1992, deal with *ex officio* members of the Assembly, who are the Moderator, the immediate past Moderator, the Clerks, Procurator and Law Agent (the Solicitor), and the Convener and Vice-Convener of the Business Committee.

There are also corresponding members, with the right to speak but not to vote, as detailed in the Standing Orders. Those appointed by Committees may speak only on business relating to such Committees. The General Treasurer of the Church although appointed by the Assembly, is a corresponding member, not an *ex officio* member.

Persons entitled to be in the Assembly in pursuance of their duties, even if not members, are the Assembly Officer, the Precentor, the Moderator's Chaplains, and a Medical Officer. Conveners may be accompanied by members of departmental staff, who may, with the permission of the Assembly, answer questions. Conveners who are not commissioners are entitled to attend and speak to their Reports, but not to move motions or to vote. The normal practice is for one of the Clerks to move the deliverance formally on behalf any such convener. The Clerks are not thereby prevented from moving amendments or counter-motions subsequently.

Delegates from other Churches and ecumenical bodies are accorded the same status as corresponding members, and may speak on any matter except judicial cases.

Visitors from other Churches are entitled to be present in the Assembly, but not to speak or vote.

6. Meetings

The Assembly meets for one week each year, towards the end of May. On each day there is usually one Session, but the opening and closing days usually have two Sessions. Each Session is constituted by an act of devotion, and ends with an adjournment to the next Session, and the Benediction. In the course of a Session, there may be a break, or more than one break, for which the Session is suspended without formality, and business resumes by the Moderator calling the Assembly to order. At the closing Session, the Assembly passes an Act appointing the next Assembly.

7. Business

a) Formal

Formal business is conducted at the opening Session, and includes the election of the Moderator, the reading of the Commission of the Lord High Commissioner and of the Queen's Letter to the Assembly, and an address by the Lord High Commissioner. The Lord High Commissioner addresses the Assembly again at the closing Session.

b) Cases

Cases are usually heard at the end of a Session, with an Order of the Day at about 7 p.m. This is because the time limits on speeches do not apply in judicial proceedings, and therefore the time they will take is unpredictable, so that to allocate them to an earlier part of the day would make the timing of the business of the rest of the day very uncertain.

c) Reports

Most of the Assembly's time is spent on the reports of standing committees (which is a generic term for boards and panels as well as committees), and reports of any special or *ad hoc* committees or commissions.

Reports must be submitted to the Clerks in writing, in time for them to be included in the Volume of Reports (colloquially known as "The Blue Book") and issued to all commissioners before the Assembly begins.

Oral reports, and minority reports, are not in order.

Although there is no official provision for "supplementary reports", it is the practice for such reports, dealing with matters which have arisen too late to be included in the main reports, to be issued either in the Order of Proceedings or in the Daily Papers.

Each report contains a "Proposed Deliverance", in numbered sections. These are properly referred to as, say, "Section ten of the deliverance", not "Deliverance ten." When the report has been presented and spoken to, and the deliverance moved and seconded, there is an opportunity to question the convener before passing to the deliverance. Each section is a motion, which is put to the Assembly, with or without debate. Any commissioner may move an amendment of, or counter-motion to, any section.

The first section is always a motion to receive the report, and is not normally contested, since it would be unreasonable not to receive a report which the Assembly has required; but a report may be received with the exception of part or parts of it if, for example, the committee has included matter which properly belongs to the remit of another committee, or if it is considered to be inappropriate for the Assembly to deal with such part or parts.

A commissioner who wishes to make a general comment on the report as a whole may be permitted to do so when the first section is put. Technically such a commissioner is speaking to the motion to receive the report. It was recently argued in the Assembly that it was not competent to discuss a report before it had been received, but in the past, when there was specific provision for general discussion as well as for questions, this took place before the first section of the proposed deliverance had been put, as is still the case with questions. It is however incompetent to move any motion on any other section of the proposed deliverance before the report has been received, and if any part of a report is not received, any section relating to that part automatically falls.

The specific provision for general discussion was departed from in order to discourage commissioners from making speeches in general discussion, and then making substantially the same points in relation to a specific section. The fact that this provision was departed from does not render making general comment on the first section incompetent, but it does mean that this should be done responsibly.

When every section has been considered, and approved, deleted, amended or replaced, as the case may be, the deliverance as a whole is put to the Assembly.

In this way the Assembly oversees the work of the committees, and gives remits and instructions to them for the following year.

d) Overtures

Overture is the way by which a Presbytery, or a group of commissioners (a minimum number of twelve is sometimes quoted, but it is not in Standing Orders) place business on the agenda of the Assembly. It is distinguished from a petition in that it is about a matter of concern to the whole Church rather than a particular interest of a petitioner.

The form of an overture is simple:

It is humbly overtured by........., to the Venerable the General Assembly, to............

It may have a preamble, giving reasons, and it must have a proposed deliverance.

8. Standing Orders

Details of Assembly business and procedure are in the Standing Orders of the Assembly, which are not reproduced here, as they are fairly frequently amended. As indicated above, they are issued in the Order of Proceedings to every commissioner, so they are reasonably accessible. Copies may be obtained from the office of the Principal Clerk.

XIV. PRESBYTERY

1. Presbyterian Government

The Presbytery was the latest of the church courts to evolve, and the Church was presbyterian before it had Presbyteries, the essence of presbyterian government being a conciliar system of superior and inferior courts, by whatever name these courts are known.

The Presbytery's rôle, as part of the structure of discipline in the broad sense, is the repression of vice and the nourishment of virtue (see p. 62) within its bounds. Its basic function is to give spiritual leadership and encouragement to the ministers, office-bearers, and congregations, and it should be recognised that, apart from duties prescribed by law, or instructed by the Assembly, it should always be seeking other ways of promoting the advancement of Christ's kingdom.

2. Moderator

Act XXI, 1944, was amended by Act VIII, 1996, to the effect that a Presbytery no longer has to choose its Moderator from among its ministerial members. While this change means that an elder or deacon may be appointed as Moderator, it does not have the effect of conferring ministerial functions on such a Moderator, who will therefore not be able to officiate at a Presbytery communion service. With regard to ordination care should be taken to ensure that the ordination prayer is given by a minister, and a non-ministerial Moderator will not be able to participate in the laying on of hands.

Normally the task of nominating a Moderator is entrusted to a committee, and the Moderator is elected by the Presbytery, to hold office for a year.

3. Clerk

Every Presbytery must appoint a Clerk, who takes the oath *de fideli* (see Chapter XIII, p. 90) on appointment. In the absence of the Clerk, the Presbytery must appoint a temporary Clerk, who must take the oath. The Clerk need not be a member of the Presbytery. It is possible for a Presbytery to have two or more Clerks.

The main duties of the Clerk are to prepare the minutes and keep them in the minute book, to issue extract minutes when so instructed, to ensure the safe custody of all official records, and to deal with all correspondence, including extract minutes from the Assembly and its committees. It is important that any document received by the Clerk for the court should be submitted to the court at its next meeting.

At meetings, one function of the Clerk is to give guidance to the Moderator and the court on matters of procedure and church law.

A Clerk who signs any document and designates himself or herself as Presbytery Clerk is presumed to be acting with the full authority of the court (cf. p. 91).

4. Membership

Act III, 1992, deals with membership of Presbyteries, and should be referred to for its terms. It should be noted that, as far as ministers and deacons are concerned, a Presbytery has no control over who shall be members. It cannot reject any who are entitled to membership in terms of the Act, nor can it accept as members any who are not so entitled. Similarly, the Presbytery has no control over who shall be elected as representative elders by Kirk Sessions, but it is entitled itself to choose additional elders. The choice of corresponding members is also a matter for the Presbytery.

Act III, 1956, deals with the ordination of licentiates appointed to theological chairs and lectureships in Scottish Universities or Church Colleges. On being ordained, they are qualified to be members of Presbytery in terms of Act III, 1992. On appointment to a chair, or to be principal of a Church College, a minister is inducted to office by the Presbytery.

5. Meetings

a) Ordinary

A Presbytery always, at the end of an ordinary meeting, adjourns to meet on a specified date at a specified time and place, even when this is in accordance with a scheme of meeting on e.g. "the first Tuesday of every month except . . .", or some such formula.

A notice in writing giving the time and place of the next meeting of a Presbytery is technically a reminder of the time and place already appointed, and should not purport to be a "call notice." It will usually be accompanied by a proposed agenda, a copy of the minute of the previous meeting or meetings, and any papers relating to the proposed agenda. At an early stage after the court has been constituted, the proposed agenda will be submitted, adjusted if necessary, and approved. After that, no other business will be competent, except as provided for by standing orders. For example, standing orders may allow notice of motion for the next meeting to be submitted before a meeting is closed.

b) In hunc effectum and Pro re nata

Apart from ordinary meetings, Presbyteries may meet *in hunc effectum* (for this purpose) or *pro re nata* (for a thing which has arisen). The purpose of such meetings is to enable the Presbytery to deal expeditiously with matters in which the interests of the Church would suffer if they were left until the next ordinary meeting.

A Presbytery itself appoints a meeting *in hunc effectum*, specifying the business to be transacted, and only business so specified may be transacted.

A meeting *pro re nata* is for the transaction of urgent business which has arisen since the last ordinary meeting and cannot wait until the next. It is called by the Moderator, on his own initiative or at the formal request of at least three members of Presbytery. There must be written notice of the meeting, and of the business to be transacted, and again only business so specified may be transacted. When the Presbytery meets, it must approve the action of the Moderator in calling the meeting before it can deal with the business.

Minutes of meetings *in hunc effectum* and *pro re nata* are normally submitted for approval to the next ordinary meeting, but they may be read over and approved at the end of the meeting itself, the approved minutes being circulated with the papers for the next ordinary meeting.

c) Funerals of Ministers

Act XX, 1931, requires a Presbytery to meet, "without formal summons" immediately after the funeral of a parish minister, in order to appoint an Interim Moderator and deal with any necessary vacancy business, unless due intimation is made to the contrary. The Presbytery is responsible for the funeral service of a parish minister, the Moderator and Clerk making arrangements in consultation with the family.

6. Supervision

Each Presbytery exercises supervision over all ministers (including probationers, licentiates, and ministers who are not members of Presbytery, but excluding those who are members of another Presbytery), deacons, Kirk Sessions, financial boards, and congregations within their bounds, but the supervision of individual elders and members is a function of Kirk Sessions. This supervision (επισκοπη: *episcopé*) is similar in some ways to that exercised by a bishop in episcopal government (the word "bishop", earlier "biscop", being derived from επισκοπος: *episcopos*), but there are significant differences. For example, a Presbytery has no rôle in confirmation as does a bishop. In fact the differences are greater than the similarities, but the main point of the comparison is that presbyterian Churches are at one with episcopal Churches in recognising the fundamental importance of supervision as such, whether it is exercised by Presbyteries or bishops.

7. Quinquennial Visitation

The main instrument of presbyterial supervision is the Quinquennial Visitation, which is regulated by Act II, 1984 (as amended by Act VI, 1992). This is a form of "spiritual audit", whereby a team from the Presbytery visits a congregation, meeting with the minister, Kirk Session, and financial board, and the leader of the team addresses the congregation at public worship or at a congregational meeting. The general purpose of the visit is to give counsel and encouragement, and to report difficulties to the Presbytery in order that supportive or remedial action may be taken.

Arrangements for such visitations are usually made by a superintendence committee, to which the visitors report in the first instance, and which then reports to the Presbytery.

A difficulty about supervision being exercised by a corporate body is that it cannot easily intervene confidentially in the pastoral care of a minister at an early stage, before a situation develops in such a way as to require more formal action. Who can effectively be a *pastor pastorum* (pastor of the pastors)? Some Presbyteries have appointed senior ministers to be pastoral counsellors. A Presbytery may, after the induction of a minister to a first charge, appoint the Interim Moderator to continue for a period as pastoral counsellor to that minister. The Presbytery Clerk may be consulted by a minister in difficulty, but should be careful not to become too personally involved in a matter which may lead to more formal proceedings, when the Clerk may be required to give impartial advice to the Presbytery.

A superintendence committee, sometimes acting informally through its convener, can often act helpfully in such situations, as can the Ministry Department in the Church Offices, acting through its secretary.

If a minister is willing to seek and take advice early enough, any difficulty may be more easily resolved; but if the minister is not so willing, the convener of the Presbytery's superintendence committee may take a more formal initiative, and if this meets with a rebuff, the authority of the Presbytery for a more formal visit may be sought.

8. Inspection of Records

Presbyteries are responsible for ensuring that all records of congregations within their bounds are properly kept, and to this end each Presbytery requires such records to be submitted annually for inspection.

With regard to their own records, Acts VI, 1992, and II, 1996, provide for the Presbyteries themselves to examine these. This was a consequence of the abolition of Synods, which had previously examined Presbytery records. An extract minute showing that the examination has taken place must be submitted annually to the Board of Practice and Procedure, which reports appropriately to the Assembly.

Presbyteries are also required to ensure that their records are in due course sent or delivered to the Principal Clerk for transmission to the Scottish Record Office (see Chapter VI, p. 40).

9. Summary

A Presbytery is responsible for all spiritual matters within its bounds, and should be alert to take suitable initiatives for the advancement of Christ's kingdom, even if these are neither prescribed by law nor instructed by the Assembly; but a useful summary of its specific duties within its bounds is as follows:

(a) determine the number of charges
(b) set parish boundaries
(c) dispose of calls to ministers and from congregations
(d) consider levels of parish assistance
(e) accept demissions and resignations
(f) record tributes to deceased members
(g) deal with commissions from Kirk Sessions
(h) admit to membership of the Presbytery (of those qualified) and, on the instructions of the Assembly, to the ministry of the Church of Scotland
(i) nominate and supervise candidates for the ministry, the auxiliary ministry, the diaconate, and the readership, and encourage recruitment
(j) carry out trials for licence
(k) arrange and conduct services of ordination, licensing, induction, commissioning, setting apart, union or linking, and dedication
(l) determine ministerial stipends in conjunction with the Committee on the Maintenance of the Ministry
(m) determine Mission and Aid allocations in conjunction with the Board of Stewardship and Finance
(n) arrange and carry out Quinquennial Visitations
(o) arrange for the Quinquennial Inspection of church property
(p) process applications for work on property
(q) examine congregational records and accounts
(r) attest Presbytery records
(s) appoint commissioners to the Assembly
(t) consider Assembly remits
(u) consider matters of public interest, locally, nationally, and internationally
(v) deal with petitions and overtures
(w) discharge its disciplinary functions
(x) act as a court of appeal
(y) ensure that the laws and accepted practices of the Church are observed

The above list, only slightly modified, has been taken, by kind permission, from *An Introduction to Practice and Procedure in the Church of Scotland*, privately published by the Rev. A. Gordon McGillivray, former Depute Clerk, Principal Clerk, and Clerk to the Presbytery of Edinburgh.

XV. KIRK SESSION

1. Spiritual Responsibility

The Kirk Session is the lowest court of the Church. It has spiritual responsibility for the congregation and parish, and spiritual jurisdiction over all the members of the congregation, including its own members, but with the exception of its Moderator and of any other ministers who are members of the congregation, all ministers being subject to the Presbytery.

As with other courts, spiritual responsibility should be regarded in broad terms. It involves leadership, nurturing the spirituality of the congregation and its members, caring for the spiritual welfare of the parish and parishioners, encouraging members to participate in the worship and life of the congregation, and promoting mission and evangelism in the parish. To see the function of the Kirk Session in such terms is to realise that it has not completely fulfilled its purpose when it has carried out all the specific duties laid upon it by law.

Some specific duties are set out in Act XVII, 1931.

2. Moderator

The minister of a congregation is *ex officio* the Moderator of its Kirk Session. When the congregation is vacant, or when the minister is absent, on sick leave, or having been granted leave of absence for other reasons, or being under suspension, the Presbytery appoints an Interim Moderator, who has all the powers and functions of Moderator. An Interim Moderator may be appointed in anticipation of an impending vacancy, to deal with vacancy business, while the minister is still in office.

Act X, 1933, provides that the minister or Interim Moderator may authorise another minister to act as Moderator, provided that the authority is given in writing, specifying the meeting or meetings to which it applies, and the business to be conducted. No other business is competent in such a situation.

There are two exceptional cases. First, if a meeting is called in connection with readjustment, the Presbytery appoints a minister or elder to preside (Act IV, 1984). Second, a minister of another Church may act as Moderator when he or she is one of an ecumenical team (Act X, 1992).

The Moderator in the chair has a casting vote, but no deliberative vote, but, unlike Moderators of other courts, may introduce items of business and speak to them. (see also Chapter XII, p. 85 — Tied Votes; and Chapter XVI, p. 118 — Joint Ministry.)

3. Other Ministers

In joint, shared, or team ministries, where the ministers have equal status, each is entitled to act as Moderator, usually by rota or on another basis by agreement. This does not apply to associate ministers. Those appointed in terms of Act IV, 1984, are members of the Kirk Session, but others are not, unless there is specific provision for this in their terms of appointment (see Chapter XVI, p. 119). Any other minister who is a member of the congregation may, if invited by the Kirk Session, be associated in its practical work, with the right to attend meetings and to speak, but not to vote (Act III, 1992, Section 15).

Probationers and other assistant ministers who are not ordained have no right to attend meetings, but they may be invited to do so, in which case they may also be invited to speak on specific items of business.

4. Deacons

A deacon working in a parish is entitled to be a corresponding member of the Kirk Session. Any other deacon who is a member of the congregation may be associated with the practical work of the Kirk Session. Although Act III, 1992, does not, in Section 23, specify the right to attend meetings and speak, as it does in the case of ministers, it would be possible to construe the additional part of Section 15 as being partially definitive of the meaning of being "associated" with the practical work. In practice this should not be a major difficulty, as the Kirk Session can in any event invite such a person to attend and speak. The only difference between being a corresponding member and being associated with the practical work is that the corresponding member has this status *ex officio*, whereas association with the practical work is by invitation only.

5. Elders

All communicant members of the congregation aged 21 or over are eligible to be ordained and admitted as elders. Act XXVIII, 1966, declared that women are eligible for the eldership on the same terms and conditions as men, and the

Assembly has subsequently ruled that this means that, while every Kirk Session is not required to have women in its membership, no Kirk Session has the right to decide as a matter of policy or principle that it will appoint no women. The declared equal eligibility of women and men in the matter is not to be infringed by failing to give the same consideration to individual women as is given to individual men in considering their suitability, as distinct from eligibility, for appointment.

Ministers and deacons are not eligible to be appointed as elders, even if they previously had that status. This applies to auxiliary ministers, even when not in designated appointments.

The procedures for appointing elders are set out in Act X, 1932. This Act was repealed by Act XXVIII, 1966, "in so far as it is inconsistent with this Act", but the only changes actually required were minor ones, such as adding "or her" after "his". It should be noted that the persons considered must have attained 21 years of age, although Herron (pp. 281-2) mistakenly says 18. It would surely be wrong to declare a solemn act of ordination null and void, if a person under 21 has been ordained in good faith on the strength of this, but admission to the Kirk Session could be withdrawn until he or she reached the proper age.

A new elder is ordained to office, and admitted to the Kirk Session. An elder who leaves a congregation ceases to be a member of its Kirk Session but retains ordained status, and, on becoming a member of another congregation, does not *ipso facto* become a member of its Kirk Session. If invited to become a member, such an elder is admitted, but not re-ordained.

Ordination and admission both take place at a service of public worship.

6. Assessors

When a Kirk Session has become too small to have a quorum, which is three, including the Moderator, the Presbytery should appoint Assessors to act with it. These may be ministers or elders. The first duty of a Kirk Session so supplemented is to appoint more elders. When this has been done, the Assessors should report accordingly to the Presbytery, and ask to be discharged.

The most frequent use of Assessors is at the beginning of a Church Extension charge, when there is no extant Kirk Session.

There is another use of Assessors, namely "in cases of difficulty, at the discretion of the Presbytery" (see p. 169). In such a case the Assessors will remain in place until the difficulty has been resolved, or until the Presbytery resolves to seek to deal with it in some other way.

In appointing Assessors for any reason, the Presbytery should state whether or not they will have the right to vote.

7. Session Clerk

Each Kirk Session must appoint a Clerk, known as the Session Clerk, who need not be an elder, but almost invariably is. On appointment the Clerk must take the oath *de fideli* (see Chapter XIII, p. 90). In the absence of the Clerk, a temporary Clerk must be appointed, who must take the oath.

In any case of failure to appoint a Clerk, the duties devolve on the Moderator, but this should be regarded as a last resort, and it is better to appoint a person who is not an elder, or an elder from a neighbouring Kirk Session, rather than have the two offices combined for any significant time.

Two or more may be appointed to fulfil the duties involved, in which case the basis on which the duties are divided should be recorded in the minutes.

The Clerk's duties are to prepare the minutes and keep them in the minute book, to issue extract minutes when so instructed, to ensure the safe custody of all official records, and to deal with all correspondence, including extract minutes from other courts and committees. It is important that any document received by the Clerk for the court should be submitted to the court at its next meeting.

A Clerk who signs any document and designates himself or herself as Session Clerk is presumed to be acting with the full authority of the court (cf. p. 91).

The Session Clerk is also the one on whom the duty of taking emergency action in the absence of the minister devolves. For example, Act II, 1986, provides that, if the minister fails to appear at the time of public worship, the Session Clerk should lead the congregation in an act of devotion, or ask someone else to do so.

8. Other Appointments

The Kirk Session in a *quoad omnia* (see p. 130) charge requires also to appoint a Treasurer, and in other charges it may also do so if it has separate funds, such as benevolent funds, which are not the responsibility of the financial board.

The Kirk Session also appoints the organist (or precentor, or leader of the praise) and the beadle (or church officer), but the financial board is responsible for their salaries.

Although a minister is not entitled to fees for weddings or funerals, these being among the duties of the full-time office for which a stipend is paid, organists and beadles are entitled to fees, as they are part-time employees and such services are additional to their regular work. If a marriage service is being recorded, the organist is entitled to an additional fee for the recording, in respect of performing rights.

Care should be taken with contracts for these appointees, as these are matters of civil law, although the application of industrial relations legislation will depend on the length of service and the weekly hours worked. It would be wise to consult the Law Department of the Church unless appropriate legal advice is available locally. Whether the employer is formally the Kirk Session or the financial board, both bodies should approve it, and Act XVI, 1931 requires the terms of it to be recorded in the Kirk Session minute book. Advice is available from the Secretary of the Panel on Worship about appropriate fees for organists.

Act XVI, 1931, also provides that in the conduct of public worship the organist is under the control and direction of the minister. This is a matter in which the spirit of the law is best fulfilled by the minister establishing a good rapport with the organist.

The Kirk Session may also appoint a Session Officer, but it is more usual for the beadle to undertake the duties of such an appointment.

9. Meetings

A pattern of meetings, e.g. on the second Tuesday of each month, is usual for a Kirk Session, but such meetings must each be called by pulpit intimation or written notice. In an emergency a meeting could be called by telephone or by personal visitation. The adequacy of such notice will depend on the circumstances. The meeting should be asked at the outset to agree that the notice was adequate, and such agreement should be minuted. If there is no such agreement, the meeting should not proceed. When the minute of a meeting called at short notice is submitted for approval at the next regularly called meeting, that meeting may, for the avoidance of doubt, agree to homologate the decisions recorded.

A rigourous pursuit of every possible hypothesis in this area would have to deal with such questions as what happens if an emergency meeting of a Kirk Session, called at short notice by pulpit intimation, decides that the notice was adequate, but the subsequent regular meeting, with members attending who were not present to hear the intimation, decides that the notice was not adequate. The general answer to that hypothetical question, which might be applied *mutatis mutandis* to others, is that the Kirk Session could take the matter by reference to the Presbytery, or aggrieved members could petition the Presbytery.

Kirk Sessions do not normally adjourn, but they may do so, in order to continue a particular piece of business. The normal practice is to close each meeting with prayer, the next meeting being called in the usual way.

10. Spiritual Oversight

Among the specific responsibilities of the Kirk Session is the spiritual oversight of the congregation. Act VI, 1938, and subsequent amending Acts, provide for the keeping of the Roll of Communicants. Provision has been made for loose-leaf and computerised records (see Appendix F). Normally a roll-keeper is appointed by the Kirk Session, failing which the duty devolves on the Session Clerk.

In 1995 the Assembly agreed to a recommendation that only one roll be kept, "but in such a way that names can be coded or annotated so as to identify members, adherents, children attending communion, children not attending communion, persons on the supplementary roll, and any other categories a Kirk Session may choose."

The names of ministers of congregations should be on the roll, and other ministers who are not in parishes may join congregations as members, their names also being on the roll. This is without prejudice to the fact that ministers are not under the spiritual jurisdiction of Kirk Sessions.

Pastoral care of the members is part of spiritual supervision, and for this purpose the congregation should be divided into districts, with one or more elders being responsible for each district. For each district there should be an elder's roll book, containing the names and addresses of the members in the district, and other relevant information from the communion roll. Elders should visit the members in their districts regularly, and bring to the notice of the roll-keeper any changes of address or other amendments which should be made to the roll. If they encounter a pastoral situation which requires action they cannot themselves undertake, they should draw this to the attention of the minister or of the Kirk Session.

11. Worship

While the responsibility for the conduct of worship belongs exclusively to the minister, subject to the Presbytery, the Kirk Session, with the concurrence of the minister, appoints the times for diets of worship, including communion services.

While the repair and maintenance of the church building is the responsibility of the financial board, major matters such as a renovation which includes changes in the layout of the building, or the installation of a new organ, are spiritual matters which, in *quoad sacra* charges, require the approval of the Kirk Session. In such matters the financial board is obviously also involved because of the financial implications. When there is a proposal involving both the Kirk Session and the financial board, the only safe basis on which to proceed is with the approval of both. If such a matter is considered at a joint meeting, care must be taken to ensure that any vote for approval contains a majority of both bodies.

12. Baptism

While baptism, as a sacrament, is a ministerial act, it is the responsibility of elders to encourage parents to bring their children for baptism. In the event of parents, neither of whom is a communicant member but who express a willingness to become members, seeking baptism of a child, the baptism may take place immediately, but the Kirk Session is required to appoint an elder to shepherd them into membership.

It is also the responsibility of the Kirk Session to keep a roll of all baptisms, but the usual practice is for the minister to act on behalf of the Session in this matter.

It occasionally happens that an "emergency" baptism is administered to an infant by a hospital chaplain, in which case it is the responsibility of the chaplain to ensure that the baptism is recorded in the appropriate roll, which is that of the congregation to which the parents belong, or that of the parish in which they reside. (1954, Sess. 1) There is no authorisation for a chaplain to keep a separate baptismal roll. If a chaplain does so, it should be submitted annually to the Presbytery and in due course submitted to the Principal Clerk for onward transmission to the Scottish Record Office; but this does not relieve the chaplain from the duty of ensuring that baptisms are recorded in a congregation's baptismal roll.

The only authorised exception to the rule that baptisms must be recorded in a congregation's baptismal roll is the Forces Register of Baptisms (see Chapter XVI, p. 123).

Act XVII, 1963, governs the administration of baptism to infants, and Act IV, 1975, specifies those who may administer the sacraments.

13. Communion

The Sacrament of the Lord's Supper, or Holy Communion, is a ministerial act, for which the Kirk Session does not require to be constituted, although it is normally the function of the elders to assist in the distribution of the elements. The minister may invite others to do this, but would be wise, in normal circumstances, to seek the concurrence of the Kirk Session.

The issuing of communion cards is not obligatory, as it is no longer necessary to record attendances at communion, but it is still a fairly common practice (cf. communion tokens, p 126).

Members of other Christian Churches are eligible to take communion in the Church of Scotland. If communion cards are in use, such persons may be given visitors' cards at the church door.

Strictly speaking, members are entitled to communion by the common cup, and to the ordinary elements of bread and wine (1909, Sess. 11 & 13) but the individual cup and unfermented wine are permitted and are in use in many congregations. Kirk Sessions should be cautious about making any change in these matters. Occasionally sections of a church are designated for those who prefer fermented or unfermented wine, or the common or individual cup, but this would appear to be divisive of a congregation at a sacrament which is, among other things, symbolic of unity. Nevertheless, it may be expedient.

Act XV, 1992, governs the admission of children to Communion, and Act III, 1985 the admission of mentally handicapped persons.

14. Other Functions

For the functions of the Kirk Session in relation to vacancy procedure, Act V, 1984, should be consulted.

It should be noted that, while various records, especially the minute book, the baptismal roll, and the roll of communicants, must be submitted annually to the Presbytery for inspection, it is the responsibility of the Kirk Session itself to ensure that they are kept safely, to attest them accordingly, and in due course to ensure that they are sent or delivered to the Principal Clerk, for onward transmission to the Scottish Record Office (see Chapter VI, p. 40).

XVI. MINISTRY

1. Ordination

"Ordination is the solemn setting apart of a person to some public church office" *(The Form of Presbyterial Church Government, 1645)*. Authority to ordain ministers is vested in Presbyteries, and the terms and conditions under which this may be done, are set out in Act II, 1987.

This Act also states the basic functions of ministry, and the conditions under which these functions may be exercised.

"No man ought to take upon him the office of a minister of the word without a lawful calling" *(The Form of Presbyterial Church Government, 1645)*. It is not sufficient that a person believes that he or she has been called by God to the ministry. A call must be tested by the Church. That is done (a) by a "selection school" process, arranged by the Committee on Education for the Ministry, and (b) by the Presbytery within whose jurisdiction the person is. In the case of parish ministry, the "lawful calling" is confirmed by the call of a congregation.

Procedure for the admission of ministers already ordained in other Churches is set out in Act III, 1995.

2. Education

This Church has always believed in an educated ministry, the education being both general and theological. The norm has been a first degree in Arts, or other degree held to be equivalent for this purpose, followed by a degree in Divinity in the University of St. Andrews, Glasgow, Aberdeen, or Edinburgh. There are now many exceptions to this norm, but they all conform to the basic concept of an educated ministry.

Historically, the Church has had close links with the above Universities, and has relied on them to teach theology to an acceptable standard. It has not set up seminaries of its own. An apparent exception was the establishment by the Free Church, after the Disruption, of its own colleges: Trinity College (Glasgow), Christ's College (Aberdeen), and New College (Edinburgh). After the 1929 Union, however, these Colleges were amalgamated with the Faculties of Divinity in the Universities of Glasgow, Aberdeen, and Edinburgh respectively, although there are still some respects in which they retain separate legal identities.

The Universities have undertaken to provide courses acceptable to the Church, and the Church participates in the appointment of professors, through the Boards of Nomination to Church Chairs.

3. Probationary Period

On satisfactory completion of a prescribed course of education, a candidate is taken on Trials for Licence by his or her Presbytery, and may then be licensed by the Presbytery. Normally a Licentiate then becomes a Probationer, entering on a probationary period as assistant minister in a charge. If the probationary period is sustained, he or she is eligible to be called to a charge.

Relevant legislation is to be found in Acts V, 1985, and XI, 1994. The Preamble, Questions, and Formula to be used at licensing are in Act XI, 1932, but it speaks of "licensing of Probationers", presumably on the assumption that a Licentiate will *ipso facto* be a Probationer, which is not now the case (XI, 1994).

Proposals for significant change in this area are being brought to the 1997 Assembly. Meanwhile, further information may be obtained from the Committee on Education for the Ministry, and from the Committee on Probationers.

4. Parish Ministry

The Church's obligation to provide religious services for the people of Scotland through a territorial ministry is fulfilled by parish ministers; and this is the ministry to which the process of selection, education, and probation normally leads.

The right of a congregation to call its own minister, rather than have one imposed on it, is regarded as a fundamental one in the Church. Historically, this was a right claimed by the Church, and included the right of Presbyteries to adjudicate on calls, the denial of which by civil authorities in the interests of the patronage exercised by heritors, was one of the causes of the Disruption. It is now regarded as a right of congregations. It does not apply to Church Extension charges, and has been considerably modified by regulations governing the appointment of ministers to charges in the Presbytery of Shetland.

It is important to note that the congregation's right of call is not absolute, in that it comes into effect only after permission to call has been granted, following the completion of the procedures for dealing with the question of readjustment; and if a congregation fails to call a minister within the prescribed time limit of six months, which may be extended by the Presbytery, the *ius devolutum* (devolved right) applies, and the Presbytery may appoint a minister.

It is true that the congregation nominates and calls, and the Presbytery inducts; but only very seldom and in most unusual circumstances has a Presbytery declined to induct a minister chosen by a congregation.

It is also true that, on one interpretation, Act IV, 1984, appears to give the Presbytery power to impose on a united congregation the minister of one of two congregations being united, but it is questionable (a) whether that interpretation is correct (see discussion under Interpretation, p 60.), (b) whether, even if it is correct, a Presbytery would choose to exercise such power, and (c) whether the Assembly, on appeal, would sustain such exercise of power.

5. Vacancy Procedure

The whole matter of vacancy procedure is contained in detail in Act V, 1984, which should be referred to for its terms. What follows is in no way a summary of the Act, but merely draws attention to some of its provisions.

a) Anticipating a Vacancy

If sufficiently long notice is given of an impending vacancy, for example when the date of a minister's demission is known well in advance, it is possible for much vacancy procedure to be carried out, such as the settlement of the question of readjustment, and the appointment of a vacancy committee which, with the permission of the Presbytery, may carry out all its duties prior to reporting the name of a sole nominee to the Kirk Session, before the charge is actually vacant. This can significantly shorten the time during which a congregation is vacant.

It should be recognised however that the fact that the minister of another charge is being considered by a vacancy committee should be a matter of strict confidentiality in the interests of that minister, and should continue to be so unless and until that minister is invited to be sole nominee. In such a case the ability of that minister to give long notice of impending translation is limited.

b) Withdrawal

While there is provision for a sole nominee to withdraw, and even for a minister who has been elected and called to decline the appointment, ministers ought to be careful to act responsibly in this matter. They should discover all relevant information which might lead to withdrawal at the earliest possible stage. For example, if a minister agrees to be sole nominee without ever seeing the manse, visits it on the day of his preaching as sole nominee, and his election, and then withdraws because he does not like the manse, that can only be called unreasonable behaviour, although it is lawful. It is also unreasonable for a minister, at the last moment, to indicate acceptance on condition that a different house is provided for a manse. Manses belong to congregations, not to ministers, and must be chosen by congregations. If at an earlier stage a minister indicates dissatisfaction with the manse, the vacancy committee can take that into account in choosing a sole nominee.

Such considerations may not be matters of law, but they are related to the fundamental precepts of law and morality nevertheless. The precept "to injure no-one" (see Chapter I, p. 2) should constrain candidates in a vacancy not to act in ways which will cause considerable inconvenience to others, unless very grave and exceptional reasons make this the lesser of two evils; but the lesser of two evils is still evil, and the situation should be avoided by wise anticipation as far as possible.

c) Undue Influence

The Assembly has declared that an Interim Moderator or a *locum tenens* in a vacant congregation is not *ipso facto* debarred from receiving a call to be minister of that congregation (1988, Sess. 1). The reason for this was that there was doubt about whether ministers in such positions could give the necessary assurance that they had used no undue influence to secure the call.

The requirement to give this assurance is a relic of the 1888 Act on Simonaical Practices. The term "simony" is derived from the story of Simon trying to buy from the apostles the power to give the Holy Ghost (Acts 8:18-24), and is used of purchasing or attempting to purchase ecclesiastical appointments. The 1904 Act on Offences in the Election and Appointment of Ministers, from which the phrase "undue influence" comes, lists offences as "all bribing or treating of electors in order to induce them to vote or abstain from voting; promising them employment; paying, or promising to pay, them for loss of time, wages, travelling expenses, or conveyance to the poll; all undue influence, or the doing or threatening of any injury." By the legal *eiusdem generis* (of the same kind) rule, undue influence would be construed as actions of the same kind as those more specifically listed. It is clear that being an Interim Moderator or *locum tenens* does not come into such a category, but the force of "*ipso facto*" is that people in such positions might have more opportunity to use undue influence, so they still have to give the assurance. It might also appear that being regularly among the people gave such a person an advantage over other candidates, or it might be a disadvantage, and in any case it is wise for anyone in such a position to withdraw from it as soon as he or she forms an interest in being a candidate in the vacancy.

Similar reasoning could apply to an assistant minister or an associate minister in a vacant charge, although it would be more difficult for them to withdraw from positions on which their livelihood depended. It is also possible for a minister in a terminable tenure, whose appointment has been terminated to facilitate union, to be a candidate in the vacancy in the newly united charge, but if the Basis of Union has not provided for him or her to be the minister, it is wiser to seek another charge or appointment.

d) Other Procedures

Regulations 3, 1995, make provision for appointments to Church Extension charges. Special procedure for appointing ministers in the Presbytery of Shetland is to be found in Regulations I, 1995. The Presbytery of Europe is specially provided for in Act III, 1996, and the Presbytery of Jerusalem in Act VIII, 1979.

6. Induction

The procedure for induction of a parish minister, as well as for nomination, election, and call, is set out in detail in Act V, 1984.

Prior to induction, an edict has to be read on two Sundays to the congregation, giving opportunity for anyone, who has objections on the grounds of the life or doctrine of the minister to be inducted, to come and state these to the Presbytery at a meeting, usually just before the service of induction, "with certification that if no relevant objection be then made and immediately substantiated, the Presbytery will proceed without further delay." Any objector who appears must have convincing proof of the substance of the objection, because the consequences of delaying an induction on the basis of an allegation which turned out to be unfounded are manifestly unacceptable (See also Chapter VII, p. 50).

7. *Ad Vitam Aut Culpam*

Until 1972 ministers were inducted to charges *ad vitam aut culpam*, which meant that their tenure could be terminated only by death or by judicial process in which a sufficiently serious offence to warrant termination of tenure, suspension or deposition was proved.

It was always open to a minister to offer to demit (see below, p. 118), but before the advent of pensions retirement took the form of the appointment of a colleague and successor, or assistant and successor, the congregation providing stipends for both the minister and the colleague or assistant.

Even with the advent of pensions, while the *ad vitam aut culpam* rule was still in force, a minister could not be required to retire, which is why readjustment legislation made special provision for those retiring in the interests of readjustment, so that a minister might be induced to retire to facilitate readjustment. The same legislation was careful to provide that, when a terminable appointment was made, the charge was "suppressed" and the minister was introduced to it, but not inducted.

A major change was effected by Acts III, 1972, and XXI, 1974, whose effect was that ministers inducted after the Assembly of 1972 would be required to retire at 70 years of age. Act IV, 1995, reduced the age to 65, repealing the previous Acts. Ministers inducted before 1972 still have rights *ad vitam aut culpam*, and those inducted before 1995 retain the right to remain in their charges until the age of 70.

Other changes were made by Act IV, 1984, which provided for induction on a basis of terminable tenure; Act I, 1988, which removed the need to find fault from the legislation relating to congregations in an unsatisfactory state; and Act VI, 1984, which provided for termination of tenure without *culpa* in changed circumstances, but a minister inducted before the passing of Act VI, 1984, must give prior written notice that he or she is prepared to concur if the Presbytery decides on termination. The question whether a minister inducted *ad vitam aut culpam* can have tenure terminated under Act I, 1988, without fault being found, has not been tested in any case.

8. Stipend

A minister who has been duly inducted to a charge is paid a stipend. The fund from which stipends are paid is known as the Fund for the Maintenance of the Ministry, but its full title is "The Fund for the Maintenance of Gospel Ordinances for the People in every Parish of Scotland through a Territorial Ministry" This obviously relates to *Article III*, and makes clear the basic purpose for which ministers are paid.

Stipend is not a salary or wage or remuneration, but the way in which the Church "seeks to ensure for every minister and his dependants a reasonable maintenance." (*Stipend in the Church of Scotland*, by A. J. H. Gibson, p. 2) It is basically for the same reason that a minister is provided with a manse.

A minister is also entitled to "Listed Expenses", which are: communion expenses, fees or expenses of a visiting minister at a Communion Season, holiday pulpit supply on six Sundays, pulpit supply during attendance at the Assembly, telephone rental and cost of official calls, stationery and postage stamps for official use, and travelling expenses on ministerial duties. These must be paid by congregations which are not aid-receiving.

9. Parish

A parish is a territorial area in which the Church operates through a minister or ministers, Kirk Session, and congregation. A charge is a minister's sphere of pastoral duty. This includes the responsibilities a minister has both as parish minister and as minister of the congregation of the parish. However, it is possible for more than one minister to be inducted to a charge; and, in the case of linked congregations, one charge will include responsibility for more than one parish and congregation. Ministers are inducted to charges, but not to other spheres of pastoral duty, the exceptions being theological professors and principals of church colleges (see p. 98).

10. Parish boundaries

It is the responsibility of the Presbytery to determine the parish boundaries within its own bounds. Normally adjustments to parish boundaries are made in connection with the establishment of Church Extension charges, or in connection with readjustment, in accordance with the relevant legislation.

It is sometimes argued that, once a minister has been inducted to a charge, the boundaries of the parish may not be changed without his or her consent. Legally, however, the Presbytery does have the right to alter the boundaries without the minister's consent. The Plan of Union, 1929, provided for Presbyteries to readjust parish boundaries after the Union. This was a special situation, in that parishes had to be found for all the former United Free Church congregations, which meant that most existing parishes had to be significantly reduced, but there was no mention of any need for the consent of existing parish ministers. The clear inference is that Presbyteries have the right to make alterations.

In practice a Presbytery's ability to do so will be restricted by the possibility of appeal or dissent and complaint. If the magnitude of the proposed alteration were such that it involved considerable change, either of increase or reduction in a parish minister's responsibility, that minister could appeal, not on the grounds that the alteration was illegal, but on the grounds that it was unreasonable. If the nature of the proposed alteration seemed to be such that it amounted to a form of readjustment, an appeal might be taken on the grounds that the alteration should have been made by the appropriate procedure for readjustment.

Accordingly, Presbyteries should certainly consult the parish minister or ministers concerned before altering parish boundaries, and should be wary of making substantial alterations without the consent of such ministers.

11. Demission

Demission is the act of withdrawing from a charge, or from status as a minister, but it is not an act of resignation in that it is not unilateral. It requires the consent of the Presbytery. What the Church has conferred, it alone can remove. If, for example, there were proceedings pending against the minister, which might lead to suspension or deposition, the Presbytery might decide not to allow demission, in order that the proceedings could continue (see Chapter X, p. 72).

When a minister offers to demit, which must be done in writing, the Presbytery at its next meeting (or at a meeting *pro re nata*) appoints a committee to confer with him or her, and report to the following meeting (or a meeting *in hunc effectum*), at which the Presbytery will make a decision, and if it agrees to the demission it will appoint a date (Act V, 1984, Section 27, as amended by Act V, 1996, which is about demission of a charge, but, in the absence of other specific legislation, should also be followed for demission of status). The point of the conference is to ensure that the minister is fully aware of the consequences and implications of the proposed demission, especially if it is to be a demission of status.

When tenure is to be terminated because of age, in terms of Act IV, 1995, that is treated as if an offer to demit had been received and accepted, and there is no need for a committee to be appointed to confer with the minister.

There are special arrangements for demission in the interests of readjustment, and these are set out in Act X, 1996, which amends the provisions of Act IV, 1984, in this respect.

12. Joint Ministry

The 1994 Report of the Committee on Parish Re-appraisal states that it has defined a Joint Ministry as one in which a charge has within it another church appointment. This is a particular form of part-time ministry (see Section 16 below). The other church appointment could be a chaplaincy, under the auspices of the Board of National Mission or the Joint Prison Chaplaincies Board. Provision has to be made for agreement between the congregation and the body appointing the chaplain, so that the person chosen will be acceptable to both. There should be a Basis of Joint Ministry, setting out the terms of the joint appointment.

Different from this Joint Ministry is the arrangement set out in Section 18 of Act IV, 1984, which provides that when two congregations are united, each with a minister, these ministers both become ministers of the united congregation. This arrangement was previously known as a joint ministry.

13. Associate Ministry

There are two situations in which the term "associate minister" is used.

1) there is legal provision for Associate Ministry as a form of Joint Ministry (see above) in Act IV, 1984. An associate minister of this kind is appointed by the Committee on Parish Re-appraisal, in consultation with the minister of the charge and the Presbytery of the bounds. This will normally be a full-time appointment, and the necessary expenses will be payable from the central funds of the Church, to the extent that the congregation or congregations of the charge cannot meet them. Act III, 1992, provides that the Associate in terms of the 1984 Act will be a member of the Kirk Session or Kirk Sessions, and also of the Presbytery.

2) There is a kind of associate minister appointed by a Kirk Session, on its own initiative, but with the approval of the Presbytery, on the understanding that the Kirk Session, or other financial board, will be entirely responsible for all the expenses involved, without prejudice to its other financial commitments. There is no legislation applying directly to such appointments, and there appears to be no difference in law between an associate minister of this kind and an assistant minister.

The concept of this second form of Associate Ministry began in 1958 when steps were being taken to discontinue the collegiate charge at St. Cuthbert's, Edinburgh, and the special Act which was passed made provision for an associate minister. A similar Act was passed in the case of Glasgow St. James' (Pollok) in 1969. These specific Acts are no longer in force, but in so far as the associate ministers appointed under them may be regarded as prototypes of the second form of Associate Ministry, it is noteworthy that they did not provide for the associate ministers to be members of the Kirk Sessions. Such provision may however be incorporated in terms of appointment approved by the Presbytery.

The 1994 Model Deed (Act II, 1994) provides for "any associate minister" to be a member of the Congregational Board, but without the right to vote, except in the event of being chairman and having a casting vote. Act III, 1992, provides for an associate minister to be a member of Presbytery. The question whether these provisions apply to the second type of associate minister, in the absence of a specific legal basis for such ministry, is in these cases academic, because the "associate minister" will qualify for membership of Board and Presbytery as an ordained assistant.

The question whether such an associate minister will be a member of the Kirk Session is a different matter, for there is no legislation providing for an associate minister, other than one appointed in terms of Act IV, 1984, to be a member of Kirk Session. If however the Kirk Session itself is agreeable to the associate minister being one of its members, it may be presumed to be within the competence of the Presbytery to approve terms and conditions providing for this. (If an associate minister has been acting as a member of Kirk Session without such approval, the best advice is to seek to have the position homologated by the Presbytery as soon as possible.)

In the absence of specific legislation on associate ministry, it would be possible for a licentiate to be appointed as an associate minister, in which case the question of membership of Kirk Session and Presbytery would not arise, although the question of ordination for the appointment could be raised.

14. Team Ministry

Another form of ministry involving more than one minister is a team ministry, in which two or more ministers share a parish and congregation on an equal basis. A team ministry may be an ecumenical one, in which a minister or ministers of another Church or other Churches is or are in the team.

In such cases there will normally be a Basis and Plan of Union whereby the congregations of the participating denominations are united, and this should provide for all the necessary financial arrangements, procedure for replacing members of the team, ownership of buildings, relationship to the appropriate authorities of the denominations involved, etc. Alternatively or in addition to a Basis and Plan of Union, the ecumenical congregation may have its own constitution. For the Church of Scotland, the Presbytery, with the concurrence of the Committee on Parish Re-appraisal, may approve such a constitution, provided that it is not at variance with any law of this Church, but if any part of it is at variance with the law, an Act of Assembly will be required.

Act X, 1992, makes exceptional provision for a minister of another Church to act as Moderator of a Kirk Session, when a member of an ecumenical team which includes a minister or ministers of this Church.

15. Shared Ministry

When there is provision for only one ministerial appointment to a charge, two ministers may nevertheless be inducted on the basis that they will share the one appointment. In such a case the Presbytery should, before induction, prepare a Basis of Shared Ministry, which should clearly set out the terms on which the ministry will be shared. Amongst other things, the Basis should provide for the moderating of the Kirk Session, such eventualities as the departure of one of the ministers, e.g. by death, retirement, translation, demission, etc., for it must be clear from the outset whether such departure will *ipso facto* terminate the ministry, thus creating a vacancy, or whether the remaining minister will become the sole minister of the charge, or whether another minister may be called to share the ministry with the remaining minister.

Both ministers in a shared ministry will be members of Presbytery, but the Kirk Session will appoint only one elder to the Presbytery.

16. Part-time Ministry

A part-time ministry may be instituted as a form of readjustment. This may be a part-time parish ministry combined with another part-time ministerial appointment, such as a chaplaincy, in which case arrangements must be made in conjunction with the appointing authority for the chaplaincy or whatever the other appointment is. (This is what the Committee on Parish Re-appraisal has defined as Joint Ministry — see Section 12 above.)

A part-time ministry may also stand by itself, the remainder of the minister's time being at his or her own disposal, provided that remunerative employment even in this situation would require the approval of the Presbytery in terms of Act XXII, 1950, because the Presbytery would have to be satisfied that the nature of such employment would not interfere with parish responsibilities. A Basis of Part-time Ministry would be necessary, to provide a clear indication of the terms and conditions.

17. Severance of Pastoral Tie

A minister's pastoral tie may be severed by disciplinary action, which can be taken only on grounds of behaviour contrary to the Word of God or the law of the Church (see Chapter X, p. 65).

The law also provides a process for dealing with congregations in an unsatisfactory state, whereby the pastoral tie may be severed for reasons which are not grounds for disciplinary action (Act I, 1988).

There is also legislative provision for removing a minister when a congregation is in changed circumstances (Act VI, 1984).

Act XVI, 1933, provides for the severance of the pastoral tie on grounds of the minister's mental incapacity, when it appears that no improvement in that condition is expected.

Accordingly, unless induction has been on the basis of terminable tenure (Act IV, 1984), the pastoral tie of an inducted minister cannot be severed except by a special process provided by the law of the Church. Except in the case of mental incapacity, the process is a judicial one, and the minister has a right of appeal to the Judicial Commission, in terms of Act II, 1988, or to the Assembly or Commission of Assembly, either in terms of Act II, 1988, or where no provision is made in that Act.

If tenure has been legally terminated, either by judicial process, or in terms of a terminable tenure, the minister has no right of appeal to any civil court or tribunal. This is chiefly because civil jurisdiction is excluded by the *Declaratory Articles*, but also because an inducted minister has no contract of service (*Davies v. Presbyterian Church of Wales*, House of Lords, 1986).

18. Assistant Ministry

Strictly speaking, a probationer in a parish is there to be trained rather than to assist, although in practice what is done as a learning experience may be of great assistance to the parish minister, and the probationer is commonly called an assistant minister. The term may be applied also to one who, on completion of the probationary period, has been ordained in order to continue as assistant minister in that parish, or in another parish, or to an already ordained minister who is appointed to be an assistant minister. Occasionally a minister of another Church is appointed, in which case special permission of the Presbytery is required if he or she is to administer the Sacraments (Act IV, 1975).

A probationary period is always full-time employment, whereas other assistant ministers may be appointed on a part-time basis.

Probationers are given their placements by the Committee on Education for the Ministry, but this clearly requires the consent of the parish minister who will be the supervising minister. The appointment is intimated to the Presbytery, which is responsible for normal presbyterial supervision. On appointment, the probationer's training becomes the responsibility of the Committee on Probationers, which may prescribe additional training, and which is responsible eventually for deciding whether or not the probationary period should be sustained. Since the choice of charge in which a probationer is placed depends on its suitability for training purposes, and not on the ability of the congregation to pay all or part of a probationer's salary and expenses, these are paid from the central funds of the Church.

Other assistant ministers are appointed by Kirk Sessions, but if a minister eligible for a charge is to be appointed, the concurrence of the Presbytery should be sought. In any event, the Presbytery should be informed and, since the Kirk Session, or financial board, will be entirely responsible for the payment of an assistant minister, the Presbytery may forbid an appointment if it is liable to have an adverse effect on the congregation's ability to meet its other financial commitments.

19. Community Ministry

A community minister may be appointed by the Committee on Parish Re-appraisal, on the initiative of the Presbytery, and with its concurrence. The terms and conditions of the appointment are drawn up by the Committee in consultation with the Presbytery, and the Presbytery, in concurring in the appointment will thereby endorse its terms and conditions. Normally the community minister will operate in an area covering more than one parish, but his or her responsibilities will be to work in these parishes without having responsibility for their congregations. The community minister may be associated with the practical work of the Kirk Session or Kirk Sessions within his or her area of operation, but may not be a member of any Kirk Session.

20. Chaplaincies

In recent years there has been a considerable growth in the establishment of chaplaincies of one kind or another. Special legislation has long existed for

Chaplains to Her Majesty's Forces, but now there are also full-time appointments to university, school, hospital, industrial, and prison chaplaincies.

In so far as a chaplain is appointed in accordance with Assembly legislation, or is holding an appointment which qualifies for a seat in Presbytery in accordance with Assembly legislation, and is formally introduced to the office or accepted into membership by the Presbytery, the presumption is that authority to perform ministerial functions in pursuance of the chaplaincy is in place.

With regard to baptism and admission to church membership, special provision is made for Chaplains to Her Majesty's Forces to baptise and admit, and for appropriate records to be kept in the "Forces Register of Baptisms" and in the "Forces Register". Other chaplains must ensure that the names of those they baptise are entered in an appropriate parish record, and they must be aware that, as there is no Kirk Session in connection with their chaplaincies, they have no authority to admit to membership of the Church.

In practice it sometimes happens that a school or university chaplain will conduct the equivalent of a class for first communicants. There can be good pastoral reasons for this, in that a pupil or student may attend such classes with others in the same peer group. After that, the chaplain may furnish the person concerned with a certificate which the minister and Kirk Session of that person's home congregation or parish will accept, and so proceed to admit him or her in the normal way.

Sometimes however a school or university chaplain may proceed to a service of "confirmation" which purports to admit pupils or students to the Church. Such admission should take place only with the prior agreement of the person's home minister and Kirk Session, or of the minister and Kirk Session of the parish in which the school or university is situated.

Purported admission without the necessary prior agreement will be invalid, for only a Kirk Session may admit to membership of the Church of Scotland. The invalidity may be cured if subsequently a Kirk Session agrees to homologate the action of the chaplain and to add the person's name to the roll without further procedure. In pastoral terms, this is the only reasonable action a Kirk Session can take, because the irregularity is not the fault of the pupil or student, but of the chaplain, and the consequences of rejecting a young person at that stage are surely unacceptable pastorally. Clearly, chaplains should be careful not to put people in this kind of invidious position, and they could be subject to disciplinary proceedings if they did so.

21. Auxiliary Ministry

In 1980, the Assembly approved of the establishment of an auxiliary ministry, the relevant legislation for which is now Act III, 1987, in which an auxiliary minister is defined as "a person who has been ordained for life to a Ministry of Word and Sacrament exercisable under supervision on a part-time and non-stipendiary basis."

Recruitment to the auxiliary ministry is in the first instance a function of Presbyteries. Selection and training is under the supervision of the Committee on Education for the Ministry, in accordance with Regulations approved by the Assembly, copies of which are obtainable from that Committee.

An auxiliary minister, once ordained, functions only as provided for by a "designated appointment" drawn up by a Presbytery. No function of ministry can be exercised by an auxiliary minister who is not in a designated appointment, or without the approval of the supervising minister in a designated appointment, and the auxiliary minister is a member of Presbytery only during the period of such appointment.

Questions have sometimes been asked about the status of "retired" auxiliary ministers. The short answer is that the concept of retirement does not apply to them. There is no age limit beyond which an auxiliary minister becomes ineligible for a designated appointment. If an auxiliary minister decides, on grounds of age, to accept no further appointments, that person may no longer exercise any function of ministry, and ceases to be a member of Presbytery. However, since Presbyteries have considerable liberty in setting out the terms of designated appointments, there is nothing to prevent a Presbytery from devising an appointment with very light duties for an older auxiliary minister.

No auxiliary minister, whatever the terms of his or her designated appointment, may exercise any ministerial functions within the bounds of a Presbytery other than that responsible for the designated appointment, without the express permission of such other Presbytery.

22. Intrusion

A minister is not permitted to exercise ministerial functions in a parish other than his or her own without the prior consent of the minister of the parish (Act VIII, 1933). Although the precise terms of the Act refer only to parish ministers, it is a reasonable inference that no minister, whether or not a parish minister, may intrude into the parish of a parish minister to exercise any ministerial function.

The exceptions to this rule, in terms of the Act, are that the intruding minister is acting "under special commission or order of the Presbytery of the bounds, or of a superior court", or ministering to members of his or her congregation, or officiating at a marriage or funeral by private invitation (see Section 23 below).

The first of these will include community ministers and auxiliary ministers fulfilling the terms of their appointments. For the position of chaplains, see Section 20 above. In any case of doubt, a minister proposing to perform any ministerial function in a parish should obtain the consent of the parish minister before proceeding.

23. Private invitation

With regard to marriages by private invitation, it is necessary that the private invitation should be a *bona fide* one. Any minister who conducts a marriage in another minister's parish, without that minister's consent, of people whom he or she has not known personally or pastorally before being invited to conduct the marriage, in response to an invitation conveyed by a hotel or other commercial institution, or by the people themselves at the instance of such body, is clearly acting by commercial invitation, not private invitation. If the minister concerned has accepted a post as "chaplain" to the body concerned, this will make no difference, because such a chaplaincy has no authority from the Presbytery or from the Assembly.

If a minister is found to be conducting marriages on this kind of basis, the Presbytery should first enjoin him or her to desist forthwith from such practice, and thereafter any infringement of that injunction should be dealt with as a clear case of contumacy.

Similar considerations apply to funerals, but in view of the inevitably short notice involved, and when the parish minister cannot be reached, another minister may reasonably agree to act, so that the people concerned are not deprived of pastoral care at such a time.

24. The Diaconate

The Order of Deaconesses was originally formed to provide avenues of service within the Church for women who were not at the time eligible to be ministers or elders. The scheme has been revised several times, to include men in the diaconate, and to incorporate most of the lay missionaries. The latest scheme was approved by the Assembly (Reg. III, 1993) and details may be obtained from the Secretary of the Diaconate Committee. In 1996 the Assembly agreed that all members of the diaconate should be referred to as "deacons". There is a slight possibility of confusion with those who are deacons as members of Deacons' Courts, but the sense in which the word is used will usually be obvious from the context.

Act III, 1992, lays down the conditions on which deacons may be members of Presbyteries, and corresponding members of Kirk Sessions; and Act X, 1994, provides for their appointment as commissioners to the Assembly.

25. Readers

Readers are persons who have been trained and authorised to conduct public worship in the absence of a minister (see Act XVII, 1992 for details).

26. Jury Service

Ministers are not ineligible to serve as jurors in civil courts, but they are excusable as of right in terms of Part III of Schedule 1 to the Law Reform (Miscellaneous Provisions) (Scotland) Act 1980. This right to be excused may be claimed by a minister when cited for jury service (Section 1.(2) of the Act.).

27. Disqualifications

Act XXVII, 1959, repealed an Act of 1638, and thus removed all church restrictions on ministers being members of civil judicatories, but, under civil law, they are not eligible to be members of the House of Commons.

Act XXII, 1950, provides that no parish minister may undertake any contract for remunerative employment without the prior consent of the Presbytery or of the Assembly.

28. Pensions

Pensions for ministers, and their widows and orphans, are now the responsibility of the Retirement Scheme Committee, and detailed information is available from the Pensions Administrator at the Church Offices. For historical information about the Widows' Fund, see *The Scottish Ministers' Widows' Fund, 1743-1993*, edited by A. Ian Dunlop.

29. Ministerial Certificates

Act II, 1987, as well as dealing with ordination, provides for issuing Ministerial Certificates to ministers who take up employment which does not qualify for membership of Presbytery. Without prejudice to the validity of ordination for life, only ministerial members of Presbytery, or ministers with ministerial certificates, may perform the functions of ministry specified in the Act, and others are not entitled to use the designation "minister of the Church of Scotland" in connection with any such function.

A Ministerial Certificate is not the same thing as a Presbyterial Certificate, which is a certificate of status and good standing given to a minister who is a member of a Presbytery. It is the "satisfactory evidence" required by Section 13 of Act III, 1992.

XVII. CONGREGATION

1. Definition

Act IV, 1984 defines a congregation as "a company of persons associated together in a parish whose names are on the Communion Roll and who are under the pastoral oversight of a minister or ministers and a Kirk Session, for Christian worship, fellowship, instruction, mission and service." While the Act states that this definition is "for the purposes of this Act only", there is no other definition in any other Act, and this one may safely be used in most legal contexts, the chief exception being the inclusion of adherents in vacancy procedures (Act V, 1984). For pastoral purposes, adherents and the children of members should be regarded as belonging to a congregation.

The congregation is the basic organisational unit of the Church. While its members may not all live in its parish, it has a corporate rôle, along with the minister and Kirk Session, in the Church's "distinctive call and duty to bring the ordinances of religion to the people in every parish of Scotland through a territorial ministry" (*Article III*).

2. Membership

The process whereby people become members of the Church has evolved over the years. What became the normal practice acquired legal force by consuetude, but with no actual legislative support.

After the Reformation, the practice grew of catechising the people of the parish before each Communion, and of issuing communion tokens (for admission to Communion) to those who answered the questions satisfactorily. This eventually gave way to the practice of public profession of faith by first communicants, who were then admitted to communicant membership of the congregation. This practice was tacitly recognised in Act XVII, 1931, which stated that it was one of the duties of the minister to prepare young communicants.

In 1985 this practice was embodied in the law of the Church by a Declaratory Act (III, 1985), and repeated in practically the same terms in Act XV, 1992, as follows:

> In accordance with the law and practice of this Church, a Kirk Session is obliged to test the response in faith of a baptised person before authorising admission to the Lord's Table. The Kirk Session normally requires to be satisfied that the baptised person has received instruction in the faith and order of the Church, is of Christian character, and is ready to make public profession of faith, whereupon such person is admitted to the Lord's Table and his or her name is added to the Communion Roll.

In 1985 the context was a clarification that mentally handicapped persons were not disqualified from communicant membership; and in 1992 the context was the admission of children to Communion without their *ipso facto* becoming communicant members.

3. Public Profession

The public profession of those who seek membership is normally made at a diet of worship, in a Service of Admission, sometimes called Confirmation. The Kirk Session is normally constituted before the Service, hears a report from the minister to the effect that the candidates have received the necessary instruction, and resolves to proceed to their admission. After the Service, the Kirk Session, still being constituted, resolves to add their names to the Communion Roll. There is however no reason why the Kirk Session should not have made the necessary resolution to proceed at a meeting before the day of the Service, and the resolution to add the names to the Roll may be at a subsequent meeting, in which case it would not have to be constituted at the time of public profession. Nevertheless, it would be good practice for the Kirk Session to be formally present to witness the profession of faith on which its subsequent resolution to add names to the Roll will be based, and it is normal for the elders, or some of them, to join with the minister in giving "the right hand of fellowship."

4. Supervision

Act VI, 1938 and subsequent amending Acts should be referred to for the supervisory rôle of the Kirk Session with regard to membership, and for the procedure for removing names from the Roll.

When the name of a person who continues to live in or near the parish is removed, a record of that name is kept on the Supplementary Roll, "with a view to continued supervision".

5. Transference

When a member whose name is on the Roll wishes to move to another congregation, a Certificate of Transference (valid for one year) is issued by authority of the Kirk Session. This function is normally delegated to the minister or to one or more office-bearers. When a Certificate of Transference is presented, it is for the Kirk Session of the new congregation to decide to admit the person concerned to its Roll. Certificates from congregations of other Churches (Congregational, Methodist, United Free, and United Reformed) with whom the Church of Scotland has an agreement about mutual recognition of members are treated in the same way. In 1987 the Assembly commended the use of a form of certificate common to all the Churches.

6. Resolution of Kirk Session

Members may also be admitted by resolution of the Kirk Session. Usually this is a matter of restoring to the Roll a lapsed member whose name has been removed; but the Kirk Session has a wide discretionary power, and may competently resolve to admit, for example, a person who has mislaid a Certificate of Transference, or whose Certificate is out of date, or who comes from another denomination of the Church which is not one of those with which there is an agreement about mutual recognition of membership.

7. Adherents

Adherents are people who are associated with a congregation without becoming communicant members. The Kirk Session decides who shall be enrolled as adherents, and on this its decision is final.

In some areas the number of adherents is large because of a traditional reluctance to become communicants.

8. Spiritual Matters

Every congregation has a Kirk Session which is responsible, with the minister or ministers, for spiritual matters in the parish and congregation (see Chapter XV).

9. Temporal Matters

In *quoad omnia* charges, the Kirk Session is responsible for temporal as well as spiritual matters. In other charges, a separate financial board deals with temporal matters, namely finance and property, i.e. a Congregational Board, Deacons' Court, or Committee of Management. A general reference to financial boards includes a *quoad omnia* Kirk Session.

a) Historical Background

These differences in methods of administration have their origins in the history of the Church. Originally, parishes were civil as well as ecclesiastical areas, and the Kirk Session was the only body with ecclesiastical jurisdiction; but it was also responsible for the care of the poor of the parish, for the establishment and maintenance of schools, and for hospitals, responsibility for which has now passed to civil authorities.

When changes in population or other circumstances made it necessary to provide additional churches, the Church sought ways of providing these without having to go through the civil procedures for the creation of new parishes. One method was the establishment of chapels, or chapels of ease (to ease the situation). These chapels were subject to the jurisdiction of the Kirk Session of the parish within which they were formed, but the congregations were empowered to appoint trustees to manage their finance and property. Their ministers were not members of the Kirk Session, nor of the Presbytery, nor of the Synod, and thus not eligible to be commissioners to the Assembly.

The Assembly passed the Chapels Act in 1834, claiming the power to establish ecclesiastical parishes, with Kirk Sessions, and whose ministers were to be members of church courts. This was declared to be *ultra vires* by the Court of Session in 1839, and this was one of the issues between Church and State which gave rise to the Disruption.

Eventually, the right of the Church to create new parishes for ecclesiastical purposes (*quoad sacra*) was recognised, and the trustees of former chapels of ease were replaced by Congregational Boards. Thus the Congregational Board had its origin in parishes *quoad sacra*, as distinct from the original parishes *quoad omnia* (for all purposes) in which the Kirk Session dealt with temporal as well as spiritual matters. Although in practice all parishes are now ecclesiastical, the term *quoad omnia* is still used to denote a parish in which there is no separate financial board, and temporal as well as spiritual matters are dealt with by a Kirk Session.

After the union of 1929 a Model Deed of Constitution, providing for a **Congregational Board**, was drawn up, and has been subsequently revised, the latest version at time of writing being in Act II, 1994.

In the Free Church, the **Deacons' Court** was the body appointed to deal with finance and property. In spite of its name, it is not a court of the Church. The appointment of deacons is regulated by Act X, 1932.

In the United Presbyterian Church, the **Committee of Management** was the body appointed to deal with finance and property.

There are a few exceptions, such as Congregational Boards carried on from the United Free Church, congregations with constitutions approved by a superior court, and ecumenical parishes; and it should be noted that the constitutions of former U.P. congregations are not all the same.

b) Changing Constitutions

In order to implement the post-1929 policy of moving towards the Model Constitution, the Assembly has encouraged all congregations to change to the *quoad sacra* system, especially by Act XIX, 1964, which simplified the procedure for making this change. Thus, while this constitution belonged originally to parishes *quoad sacra*, it has now been adopted by many congregations which were formerly *quoad omnia*, or Free Church, or United Presbyterian.

There is also a procedure for changing to a form of constitution other than the Model Constitution (Act XXIV, 1933), but this involves approval by the Presbytery of the bounds, which must then refer the case to the Assembly. Since such a change would be a departure from the declared policy of the Assembly, it is not likely to succeed, and in 1995 the Assembly declined to sanction such a change.

c) Financial Boards

While financial boards are concerned with temporal as distinct from spiritual affairs, they are expected to apply spiritual principles to the administration of finance and fabric. The principles of Christian stewardship are especially relevant, for all the matters with which such boards deal are to be regarded as gifts from God, of which they are stewards.

The financial function of a board is not just to manage the available funds, but to encourage members of the congregation to contribute to these at a level which will enable all bills to be paid and all commitments met.

With regard to fabric, the task of the board is to see that all buildings belonging to the congregation are properly maintained and fully insured. This includes the manse, which belongs to the congregation, and must be kept in a good state of repair and decoration. Regular inspections of buildings are obligatory, as is the keeping of a Property Register.

d) Buildings: Use and Sale

Rules about the use of church buildings are set out in Act XVII, 1932; and procedure for the sale of buildings is laid down in Acts XXVI, 1933, and VII, 1995 (as amended by Act XIII, 1996) (see also Chapter XIX).

The Assembly has ruled that the funds of church courts and committees are not to be used for the purchase of alcohol, and has recommended that alcohol is not to be served in church buildings.

10. Woman's Guild

The congregational branch of the Woman's Guild is subject to the spiritual supervision of the Kirk Session. The Guild also has a national structure, with a constitution approved by the Assembly, to whose terms branches should be careful to adhere. A proposed revision of the constitution is due to be brought to the 1997 Assembly.

11. Sunday Schools

The Sunday School, by whatever name it may be known, is under the supervision of the Kirk Session. The minister is head of the Sunday School, even when a superintendent is in office. The financial board should not only supervise the finances of the Sunday School but also ensure that sufficient funds are made available to it.

12. Other organisations

All other organisations attached to the congregation are under the spiritual supervision of the Kirk Session and under the financial supervision of the financial board. Their accounts should be audited annually, and appended to the congregational accounts presented to the annual meeting.

13. Congregational Meetings

Meetings of congregations are for ecclesiastical (spiritual) purposes or for temporal purposes.

A meeting for ecclesiastical purposes is normally called by the Kirk Session and presided over by the Moderator, the Interim Moderator, or the duly appointed deputy of either, but a Presbytery may call such a meeting and appoint one of its members to preside. Minutes are kept by the Session Clerk, in whose absence the meeting appoints a Clerk, and entered in the minute book of the Kirk Session.

A meeting for temporal purposes is normally called by the financial board and presided over by its chairman, in whose absence either a person authorised by him or her, or a person chosen by the meeting, may preside. The Clerk of the board, or a person appointed by the meeting, takes the minutes, which are entered in the minute book of the board.

Act XVIII, 1932, deals in detail with congregational meetings, and should be referred to. Act III, 1994, provides that all congregations must have an annual meeting to approve the annual accounts. Before that date, *quoad omnia* congregations were not required to have annual meetings, and the change was made in connection with designation under the Law Reform (Miscellaneous Provisions) (Scotland) Act, 1990. (see Chapter XVIII p. 139)

a) Calling

Meetings of any kind must be properly called. In most cases the law requires pulpit intimation on two Sundays, but meetings for which only one

Sunday's intimation is required are specified in Section 7 of Act XVIII, 1932 (briefly: annual meetings, meetings in connection with appointment and call of a minister, and meetings in connection with readjustment, but see the Act for details). When two Sundays are prescribed, and the meeting is to be held after morning worship on a Sunday, that Sunday may be regarded as the second one on which the meeting should be intimated. It would not however be right to apply the same criterion to intimation on only one Sunday, so that the only intimation would be on the day of the meeting, but notice in such cases of a meeting to be held during the following week would be adequate on one Sunday. What is essential for all meetings is that the members should have adequate notice of the meeting, and of the business to be transacted.

b) Timeous Notice
When pulpit intimation of a meeting is legally required, it should not be omitted, and a printed notice on an order of service is not to be regarded as a pulpit intimation, although a brief reference from the pulpit to the printed notice could reasonably be held to be sufficient.

It is always possible to give more notice than that which is legally required, and in some matters, if time and resources allow, it will be good policy to do so. For example, if a Kirk Session decides to call a congregational meeting on a controversial question, there is nothing to prevent the elders from delivering relevant papers to the members in their districts, to supplement the necessary pulpit intimations. A financial board, in calling a meeting to receive the annual statement of accounts, may very properly circulate copies of the accounts beforehand.

14. Comparative Table
There follows overleaf a comparative table of what appear to be the salient differences between the main forms of financial board.

Kirk Session	Congregational Board
Membership	
Minister(s) and elders. Deacons (Diaconate) are corresponding members.	Minister and either all elders or number of elders elected by Kirk Session, together with members elected by and from congregation. Number determined by Model Deed.
Meetings	
Called by authority of Moderator or superior court by pulpit intimation or written notice. One third of elders may requisition.	Called by authority of chairman, by pulpit intimation or personal notice. Quorum may requisition.
Chair	
Minister is Moderator (or Interim Moderator, or deputy authorised in writing). A Minister of another Church in an ecumenical team may moderate.	Minister is chairman *ex officio* but may decline, in which case board elects one of its number to be chairman for year. In absence of chairman, board appoints one of its number to act as chairman.
Votes from Chair	
Moderator has casting vote only. May introduce business and speak to it.	Chairman has casting vote only. May be presumed to have the right to introduce business and speak to it.
Office-bearers	
Kirk Session elects Clerk (who need not be an elder) and treasurer, and one person may hold both offices.	Board elects Clerk and treasurer, who need not be members of board, and one person may hold both offices.
Quorum	
The quorum is three, of whom one must be the Moderator, or Interim Moderator etc. as above.	The quorum is three if the membership does not exceed nine, five if it exceeds nine but does not exceed twenty, and seven if it exceeds twenty.
Review	
Subject to the jurisdiction of the Presbytery.	Presbytery may intervene where board disregards terms of constitution.

Deacons' Court	Committee of Management
Minister and all elders are members, together with deacons elected by and from congregation, either appointed for life and ordained by Kirk Session, or elected for three year term of office. Number determined by Kirk Session.	Members elected by and from congregation for three year term of office. Number determined by congregation. Minister is not a member unless elected.
Called by authority of minister, by pulpit intimation or notice to members. Any three members may requisition.	Called by authority of chairman, whom failing Clerk, by pulpit intimation or written notice. One third of members may requisition.
Minister presides when present, but court chooses one of its own number to preside if minister is absent	Congregation elects Preses (chairman) or authorises committee to do so. Managers may choose one of their number to preside in the absence of the Preses.
Chairman has casting vote only, may not move motions, but may introduce business and speak to it.	Preses has deliberative as well as casting vote, and may introduce business and speak to it.
Court elects Clerk and treasurer from its own members.	Congregation elects Clerk and treasurer, or empowers managers to do so from their own number.
The quorum is three, and need not include the minister.	The quorum is three, or not less than one-third of the managers, whichever is greater, unless otherwise provided by the constitution.
Answerable to Presbytery for censurable or illegal actions.	Kirk Session may interpose whenever, in its opinion, the welfare of the congregation so requires. Subject to Presbytery.

XVIII. FINANCE

1. General Principles

The Church depends mainly on the givings of its members for the money it requires. Each congregation is expected, as far as it can, to meet its own needs, and to contribute to the wider work of the Church.

When a congregation is unable to meet its own financial needs from the givings of its members, provision for stipend is made from central funds. The Mission and Aid Fund is the fund from which aid is given, to ensure that no minister receives less than the declared Minimum Stipend. This fund also provides for the wider work which is administered by committees of the Assembly.

The Mission and Aid Fund is largely made up of contributions from the congregations which are able to give to it, and thus the "Mission" element in it represents the acceptance by the Church of obligations for mission and service in Scotland and in the world, beyond what can be done in each parish, while the "Aid" element is the means whereby stronger congregations, in financial terms, help the weaker ones.

Accountability is obviously important in the administration of Church finance, and there are regulations governing such matters as submission of annual audited accounts to congregational meetings, and inspection of these accounts by Presbyteries; and financial information, entered in standard schedules, must be submitted to Presbyteries and to the Board of Stewardship and Finance.

2. Christian Liberality

The givings of members are often referred to as "Christian Liberality", which reflects the fact that giving to the Church is not just a matter of providing for the work of the Church, but primarily a grateful response to what God has done for his people in Jesus Christ.

Money given or raised for Church purposes must not be used for any other purpose (Act V, 1989).

Giving may simply be a matter of placing money in the offering at services of worship, but there is provision for more structured and planned giving in the Weekly Free-will Offering system, whereby members undertake to give a regular amount weekly, and receive envelopes in which to place this amount. This enables members to plan their giving, and to put their offerings aside on the Sundays they cannot attend worship. It also helps the financial board to place a realistic figure for income in its annual budget. The envelopes are marked with numbers rather than names, the key to members' numbers being in a confidential list in the care of a WFO Treasurer, to whom alone the amount anyone gives is known.

The Church, as a charity, can benefit from forms of giving which enable it to recover the Income Tax paid on the amounts given, the main form of this being the Deed of Covenant. This also is administered in such a way that the amount anyone gives is confidential.

It is fully recognised that a member who has made a commitment under the WFO system, or by Deed of Covenant, may review this commitment in the light of changed circumstances.

Detailed information on methods of giving, and the administration of these, is available from the Board of Stewardship and Finance. Congregational Treasurers receive a *Treasurer's Handbook* containing this and other information.

3. Endowments and Investments

In anticipation of the Union of 1929, the Church of Scotland (Property and Endowments) Act 1925 was passed, its most important provision being the constitution of the General Trustees as the body in which most Church property is vested; but it also provided for such things as stipend, teinds, and endowments, in such a way that these are now of mainly historical interest, although the Church still has some sources of income derived from them. Enquiries on particular points related to these should be addressed to the Secretary and Clerk to the General Trustees.

The Church also makes provision for congregations with surplus funds in any year to apply such funds to endowment for stipend.

There are also invested funds, nationally and locally, which provide income. Usually these are the product of the submission of Christian liberality of members in past years.

The income from endowments and investments must be applied to the purposes for which they have been officially designated, and cannot be applied to any purpose which is not a church purpose.

4. Legacies and Gifts

Many of the Church's investments are the result of legacies and gifts, but legacies and gifts may be applied also to capital projects. Where they have been given for specific purposes, they must be applied to these. For example, a legacy to augment the Fabric Fund of a congregation cannot be used as a contribution to stipend.

Difficulties have occasionally arisen in relation to legacies left to be invested and the income used to augment the stipend of a parish minister. It is obviously unreasonable that, if a congregation is aid-receiving, so that other congregations have paid to bring the stipend up to the minimum, the minister should then receive an additional amount as a result of such a legacy.

Even in the case of self-supporting congregations, a legacy or gift designed to provide an addition to a minister's stipend may be at variance with the policy of the Church with regard to Appropriate Stipends, and a question of principle arises as to the extent to which an individual testator or donor may be allowed to impose his or her wish in a manner contrary to the policy of the Church.

This is not the place to discuss the legal complexities which may arise in individual cases, because much may depend on the precise terms of a particular legacy.

The whole question of "earmarked" donations is a difficult one. If a Kirk Session is determined to continue the use of the common cup at Communion, what does it do with a donation of individual glasses? If a financial board is offered money to replace existing plain lights in the church with chandeliers which it does not like, what can it do? The simple answer is that unacceptable gifts need not be accepted; but if the offer is of a gift from a living person, rather than a legacy, a tactful pastoral approach may resolve the situation.

The best advice to those who propose to give to the Church by legacy or gift is that true generosity will not seek to restrict the purposes for which the money may be used.

It should be noted that, if a financial board receives an unrestricted legacy or gift, and decides to invest it to provide income for the Fabric Fund, it is not thereby prevented from revoking that decision later. Indeed, a financial board is not entitled to retain money of this kind in its Fabric Fund if there are no other funds available to meet its Mission and Aid allocation.

5. Appeals for Funds

Act V, 1989, governs the matter of appeals for funds by church bodies generally, and should be referred to for its terms.

It should be noted that, if an appeal or money-raising event is stated to be for a specific purpose, the resultant money cannot be used for any other purpose. This means that, if funds are gathered for a project which cannot in the end be implemented, there will be serious difficulties about how such funds may be used. Care should therefore be taken about the way in which the purpose of an appeal is stated.

6. Mission and Aid

The Mission and Aid Fund is a development from what began in 1960 as the Co-ordinated Appeal, which replaced the previous practice whereby

Assembly committees each made their own appeals to congregations for funds. Under the new arrangement there was to be one appeal, and provision was made for the income to be distributed amongst the various committees on an equitable basis.

The name, while being descriptive of the process, was in due course considered to be unsatisfactory, and was changed to the "Mission and Service Fund", which was descriptive of the purposes of the fund.

The Committee on the Maintenance of the Ministry originally opted out of the new fund, and continued to make a separate assessment of congregations for the amounts necessary to provide the Minimum Stipend. There were also separate assessments of congregations for the General Purposes Fund, which provided *inter alia* for the expenses of the Assembly. All these assessments were combined in the Mission and Aid Fund by decision of the Assembly in 1986.

The process by which each congregation is given each year an allocation, which is to be its contribution to central funds, has varied over the years, and will no doubt continue to be revised from time to time, as the Church seeks to cope with the various problems involved. It has proved very difficult in practice, for example, to reconcile the difference between what, on various criteria, a congregation ought to pay, and what in practice it is going to be able to pay. Let it suffice to say that current procedures involve Presbyteries, the Board of Stewardship and Finance, and the Committee on the Maintenance of the Ministry; and Presbyteries consult with congregations where appropriate.

When a congregation's allocation has been decided, that is the *minimum* amount which that congregation is *required* to provide. It is a legal requirement, not a target at which it should aim. Until recently, there was however no effective sanction which could be applied to congregations which consistently failed to meet their allocations in full, and arrears were simply written off each year. Visits were however made by Presbyteries to congregations concerned, in order by persuasion, encouragement and help, to remedy the situation.

In 1995 however the Assembly decided that arrears should not be written off, and that the congregations concerned should be required to meet their shortfalls. A sanction was introduced in that year by an Interim Act, which, after being sent down under the Barrier Act, became Act IX, 1996. This amended Act V, 1984, to the extent of providing that, when a vacancy occurs in a congregation with current or accumulated shortfalls to central funds, the Presbytery has to determine whether such shortfalls are justified. If they are not deemed to be justified, the Presbytery is not permitted to allow the congregation to call a minister until either the shortfalls have been met to an extent determined by the Presbytery, or the congregation has been linked or united.

7. Accountability
While accountability in matters of finance has always been an important principle, the Law Reform (Miscellaneous Provisions) (Scotland) Act, 1990,

imposed a new and detailed code of law on charities in general. In terms of the Act, the Church applied for and received a designation by the Secretary of State for Scotland, which gave it exemption from some of the provisions of the Act, but this designation was granted in the light of undertakings given by the Board of Stewardship and Finance. As a result of these undertakings, new regulations were approved by the Assembly (Reg. I, 1994). The Assembly also approved an appropriate revision of the financial provisions of the Model Deed of Constitution, but the new regulations apply to all congregations irrespective of their forms of constitution.

The essence of the undertakings given, and the effect of the new regulations, is that the Church itself will adequately supervise the administration of its finances at every level. The regulations must therefore be complied with, both because they have the authority of the Assembly, and because failure to comply with them would jeopardise the Church's designation and consequent exemption mentioned above.

While it is recognised that the Church depends on volunteers who accept congregational treasurerships, and some of these may have had no financial training, while others with professional qualifications may feel that their accustomed way of setting out accounts is better than the way required by the regulations, so that there may therefore be some difficulties at congregational level in applying the regulations, the serious consequences of failure to do so must be stressed.

In this connection reference is again made to the *Treasurer's Handbook*. This provides all necessary guidance on the regulations and their application. Questions on its contents may be addressed to the Board of Stewardship and Finance. Because this handbook is readily available to those directly involved, the regulations are not printed in this volume.

8. Lotteries and Raffles

The General Assembly has instructed all congregations, church committees and institutions to avoid recourse to lotteries, raffles or any such means of raising money for Christian purposes (1975, Sess. 3). This instruction is based on two considerations: first, that gambling is morally wrong; and second, that minor gambling which may not involve serious immorality is a trivial and unworthy way of raising money for the Church.

The General Assembly has endorsed the view that participation in the National Lottery would be contrary to the Church's position opposing gambling in all its forms (1994, Sess. 7). In 1996 it was remitted to the Board of Practice and Procedure to produce a statement and to report on this matter.

XIX. PROPERTY

1. Ownership

The ecclesiastical buildings belonging to congregations are held for them by trustees. These may be the General Trustees, or local trustees, and in the latter case they may be trustees *ex officiis*, that is to say people specified by their offices, such as the minister, in which case there is usually no difficulty about their continuity (unless the congregation is to be dissolved, in which case they should transfer the property to named trustees before the date of dissolution), or they may be named trustees, in which case meetings have to be held to elect new trustees every so often, so that the trust remains in being.

Buildings formerly vested in the heritors were transferred to the General Trustees, set up under the Church of Scotland (Property and Endowments) Act, 1925. Other congregations have an option to transfer their buildings from local trustees to the General Trustees, and there are certain advantages in doing so, especially with regard to qualifying for grants and loans for the maintenance of the property.

Most property is held specifically for congregations of the Church of Scotland, whether vested in the General Trustees or in local trustees, and so cannot be alienated from this Church if, for example, the congregation decides to secede. It should be borne in mind in this connection that when a congregation's property is vested in local trustees, and the title deeds are held by the congregation, these factors in themselves do not mean that the property can be alienated from the Church of Scotland. What matters is not who holds the title deeds, but what the title deeds contain.

2. General Trustees

The General Trustees have certain powers in connection with church property, even when it is not vested in them. Until comparatively recently, the sale of a building of the former United Free Church required an Act of the Assembly, but the Assembly has now given power to the General Trustees to approve such sales in its name. They also have power to make determinations about the use to which the proceeds of sale shall be applied.

3. Maintenance

The congregation is responsible for the maintenance of its buildings. It is required to hold an annual inspection of its property, and to keep a Property Register in which the inspections are recorded, and a note of all work done on the buildings is kept. This has to be submitted annually to the Presbytery, and the Presbytery also instructs full inspections every five years (see Act IX, 1979).

If a congregation proposes to carry out work on a building it requires the approval of the Presbytery, but the Presbytery may waive this requirement, provided that the work will not cost more than the "Financial Limit", which is a figure fixed by the Assembly from time to time, on the recommendation of the General Trustees. If work costing more than this figure is approved, the Presbytery must refer the matter to the Consultative Committee on Church Properties, whose recommendation must be given due consideration by the Presbytery, but is not binding on it.

4. Necessary Buildings

While it is a major concern of the Church that all properties be kept in a good state of repair, and congregations are under obligation to achieve this, it is also part of its stewardship of property that large amounts should not be spent repairing or renovating buildings which may shortly be surplus to the Church's requirements. Accordingly, one factor which a Presbytery must take into account in relation to an application to undertake work costing more than the Financial Limit is whether or not the building is "a necessary building in terms of the ongoing missionary strategy of the Church." It is clear that this question is closely related to questions of readjustment.

Difficult problems have already arisen about the precise relationship between readjustment plans and the question of necessary buildings. It may be safely predicted that there will be further legislation in this area sooner rather than later, and therefore it would be unwise, and potentially misleading, to go into further detail here. Congregations planning work on buildings are advised to consult the Presbytery Clerk at an early stage for information about current regulations.

5. Sale

Acts XXVI, 1933, and VII, 1995 (as amended by Act XIII, 1996) lay down procedures for the sale of buildings.

6. Insurance

Congregations are required to have their buildings adequately insured. Detailed information about insurance is available to congregations through the *Treasurer's Handbook*, obtainable from the General Treasurer's office.

7. Further Information

Information about property is available from the office of the General Trustees. Those with particular questions about their own church property should communicate with that office.

For those seeking more general information about church property, the relevant section in the *Stair Memorial Encyclopedia* is recommended (Vol 3, Paragraphs 1574-1607).

XX. READJUSTMENT

1. Rationale of Readjustment

Article III of the *Declaratory Articles* states that the Church of Scotland, "as a national Church . . . . acknowledges its distinctive call and duty to bring the ordinances of religion to the people in every parish of Scotland through a territorial ministry."

It is therefore important that there should be no part of Scotland which is not in a parish, and that each parish should have a minister, a Kirk Session, and a congregation. These together constitute a Christian presence, which is there to witness to the Gospel and to provide religious services to all who seek them.

The basic purpose of readjustment is to enable the Church to ensure that limited resources are deployed in such a way that this Christian presence may be maintained throughout Scotland.

2. Historical Reasons

Because of the process of union following the various secessions, and the Disruption in particular, the Church of Scotland had, in 1929, more congregations, and more church buildings, than the population actually required in terms of parishes, although many of these might for a time justify their existence as "gathered congregations" which were self-supporting.

Since then, population growth in new towns and new housing areas, and depopulation in country and highland areas, has produced a situation in which, for example, a large new housing area might have only one church to cater for a population vastly in excess of a country town which might have four or five churches.

In sparsely populated areas many congregations cannot be large enough to be able to pay the minimum stipend, and become aid-receiving. Without a process of readjustment, the number of aid-receiving congregations would be such that the number of aid-giving congregations would not be sufficient to provide enough aid to maintain ministers in all the parishes in Scotland.

3. National Strategy

This process, now known as Parish Re-appraisal, although the relevant legislation is still in terms of unions and readjustments, is the way in which the Church has sought to implement a national strategy to rationalise the deployment of its limited resources, in terms of the availability of ministers, and the costs of ministry and of maintaining buildings.

Although "unions and readjustments" has been the formal nomenclature, union is a form of readjustment, and the term "readjustment" is therefore inclusive.

4. Readjustment Procedure

Normally the question of readjustment arises on the occurrence of a vacancy, and is dealt with first in terms of Act V, 1984, Section 3, as amended by Act IX, 1996. If it is decided to pursue the question of readjustment, the procedure to be followed is set out in Act IV, 1984. This Act provides for various forms of readjustment, and also recognises that other forms may be devised to meet particular situations. Further, it makes provision for readjustment to be implemented when there is no vacancy.

The initiative is with the Presbytery, which knows the local situation, but it should proceed in consultation with the Committee on Parish Re-appraisal, whose concern is to apply a consistent policy throughout Scotland.

The requirements of any Act should always be carefully followed, but in the case of this Act it should be remembered that readjustment is often an emotive matter, and vacant congregations feel vulnerable. Every effort should be made by Presbyteries, and by the Committee on Parish Re-appraisal, not only (a) to observe the Act meticulously but also (b) to explain the procedures, and the reasons for them, to all concerned, although it must be added that (b) is a counsel of wisdom, not a legal requirement. It is nevertheless an obvious part of the consultation with local parties which is legally required, and with the provision that "it shall be the duty of the Presbytery to make every effort to secure the approval of the congregations involved."

When the Presbytery has made a decision on a form of readjustment to be implemented, or to allow a free call, the concurrence of the Committee on Parish Re-appraisal is required before it can be effected. If the Committee does not concur the matter must be taken to the Assembly by Reference (see Chapter VII, p. 52). Non-concurrence is not therefore a veto applied by a committee to a judgement of a court of the Church; it is a way of ensuring that the final decision will be taken by the supreme court.

(See also Chapter VIII, p. 60, for comment on interpretation of Section 4(e) of Act IV, 1984.)

5. Review

Ideally, readjustment will be effected by a Presbytery, with the concurrence of the Committee on Parish Re-appraisal, and with the consent of all parties. Where there is disagreement, provision is made for review by the Assembly, either by Reference as above or by Appeal if the Presbytery and the Committee are in agreement but a party seeks review.

The possibility of review is another reason for being meticulous about proper procedure. The main issue in readjustment cases is usually one of policy and principle, and that issue can be confused if review proceeds on the basis of alleged procedural irregularities.

6. Arbitration

When two congregations are to be united, one of the most difficult questions is often that of which buildings will be used. Ideally this will be decided by agreement of all parties, and included in the Basis of Union. If agreement cannot be reached, provision is made for arbitration, and this is included in the Basis, always stating that the decision of the arbiters will be final. This means that the decision cannot be taken for review to the Assembly. As noted in Herron, however (pp. 50-51), the united congregation can subsequently reach a different decision about the use of buildings, "under authority of the Presbytery", in terms of the usual final clause in every Basis of Union.

That is true, but the Presbytery, in such a situation, has been a party to the Basis of Union, and has deliberately agreed that the decision of the arbiters should be final. It would therefore be in the position of reviewing its own decision in that respect, if it were to give authority to a departure from the decision of the arbiters. Accordingly, it could do this only if a substantial element of *res noviter* had been brought to its notice; that is to say, it would be necessary for anyone seeking such action from the Presbytery to be able to show, not that the arbiters had made a wrong decision, but that some new factor had come to light since that decision, of such magnitude and importance that it would be unreasonable not to make and authorise a new decision in the new situation thereby created.

If a Presbytery declined to give its authority, an appeal could be taken to the Assembly against that judgement of the Presbytery, for such an appeal would not be an appeal against the decision of the arbiters, but the likelihood of the Assembly sustaining such an appeal, in the absence of *res noviter*, is remote.

Those who have agreed to accept an arbiters' decision as final are in honour bound to do so, and it would be contrary to the agreement of all parties to the Basis of Union if only the factors and arguments submitted to the arbiters were to be rehearsed before the Presbytery.

Dr. Herron is careful not to suggest that the possibility of acting under the final clause of a Basis of Union should be regarded as a loophole, enabling an arbiters' decision to be easily set aside.

The best advice to congregations, and Presbyteries, in this matter is therefore that congregations should not agree to a Basis with an arbitration clause if they are doing so only in the belief that the arbiters will choose their building and are not really prepared to accept the possibility of a different decision; and Presbyteries should be careful about advising an arbitration clause if they suspect that such an attitude is prevalent.

7. Church Extension

Closely associated with readjustment is the work of Church Extension, because it shares the same object of ensuring that the parish system adequately meets the religious needs of the people of Scotland. Its purpose is to set up new congregations in new housing areas, or new towns.

The question of creating a new congregation is normally raised by the minister and Kirk Session of the parish within whose bounds it is required, but the Presbytery may take the initiative. The proposal is next considered by the Committee on Parish Re-appraisal, in consultation with the Committee on Extension Projects.

The whole procedure is set out in detail in Regulations 3, 1995, including arrangements for appointing a minister, the appointment of Assessor Elders to form a Kirk Session, the establishment of a committee to manage temporal affairs, payment of stipend, and financial responsibilities. In due course a Church Extension charge may apply to the Assembly for full status, and if the application is granted the Assembly will raise it into a parish *quoad sacra*, passing an appropriate Act to achieve this.

Details of the Regulations are available from the Secretary of the Committee on Extension Projects, at the Church Offices.

XXI. ECUMENISM

1. The Ecumenical Movement

The ecumenical movement has been a feature of the Church in the twentieth century, and the Church of Scotland has been an active participant. It was a founding member of the World Council of Churches (WCC), the World Alliance of Reformed Churches (WARC), the Council of European Churches (CEC), the Council of Churches for Britain and Ireland (CCBI), and Action of Churches Together in Scotland (ACTS).

There are also local councils of Churches in most parts of Scotland, and there are some ecumenical parishes.

2. Legal Position

The legal position is that no council of Churches has jurisdiction over its member Churches, and although they may issue statements about a wide variety of issues on which they see an important Christian perspective, the member Churches are not bound by the views expressed.

When CCBI replaced the former British Council of Churches, and ACTS replaced the former Scottish Churches' Council, it was agreed that the new bodies should be so constituted that they might enable the member Churches to speak and act together, through their representatives, so far as they might be agreed, without the new bodies acquiring a separate identity of their own (although they must of course have a legal identity). They are designed to foster co-operation, and to promote joint action in areas of common concern, and their purpose is seen as engagement in a pilgrimage towards unity.

The Assembly appoints representatives to the assemblies of the various bodies. These are representatives, and not delegates: that is to say, they are not given "mandates" as to how they should speak or act, but are expected to use their own discretion in representing this Church.

3. Ecumenical Obligations

While ecumenical bodies have no jurisdiction over member Churches, they have constitutions, in terms of which member Churches have certain obligations.

There is an obligation to appoint representatives, and an obligation to make financial contributions. When an ecumenical body determines the rate of contributions, in which determination the representatives participate, these contributions are, like membership subscriptions to any organisation, obligatory payments. They are not however legally enforceable, and the ultimate sanction for failure to meet them, which would be termination of membership, is seldom, if ever, applied. They should however be regarded as moral obligations.

4. The Reformation

It is noteworthy that the idea of an international ecclesiastical body did not begin with the ecumenical movement. There were councils before the Reformation, and the idea of councils was not rejected by the Reformers. *The Scots Confession* saw two purposes for them: to refute heresies and give public profession of faith; and to constitute good policy and order in the Kirk. In *The Second Book of Discipline* reference is made to "the nationall assemblie (quhilk is generall to us)" and to "an uther mair generall kind of assemblie quhilk is of all nations or of all estaitis of personis within the kirk representing the universall kirk of Chryst quhilk may be callit properlie the generall assemblie or generall counsall of the haill kirk of God."

That such an international general assembly never came into being is not surprising in the circumstances of the aftermath of the Reformation, given the differences between the Churches which emerged, and the fact that each nation had its own Church (*cuius regio, eius religio*). The uniformity expected within each nation was such that the growth of different denominations within one nation, and the toleration of these, was a later development. The aim of the ecumenical movement is not to put the clock back to the days of uniformity, but to seek an agreed unity under Christ.

It is also remarkable that the *Westminster Confession* was produced as part of a plan to unite the Church of Scotland and the Church of England, as was *The Form of Presbyterial Church Government*, which states, "Synodical assemblies may lawfully be of several sorts, as provincial, national, and oecumenical." Oecumenical here means international rather than inter-denominational. The division of the Church into denominations is something to be overcome by the Churches on the way to the fulfilment of that oecumencial vision of a united Church. The present ecumenical bodies are not themselves the fulfilment of the vision, but seek to be agencies through which the Churches move towards unity, and in the meantime practise co-operation.

5. Ecumenical Inheritance

However remote the idea of an international or ecumenical assembly, with jurisdiction, may seem at present, it is integral to the teaching of the Reformers in Scotland. This is part of the inheritance of this Church, in that it "adheres to the Scottish Reformation" (*Article I*). Its roots are in the insistence that this Church is part of the one catholic or universal Church.

This is the basic principle behind *Article VII* which, while it arose immediately out of the experience of the legal consequences of the 1900 Union, quotes the *Scots Confession.*

Apart from the *Scots Confession, The Second Book of Discipline, The Form of Presbyterial Church Government*, and the *Declaratory Articles*, there is little in the way of actual legislation relating to ecumenism, but the Assembly passed an Act to facilitate a union of congregations, including one of the Congregational Church, in Paisley, in 1991, and Act X, 1992, made provision for ministers of other denominations in ecumenical parishes to act as Moderators of Kirk Sessions.

Theology in ecumenical discussion has legal overtones. For example, the whole discussion of presbyterianism and episcopacy is affected by the manner in which such polities are regarded by their proponents. If either is regarded as of the *esse* rather than of the *bene esse* of the Church, little progress seems possible; but the view that presbyterianism is of the *esse* is inconsistent with its place in the *Declaratory Articles*, and that is a substantial and relevant legal factor in any such discussion (see p. 7).

Another important legal factor in ecumenical engagement with other Churches is that they all have their constitutions: in canon law, standing orders, or other forms. These, as well as theological positions, have to be studied with care, because there are significant differences not only in terminology but in different meanings of the same terms. The term "confirmation" is a case in point, by which very different things are meant (see Chapter V, p. 32). Another example is the use of the word "lay", there being a fairly general opinion in other Churches that elders are lay people (see Chapter VI: Government).

When differences are merely verbal, it is comparatively easy to resolve them, but verbal agreement which conceals substantial differences leads to obfuscation.

APPENDICES

APPENDICES

APPENDIX A

THE BARRIER ACT, 1697.

The General Assembly, taking into their consideration the Overture and Act made in the last Assembly concerning innovations, and having heard the report of the several commissioners from Presbyteries to whom the consideration of the same was recommended, in order to its being more ripely advised and determined in this Assembly; and considering the frequent practice of former Assemblies of this Church, and that it will mightily conduce to the exact obedience of the Acts of Assemblies, that General Assemblies be very deliberate in making of the same, and that the whole Church have a previous knowledge thereof, and their opinion be had therein, and for preventing any sudden alteration or innovation, or other prejudice to the Church, in either doctrine or worship, or discipline, or government thereof, now happily established; do, therefore, appoint, enact, and declare, that before any General Assembly of this Church shall pass any Acts, which are to be binding Rules and Constitutions to the Church, the same Acts be first proposed as overtures to the Assembly, and, being by them passed as such, be remitted to the consideration of the several Presbyteries of this Church, and their opinions and consent reported by their commissioners to the next General Assembly following, who may then pass the same in Acts, if the more general opinion of the Church thus had agreed thereunto.

APPENDIX B

THE BASIS AND PLAN OF UNION, 1929
(Act I, 1929)

BASIS OF UNION

UNITING ACT

I

THE Church of Scotland and the United Free Church of Scotland, as branches of the Holy Catholic or Universal Church, believing that it is the will of their Lord for His disciples that they all should be one, acknowledge that the witness borne to the Lord by the Catholic Visible Church and the particular Churches which are members thereof, is obscured, and that His work is hindered by division and separation therein:

And WHEREAS in the Church of Scotland, which was reformed by Presbyters in 1560, and whose outward and visible unity continued for long time thereafter unbroken, separations have taken place among those who alike claimed to share in the common heritage and adhered to the common traditions and standards, whereby:—

In 1690 certain members thereof, being unable to consent to the Revolution Settlement of the Church, continued independent ordinances and ultimately became known as the Reformed Presbyterian Church in Scotland:

And in 1733 certain brethren, on grounds duly set forth and made public at the time, separated themselves from the jurisdiction of the Church of Scotland, and in due course formed the Secession Church in Scotland:

And in 1761 certain other brethren, for grounds and reasons similarly declared and published, formed the Relief Church in Scotland:

And in 1843 there occurred the cleavage in the Church of Scotland historically known as the Disruption, when a large section of the Church, severing ecclesiastical connection with the State on grounds set forth and recorded in the Claim, Declaration, and Protest of the General Assembly, 1842, and the Protest, 1843, formed the Free Church of Scotland:

And WHEREAS the obligation resting upon the followers of Christ to manifest their inward and spiritual unity to the world, in a common profession of faith and observance of the ordinances of Christ, has never ceased to be acknowledged by the Scottish Church throughout all her branches, so that not only were these separations contemplated and carried through with profound reluctance and in hope of ultimate reunion, but further, as the way was opened in God's Providence, various unions took place from time to time, and in particular those effected under and in terms of the several Uniting Acts following— viz., the Articles forming the Basis of Union of the United Secession and Relief Churches to form the United Presbyterian Church in 1847; the Act of Union of the Free Church of Scotland and the Reformed Presbyterian Church in 1876: and the Uniting Act with Declarations anent Union of the Free Church of Scotland and the United Presbyterian Church to form the United Free Church of Scotland in 1900:

And WHEREAS the Church of Scotland and the United Free Church of Scotland, maintaining alike the common historic heritage, and steadfastly desiring reunion, agreed, in 1909, through their General Assemblies, to enter into "unrestricted conference on the ecclesiastical situation in Scotland and the main causes which keep the Churches apart, in the earnest hope that by God's blessing, misunderstandings and hindrances may be removed, and the great object of Presbyterian reunion in Scotland be thereby advanced ":

And WHEREAS in the course of conference it appeared that the main obstacles to reunion were concerned with differences which had arisen in regard to certain aspects and applications of the principles, common throughout their history to both Churches, of the National Recognition of Religion and the Spiritual Freedom of the Church under Christ, the only King and Head thereof:

And WHEREAS in the Articles Declaratory of the Constitution of the Church of Scotland in Matters Spiritual adopted by the General Assembly of 1926, and in the United Free Church Act anent the Spiritual Independence of the Church, 1906 (which Articles and Act are appended to the present Act), these principles are reaffirmed and set forth in a manner which is in accordance with the convictions of both Churches:

And WHEREAS these Churches, deeply conscious of the evils of disunion, and being increasingly impressed with the urgent need for reunion in order to meet more adequately the religious requirements of the people, welcomed the opportunity thus afforded for the readjustment of their relations to each other, and in the General Assemblies of 1926 agreed to confer together on the formation of a Basis of Union, and generally on the whole matters to be arranged before an incorporating union could be carried through successfully:

And WHEREAS representative Committees having been appointed and having communicated to one another the existing standards, rules, and methods of the Churches, it appeared that in regard to doctrine, worship, government, and discipline as therein set forth substantial agreement obtained between them:

And WHEREAS certain further necessary adjustments have now been made; and in particular Questions and a Formula to be used at the Ordination and Induction of Ministers, the constitution of the Courts of the united Church, provision for the support and for the training of the Ministry, and arrangements for combining the methods and work of the two Churches, have been agreed upon, and have been duly authorised by the Courts of the two Churches:

Now THEREFORE THE GENERAL ASSEMBLY OF THE CHURCH OF SCOTLAND AND THE GENERAL ASSEMBLY OF THE UNITED FREE CHURCH OF SCOTLAND, devoutly acknowledging the mercy and long-suffering shown by Almighty God to themselves and to their fathers, rendering humble and hearty thanks for the gracious guidance bestowed upon them in this their endeavour to heal the divisions in His Church and to promote His glory, and entreating Him to pour out His Spirit upon His servants and upon those who shall come after them, that as good stewards of the manifold grace of God they may with growing power minister to the people of this land and to the nations that have not yet received the Gospel, DO HEREBY, in terms and in pursuance of Deliverances of their respective General Assemblies, with approval of the Presbyteries of the respective Churches in accordance with the provisions of the Barrier Act, ENACT AND DECLARE THAT THESE CHURCHES, being historic branches of the Reformed Church in Scotland, DO AND SHALL HENCEFORTH CONSTITUTE ONE CHURCH, and that the name of the united Church shall be THE CHURCH OF SCOTLAND.

II

The General Assembly of the Church of Scotland and the General Assembly of the United Free Church of Scotland enact that the Churches enter into union in view of the following DECLARATIONS, viz.:—

1. The various matters of agreement between the Churches with a view to union are accepted and enacted without prejudice to the inherent liberty of the united Church as a branch of the Church of God to determine and regulate her own constitution and laws as duty may require, in dependence on the grace of God and under the guidance of His Word and Spirit, all as more particularly set forth in the aftermentioned *Act,* 1906, and *Articles,* 1926.

2. The following are leading documents setting forth the constitution, standards, rules and methods of the united Church, viz.:—

GENERAL CONSTITUTION, including the Principles of the Spirituality and Freedom of the Church, and the National Recognition of Religion.

United Free Church Act anent Spiritual Independence (1906).

Articles Declaratory of the Constitution of the Church of Scotland in matters Spiritual (1926).

DOCTRINE
The Westminster Confession of Faith (1647).
United Presbyterian Church Declaratory Act (1879).
Free Church Declaratory Act (1892) with *Act* (1894) relative thereto.
The Church of Scotland Act on the Formula (1910).

GOVERNMENT
The Form of Presbyterial Church Government and of Ordination of Ministers (1645).

WORSHIP
A Directory for the Public Worship of God (1645).

DISCIPLINE
The Form of Process (1707).

> Which *Form of Presbyterial Church Government, Directory for the Public Worship of God,* and *Form of Process* respectively are to be regarded as generally regulative and as of validity, as these have been interpreted or modified by Acts of General Assembly or by consuetude.

3. The following *Uniting Acts* are historic documents the general principles whereof are held to be conserved in the united Church:—

> *Articles forming the Basis of Union of the United Secession and Relief Churches to form the United Presbyterian Church* (1847).
> *Act of Union of the Free Church of Scotland and the Reformed Presbyterian Church* (1876).
> *Uniting Act with Declarations anent Union of the Free Church of Scotland and the United Presbyterian Church to form the United Free Church of Scotland* (1900).

4. *The Larger and Shorter Catechisms* prepared by the Westminster Assembly of Divines, sanctioned by the General Assembly in 1648 and for long approved as manuals of instruction, continue to be held in honour in the united Church.

5. The following documents are also held in honour as having an important place in the history of Scottish Presbyterianism:—

> *Scots Confession* (1560).
> *First Book of Discipline* (1560).
> *Second Book of Discipline* (1578).
> *Book of Common Order* (1564).

6. As this Union takes place on the footing of maintaining the liberty of judgment and action heretofore recognised in either of the Churches uniting, so in particular it is hereby declared that members of both Churches shall have full right, as they shall see cause, to assert and maintain the views of truth and duty which they had liberty to maintain in the said Churches.

7. The Churches, in entering into Union, under a sense of responsibility as a branch of the Church of God, acknowledge afresh the obligation resting on the Church to provide the ordinances of religion to the people of Scotland through a territorial ministry and to labour for the universal diffusion of the Gospel, and the duty of her members to contribute, according to their ability, both by their service and their means, for the support of the ordinances of religion in this land and the extension of the Kingdom of Christ throughout the world.

III

The General Assembly of the Church of Scotland and the General Assembly of the United Free Church of Scotland enact and ordain that all previous enactments and regulations of the General Assemblies of either uniting Church in force at the passing of this Act, unless in so far as modified by the Basis and Plan of Union, shall continue in force in the same manner as prior to the passing of this Act, so long as they shall not have been repealed or amended in accordance with the law of the united Church: provided always that where any such enactments or regulations are found in conflict or where the former practice of the two Churches is materially different and has not been adjusted by the Basis and Plan of Union, any necessary legislation to which the procedure of the Barrier Act is appropriate shall be by interim Act only, which shall be transmitted to Presbyteries in accordance with the provisions of the Barrier Act for consent or suggestions before its adoption as a standing law of the Church.

IV

The General Assembly of the Church of Scotland and the General Assembly of the United Free Church of Scotland enact and ordain that the General Assembly of the Church of Scotland and the General Assembly of the United Free Church of Scotland, when they have met for the purpose of consummating the Union, and have adopted the Uniting Act, shall thereafter have the powers of a General Assembly of the united Church, and may do and authorise all things necessary or proper and lawful to be done with a view to the orderly inauguration and conduct of the affairs of the united Church, and in consistency with the terms of Union agreed upon.

APPENDIX TO UNITING ACT.

ARTICLES DECLARATORY OF THE CONSTITUTION OF THE CHURCH OF SCOTLAND IN MATTERS SPIRITUAL.

I. The Church of Scotland is part of the Holy Catholic or Universal Church; worshipping one God, Almighty, all-wise, and all-loving, in the Trinity of the Father, the Son, and the Holy Ghost, the same in substance, equal in power and glory; adoring the Father, infinite in Majesty, of whom are all things; confessing our Lord Jesus Christ, the Eternal Son, made very man for our salvation; glorying in His Cross and Resurrection, and owning obedience to Him as the Head over all things to His Church; trusting in the promised renewal and guidance of the Holy Spirit; proclaiming the forgiveness of sins and acceptance with God through faith in Christ, and the gift of Eternal Life; and labouring for the advancement of the Kingdom of God throughout the world. The Church of Scotland adheres to the Scottish Reformation; receives the Word of God which is contained in the Scriptures of the Old and New Testaments as its supreme rule of faith and life; and avows the fundamental doctrines of the Catholic faith founded thereupon.

II. The principal subordinate standard of the Church of Scotland is the Westminster Confession of Faith approved by the General Assembly of 1647, containing the sum and substance of the Faith of the Reformed Church. Its government is Presbyterian, and is exercised through Kirk Sessions, Presbyteries, [Provincial Synods deleted by Act V, 1992], and General Assemblies. Its system and principles of worship, orders, and discipline are in accordance with "The Directory for the Public Worship of God," "The Form of Presbyterial Church Government " and "The Form of Process," as these have been or may hereafter be interpreted or modified by Acts of the General Assembly or by consuetude.

III. This Church is in historical continuity with the Church of Scotland which was reformed in 1560, whose liberties were ratified in 1592, and for whose security provision was made in the Treaty of Union of 1707. The continuity and identity of the Church of Scotland are not prejudiced by the adoption of these Articles. As a national Church representative of the Christian Faith of the Scottish people it acknowledges its distinctive call and duty to bring the ordinances of religion to the people in every parish of Scotland through a territorial ministry.

IV. This Church as part of the Universal Church wherein the Lord Jesus Christ has appointed a government in the hands of Church office-bearers, receives from Him, its Divine King and Head, and From Him alone, the right and power subject to no civil authority to legislate, and to adjudicate finally, in all matters of doctrine, worship, government, and discipline in the Church, including the right to determine all questions concerning membership and office in the Church, the constitution and membership of its Courts, and the mode of election of its office-bearers, and to define the boundaries of the spheres of labour of its ministers and other office-bearers. Recognition by civil authority of the separate and independent government and jurisdiction of this Church in matters spiritual, in whatever manner such recognition be expressed, does not in any way affect the character of this government and jurisdiction as derived from the Divine Head of the Church alone or give to the civil authority any right of interference with the proceedings or judgments of the Church within the sphere of its spiritual government and jurisdiction.

V. This Church has the inherent right, free from interference by civil authority, but under the safeguards for deliberate action and legislation provided by the Church itself, to frame or adopt its subordinate standards, to declare the sense in which it understands its Confession of Faith, to modify the forms of expression therein, or to formulate other doctrinal statements, and to define the relation thereto of its office-bearers and members, but always in agreement with the Word of God and the fundamental doctrines of the Christian Faith contained in the said Confession, of which agreement the Church shall be sole judge, and with due regard to liberty of opinion in points which do not enter into the substance of the Faith.

VI. This Church acknowledges the divine appointment and authority of the civil magistrate within his own sphere, and maintains its historic testimony to the duty of the nation acting in its corporate capacity to render homage to God, to acknowledge the Lord Jesus Christ to be King over the nations, to obey His laws, to reverence His ordinances, to honour His Church, and to promote in all appropriate ways the Kingdom of God. The Church and the State owe mutual duties to each other, and acting within their respective spheres may signally promote each other's welfare. The Church and the State have the right to determine each for itself all questions concerning the extent and the continuance of their mutual relations in the discharge of these duties and the obligations arising therefrom.

VII. The Church of Scotland, believing it to be the will of Christ that His disciples should be all one in the Father and in Him, that the world may believe that the Father has sent Him, recognises the obligation to seek and promote union with other Churches in which it finds the Word to be purely preached, the sacraments administered according to Christ's ordinance, and discipline rightly exercised; and it has the right to unite with any such Church without loss of its identity on terms which this Church finds to be consistent with these Articles.

VIII. The Church has the right to interpret these Articles, and, subject to the safeguards for deliberate action and legislation provided by the Church itself, to modify or add to them; but always consistently with the provisions of the first Article hereof, adherence to which, as interpreted by the Church, is essential to its continuity and corporate life. Any proposal for a modification of or addition to these Articles which may be approved of by the General

Assembly shall, before it can be enacted by the Assembly, be transmitted by way of overture to Presbyteries in at least two immediately successive years. If the overture shall receive the approval, with or without suggested amendment, of two-thirds of the whole of the Presbyteries of the Church, the Assembly may revise the overture in the light of any suggestions by the Presbyteries, and may transmit the overture when so revised to Presbyteries for their consent. If the overture as transmitted in its final form shall receive the consent of not less than two-thirds of the whole of the Presbyteries of the Church, the General Assembly may, if it deems it expedient, modify or add to these Articles in terms of the said overture. But if the overture as transmitted in its final form shall not receive the requisite consent, the same or a similar proposal shall not be again transmitted for the consent of Presbyteries until an interval of five years after the failure to obtain the requisite consent has been reported to the General Assembly.

IX. Subject to the provisions of the foregoing Articles and the powers of amendment therein contained, the Constitution of the Church of Scotland in matters spiritual is hereby anew ratified and confirmed by the Church.

UNITED FREE CHURCH ACT ANENT
SPIRITUAL INDEPENDENCE OF THE CHURCH (1906).

WHEREAS the General Assembly judged it necessary in the circumstances of the Church• to pass the following Act, and although the principles set forth therein involve no new departure and are not in any sense a constitutional novation, but have been always accepted and maintained by this Church, yet in respect of the importance of making manifest to all that the whole Church explicitly adheres to these principles, the General Assembly deemed it right to send it down as an Overture under the Barrier Act: the General Assembly hereby, with consent of a majority of Presbyteries, declare and enact, as follows:—

Considering the situation created by the decisions of the House of Lords on 1st August 1904, in the Cases of *Bannatyne and Others v. Lord Overtoun and Others,* and *Young and Others v. Macalister and Others,* and the grounds on which these decisions were based; considering also the Resolutions relative thereto of the Commission of Assembly at its ordinary Meeting on 10th August 1904, of which Resolutions the Assembly hereby approve; and considering that it is needful to make clear the position in which the United Free Church of Scotland stands in reference to the questions thus raised, the General Assembly resolve and declare as follows:—

1. They assert and protest that those branches of the Church of Christ in Scotland now united in this Church have always claimed, and this

Church continues to claim, that the Church of Christ has under Him as her only Head independent and exclusive jurisdiction and power of legislating in all matters of doctrine, worship, discipline, and government of the Church, including therein the right from time to time to alter, change, add to, or modify, her constitution and laws, Subordinate Standards and Church Formulas, and to determine and declare what these are.

2. The General Assembly accordingly declare anew and enact that it is a fundamental principle and rule of this Church that, in dependence on the grace of God, recognising the authority of the Word of God, contained in the Scriptures of the Old and New Testaments, as the supreme unchangeable Standard, and looking to the Head of the Church for the promised guidance of the Holy Spirit, this Church has the sole and exclusive right and power from time to time, as duty may require, through her Courts to alter, change, add to, or modify, her constitution and laws, Subordinate Standards, and Formulas, and to determine and declare what these are, and to unite with other Christian Churches; always in conformity with the Word of God and also with the safeguards for deliberate action and legislation in such cases provided by the Church herself — of which conformity the Church herself, acting through her Courts, shall be the sole judge — and under a sense of direct responsibility to the ever-living Head of the Church, and of duty towards all the Church's members.

3. The General Assembly also declare and enact that in all the Courts of the Church a decision of the Court given either unanimously, or by a majority of its members present and voting, is the decision of the Court, and the decision of the General Assembly so reached is final. With respect to Acts which are to be binding Rules and Constitutions of the Church the Assembly shall have regard to the safeguards referred to in the foregoing resolution.

4. The General Assembly further declare that the Church holds her funds and property, present and future, in conformity with these principles; the Church reserving her right to accept and hold benefactions, subject to specific conditions attached to them by the donor, when and so long as she judges these conditions to be consistent with her liberty and her principles, and to be expedient in the circumstances of the time.

PREAMBLE, QUESTIONS, AND FORMULA

PREAMBLE

The Narrative shall he read and, the Ordinand having taken his place before the Presbytery, the Moderator shall declare as follows:—

In the name of the Lord Jesus Christ, the King and Head of the Church, Who, being ascended on high, <u>hath given gifts unto men</u> [*has given gifts to God's people*] for the edifying of the body of Christ, we are met here as a Presbytery to ordain A. B. to the office of the Holy Ministry by prayer and the laying on of hands by the Presbyters to whom it <u>doth belong</u> [*belongs*], and to induct him into the pastoral charge of . . . . .

In this act of ordination the Church of Scotland, as part of the Holy Catholic or Universal Church worshipping One God — Father, Son, and Holy Spirit — affirms anew its belief in the Gospel of the sovereign grace and love of God, wherein through Jesus Christ, His only Son, our Lord, Incarnate, Crucified, and Risen, He freely offers to all <u>men</u> [people], upon repentance and faith, the forgiveness of sins, renewal by the Holy Spirit, and eternal life, and calls them to labour in the fellowship of faith for the advancement of the Kingdom of God throughout the world.

The Church of Scotland acknowledges the Word of God which is contained in the Scriptures of the Old and New Testaments to be the supreme rule of faith and life.

The Church of Scotland holds as its subordinate standard the Westminster Confession of Faith, recognising liberty of opinion on such points of doctrine as do not enter into the substance of the Faith, and claiming the right, in dependence on the promised guidance of the Holy Spirit, to formulate, interpret, or modify its subordinate standards: always in agreement with the Word of God and the fundamental doctrines of the Christian Faith contained in the said Confession — of which agreement the Church itself shall be sole judge.

Then the Moderator, addressing the Ordinand or Minister to be inducted, who is to stand and make answer to the questions put to him, shall say:—

A. B., in view of this Declaration, you are now required to answer these questions:—

QUESTIONS TO BE PUT TO MINISTERS BEFORE THEIR ORDINATION OR ADMISSION TO A CHARGE

1. Do you believe in one God — Father, Son, and Holy Spirit; and do you confess anew the Lord Jesus Christ as your Saviour and Lord?

2. Do you believe the Word of God, which is contained in the Scriptures of the Old and New Testaments, to be the supreme rule of faith and life?

3. Do you believe the fundamental doctrines of the Christian faith contained in the Confession of Faith of this Church?

4. Do you acknowledge the Presbyterian Government of this Church to be agreeable to the Word of God; and do you promise to be subject in the Lord to this Presbytery and to the superior Courts of the Church, and to take your due part in the administration of its affairs?

5. Do you promise to seek the unity and peace of this Church; to uphold the doctrine, worship, government, and discipline thereof; and to cherish a spirit of brotherhood towards all the followers of the Lord [*to cherish a spirit of love towards all your brothers and sisters in Christ*]?

6. Are not zeal for the glory of God, love to the Lord Jesus Christ, and a desire for the salvation of men [*all people*], so far as you know your own heart, your great motives and chief inducements to enter into the office of the Holy Ministry?

7. Do you engage in the strength of the Lord Jesus Christ to live a godly and circumspect life; and faithfully, diligently, and cheerfully to discharge the duties of your ministry, seeking in all things the advancement of the Kingdom of God?

8. Do you accept and close with the call to be Pastor of this charge, and promise through grace to study to approve yourself a faithful Minister of the Gospel among this people?

> *The questions having been answered to the satisfaction of the Presbytery, and the Formula having been signed, the Ordinand shall kneel, and the Moderator, by prayer with laying on of hands, in which all the Ministers present join, shall ordain him to the Office of the Holy Ministry.*

> *Thereafter the Moderator, except in cases in which there is no induction to a pastoral charge or any office, shall add these words:—*

I now declare you to have been ordained to the office of the Holy Ministry, and in the Name of the Lord Jesus Christ, the King and Head of the Church, and by authority of this Presbytery, I induct you to this charge; and in token thereof we give you the right hand of fellowship.

The following Question shall then be addressed to the Congregation, who are asked to signify assent by rising and standing in their places:—

Do you, the members and adherents of this Congregation, in receiving A. B., whom you have called to be your Minister, promise him all due honour and support in the Lord; *and in view of the pastoral and missionary obligations of this congregation, do you each now agree to share with your Minister the responsibility for Christian witness and Christian service*; and will you give of your means, as the Lord shall prosper you, for the maintenance of the Christian Ministry and the furtherance of the Gospel? [The words in italics were added by Act XI, 1958.]

FORMULA

I believe the fundamental doctrines of the Christian faith contained in the Confession of Faith of this Church.

I acknowledge the Presbyterian government of this Church to be agreeable to the Word of God, and promise that I will submit thereto and concur therewith.

I promise to observe the order of worship and the administration of all public ordinances as the same are or may be allowed in this Church.

This Formula shall also be that to be signed by Elders on admission to office.

Note: Verbal modifications, mainly in the interests of inclusive language, were suggested by the Board of Practice and Procedure (1992 Reports, p. 8). In the text of the Preamble and Questions above, the original words are underlined, and the suggested modifications are in italics and enclosed in brackets. The Assembly agreed to authorise the Panel on Worship to include modifications of this kind in revisions of the *Ordinal* and of the *Book of Common Order* (see Common Order, 1994, pp. 335-6, for the Panel's modifications in the Order for the Ordination and Admission of Elders). Although the Assembly made no specific recommendation for the period before a new Ordinal is published, it would clearly be reasonable, in the spirit of the Assembly's decision, for Presbyteries to use the suggested modifications.

A similarly reasonable modification, since the abolition of Synods, would be to replace, in Question 4, the words "the superior courts of the Church" with "the General Assembly."

PLAN OF UNION

[Only selected parts of the Plan are printed here, as being still relevant, or of particular historical interest. For an outline of the contents of the Plan, see Chapter III, p. 23.]

CONSTITUTION AND POWERS OF COURTS

THE GENERAL ASSEMBLY

1. The General Assembly is the Supreme Court of the Church. In matters spiritual its decisions are final, and are not subject to review by any Civil Court.

2. The membership of the General Assembly consists of Commissioners elected by Presbyteries for each Assembly. These Commissioners, being Ministers (including Theological Professors) and Ruling Elders, are elected in proportion to the size of each Presbytery, one Minister for every four or part of four Ministers on the complete Roll of the Presbytery, and an equal number of Ruling Elders. Ministers elected as Commissioners to the General Assembly must be members of the Presbyteries by which they are elected. Elders so elected must be *bona fide* acting members of Kirk Sessions within the Church. The quorum of the General Assembly shall be 31, of whom not less than 16 shall be Ministers. [Deacons are now included in the membership of the Assembly.]

3. Each General Assembly is presided over by a Moderator elected by itself from among its own members. It is the duty of the Moderator to preside at meetings of Assembly and apply the Standing Orders for the conduct of business. He alone declares the dissolution of the Assembly and intimates the day appointed by the General Assembly for the meeting of the next Assembly. At the close of the Assembly he delivers an Address; and preaches at the opening of the next Assembly, constituting the Court, which shall then proceed to elect its Moderator. [The Moderator now preaches at the Assembly Service on the Sunday of the Assembly, and gives an address to the following Assembly.]

The Moderator of the Assembly at which Union takes place shall be nominated by mutual agreement between the Committees on Union of the Church of Scotland and the United Free Church of Scotland. The first Assembly shall nominate the Moderator of the second Assembly, and the second Assembly shall determine the future method of nomination of Moderators of Assemblies.

4. The General Assembly will loyally welcome the Sovereign should it be the royal pleasure to attend in person: or, failing the Sovereign, a Lord High

Commissioner as the royal representative. Neither the Sovereign nor the Lord High Commissioner as such is a constituent member of the Assembly.

5. The Commission of Assembly shall consist of the members of the Assembly with one member added, who shall be nominated by the Moderator; its quorum shall be the same as that of the General Assembly; it shall appoint its own Chairman, and it shall deal with such business as has been made statutory for the Commission by the law of the Church or has been remitted to it by the Assembly. [See reference to the Overture under the Barrier Act, relating to the Commission, in Chapter XIII, p. 89.]

PRESBYTERIES AND SYNODS

1. In all Presbyteries and Synods there shall be an equal number of Ministers and Elders when the Roll is fully made up. [Synods have been abolished, and the rule about equal numbers no longer applies to Presbyteries.]

2. Every Minister inducted to a charge within the bounds of the Presbytery shall be a member of the Presbytery. The Kirk Session for each charge shall elect annually a representative Elder from amongst their own number (of which intimation shall be made to the Presbytery within three months of the close of the General Assembly), or with the special permission of the Presbytery from any Kirk Session within the bounds.

3. Ministers to whom Assistants and Successors or Junior Colleagues have been appointed prior to 31st May 1932 shall continue to be members of Presbytery, as well as their Assistants and Successors or Junior Colleagues, and Ministers and Theological Professors of either the Church of Scotland or the United Free Church of Scotland who prior to the Union had demitted their charges on account of age or infirmity, and Ministers and Theological Professors so demitting their charges prior to 31st May 1932 may, if they so desire, remain members of the Presbyteries which accepted their demission (or in the case of Ministers of the Church of Scotland may, if they so desire, return as members to such Presbyteries), it being understood that the question of the extension of this right to Ministers having Junior Colleagues appointed to them or Ministers and Theological Professors so demitting their charges subsequent to 31st May 1932, is meantime reserved for determination of the General Assembly with the consent of the Presbyteries of the Church. Ministers who have demitted their charges for any other reason may remain members of the Presbyteries which accepted the demission of their charges, subject to the approval of the Synod. When the Presbytery which accepted the demission has ceased to exist, or the charge which the Minister demitted has been severed from it, "the Presbytery which accepted the demission" shall be construed as meaning the Presbytery in which after the said date his said charge is situated.

4. Theological Professors who are Ministers of the united Church shall be members of the Presbytery within whose bounds is situated the College or University in which they teach.

5. Ministers in Colonial or Continental Charges, Missionaries who are ordained Ministers, Chaplains to His Majesty's Forces, and Chaplains on the Indian Establishment who have retired from active service, may remain members of the Presbyteries of which they were members at the date of their retirement on the same conditions as Ministers of home charges.

6. Ministers of the united Church who are temporarily appointed by or with the sanction of the Presbytery for a period of not less than twelve months to the charge of congregations, shall be received as members of the Presbytery within whose bounds they labour for the period during which they hold such temporary appointment, their membership in any other Presbyteries being meantime suspended, due intimation being made to the other Presbyteries concerned.

7. In order to maintain the equal number of Ministers and Elders in the Constitution of the Court, the Presbytery shall elect as members such a number of Elders as may be necessary for this purpose, such Elders to be chosen at the will of the Presbytery from any of the Kirk Sessions within the bounds.

8. With regard to Ministers of Charges furth of Scotland, the situation shall be accepted as it exists at present, and it shall be left to the united Church to make such readjustments as may be considered advisable.

[See Act III, 1992, as amended, for current position.]

FUNCTIONS AND POWERS OF SYNODS

A Supplementary Report was sent down to Presbyteries in accordance with the Deliverance of the General Assembly. In response suggestions were received, but it has been agreed that any important change in functions and powers of Synods is a matter which would most suitably be considered and decided upon by the united Church. [It is interesting that questions were being raised about Synods as early as 1929.]

FUNCTIONS, CONSTITUTION, AND POWERS OF KIRK SESSIONS

Until otherwise determined by the united Church through its General Assembly, after due consultation with Presbyteries, the method of election to and the powers and duties of Kirk Sessions shall continue in each congregation of the united Church to be governed by the regulations presently applicable to such congregation according to the branch of the united Church to which it belonged prior to the Union, except that the Formula to be signed by Elders on admission to office shall be the Formula hereinbefore provided for Ministers.

The same shall apply to Deacons' Courts, Committees of Management, Congregational Boards, &c.

RULES AND FORMS OF PROCEDURE.

Until a Manual of Procedure has been prepared by the united Church [This was written before the first edition of "Cox".], it is understood that Presbyteries, Sessions, and Congregations are at liberty to follow any of the methods of procedure in use in either of the Churches except in so far as modified by the Plan of Union, provided always that in cases where there is uncertainty in any Congregation or Kirk Session as to which rules should be followed (as, for example, in cases of amalgamation of charges), the question shall be referred to the Presbytery, whose decision shall be final.

FUNCTION, ORDINATION, AND INDUCTION OF MINISTERS

1. The ministry of the Word, the conduct of Public Worship, and the dispensing of the Sacraments belong to the Minister, subject to the control and direction of the Presbytery.
2. The ordination of a Minister is the solemn setting apart by prayer and the laying on of hands by Presbyters of a person already licensed to preach the Gospel, to the office and function of the Holy Ministry with a view to the exercise of that Ministry in a particular sphere.
3. Induction is admission to a particular charge of one who has been previously or on the same occasion ordained in accordance with the standards of the uniting Churches.

SUNDRY MATTERS

1. *Records of Church Courts.*— Material alterations shall be attested by both Moderator and Clerk; clerical errors by the initials of the Clerk.
2. *Convening of Kirk Session.*— It is the function of the Moderator to call meetings of Kirk Session. He shall be bound to do so within ten days if requested in writing by a majority of the elders, or where these exceed nine in number by at least one-third with a minimum of five.
3. *Quorum of Kirk Session.*— This shall be three, the Moderator and two Elders.
4. *Assessors to Kirk Session.*— If there be not a sufficient number of Elders available to make a quorum, or in cases of difficulty at the discretion of the Presbytery, Assessors may be appointed by the Presbytery with or without a vote according to the terms of their appointment.
5. *Rolls, Registers, &c.*— Those persons who, at the annual revisal of the Communion Roll, are found to have been absent from Communion for three consecutive years without a sufficient reason known to the Kirk Session, shall be deemed not to be communicants, and their names

shall be removed from the Roll; and the names of such persons can be restored to the Roll only by a resolution of the Kirk Session to that effect duly recorded in its Minutes. Provided always, that if at the annual revisal of the Roll any communicant, whose address is known, is found to have been absent from Communion for two consecutive years without a sufficient reason known to the Kirk Session, it shall take such means as shall seem best to inform the said communicant of this enactment.

> A Register of Baptisms shall be kept by the Minister in each charge, and it is recommended that a Register of baptised persons, not communicants, be also kept. [The Kirk Session is responsible for the baptismal roll (Act, XVII, 1931), but in practice the Minister usually keeps it, no doubt acting for the Session.]

> The Rolls, Registers, and Records shall be examined annually by the Presbytery, and an abstract of the congregational accounts (after being audited) shall be examined and attested by the Presbytery.

> Every Presbytery shall keep a Benefice Register of the property belonging to each Charge within the bounds. [The Benefice Register has now been incorporated in the Property Register.]

6. *Presbyterial Visitation.*— The principle of periodic visitation of all Congregations is affirmed.

7. *Overtures.*— In their return to Overtures, remitted for their consideration in accordance with the provisions of the Barrier Act, *1697, IX.,* Presbyteries shall be required to state clearly and categorically whether they approve or disapprove, but they shall have the opportunity of appending remarks or suggestions. If any alteration so proposed in no way modifies the substance, sense, or intention of the Overture, it shall be competent for the General Assembly to adopt it. It shall be competent for a Presbytery among its remarks to indicate approval of the principle of an Overture while disagreeing with the method in which it is proposed to carry out that principle. In this case, however, it shall be reckoned to disapprove. When so instructed by the General Assembly, Presbyteries shall give to Kirk Sessions the opportunity of stating their opinion on Overtures.

8. *Non-residence.*— When a Manse is provided, the Minister shall reside in it unless with the express consent of the Presbytery to reside elsewhere. [For fiscal reasons, this consent is seldom given.] In all cases the Presbytery shall require him to reside within a reasonable distance of the Church and sphere of ministry. A Minister may be dealt with for non-residence,

9. *Proclamation of Banns.*— In parishes where there is more than one church, the banns shall be duly published if proclaimed in such

church or churches in the parish as shall be selected for the purpose by the Presbytery within whose jurisdiction the parish is situated. Until the Presbytery has made a selection, the existing practice shall continue, and proclamation of banns shall be made in the church or churches in the parish where it was in use to be made before Union. [Banns are no longer required for marriages in Scotland.]

10. *Parishes and Other Territorial Areas.*— For the purposes of effective pastoral work on a territorial basis, it shall be an early duty of Presbyteries after Union to readjust parochial and other areas where necessary, and assign spheres of pastoral labour and responsibility to the Ministers of particular charges.

Until this has been done (1) for the purposes of the immediately preceding article the boundaries of parishes shall remain as at the date of Union, and (2) existing arrangements, whereby parochial or other areas are assigned or recognised as spheres of pastoral labour and responsibility, shall continue.

DISCIPLINE

I. APPLICABLE TO ALL COURTS

Principles

Discipline in the government of the Church is of Scriptural authority. The ends contemplated by it are the glory of God, the purity of the Church, and the spiritual benefit of her members. It is to be administered in faithfulness, meekness, love, and tenderness.

Discipline consists in the administration of the appropriate censures of the Church to those whose conduct shall have given occasion for it.

Nothing is to be admitted as the ground of a process for censure but what is declared censurable by the Word of God, or by some Act or universal custom of this Church.

The subjects of discipline are those who hold office in the Church, communicants, and baptised persons who are adherents.

Censures

The Censures of the Church are Admonition, Rebuke, Suspension, Deposition from office, and Excommunication, and they are administered only on confession or proof of sin or offence. Private admonition, which is not a censure, may in certain cases meet the ends of Discipline.

Suspension of a person under scandal from performance of duties, or even from sealing ordinances during the investigation of the scandal, is not a Censure as long as the charge is not judicially confessed or proven.

Suspension from office *sine die* involves removal from the office held.

Record Apart

To keep the ordinary records of the courts, which have to be consulted and inspected for various purposes, free from the presence of undesirable matter, and to obviate their mutilation by the deletion of the proceedings, the principle of a Record Apart shall be adopted in all cases where moral delinquency is alleged. As far as the cases which ordinarily come before Kirk Sessions are concerned, involving communicants or baptised persons who are adherents, the desired end may be achieved by the use of a Minute Book of Discipline as mentioned in the procedure recommended below. In all other cases, such as processes against office-bearers, the court of first instance shall resolve from the first to keep the proceedings of the case in a Record Apart, and said resolution shall be minuted in the Record Apart, and not in the ordinary record.

When the judgment which finally disposes of the case, by whatever court of the Church pronounced, involves any degree of censure of the accused, then the court of first instance shall engross in its ordinary Minute Book the first Minute of the Record Apart, the libel, or a summary of each of the charges thereof, if a libel was served, and the final judgment. When a case has ended in entire acquittal, if there is a Record Apart in any court inferior to the General Assembly, it shall, with all papers in the case, so far as these do not affect the interests of third parties, be sealed up in presence of that court, docqueted with the name of the congregation and the date of final judgment, and kept *in retentis* for five years and thereafter destroyed. When a process ends in entire acquittal, the person whose innocence has been proved ought to have a certified copy of the judgment of the court delivered to him.

In every case the inferior courts shall keep an Inventory of Process, in which the Clerk shall enter and number all the documents.

Persons accused have the right of access to any productions in the case which are in the possession of the court.

Parties may appear by or have the assistance of Counsel or Agents in any process depending before the Presbytery or any higher court, unless such court shall otherwise determine. They shall not be entitled to have such assistance in any process depending before a Kirk Session except with the special permission of the Kirk Session. Any parties appearing by Counsel or Agents shall not be entitled to be heard also by themselves.

II. Processes in which the Kirk Session is the Court of First Instance

When a person under scandal refuses to submit to discipline, notwithstanding such pastoral dealing as appears to the Kirk Session sufficient, the Kirk Session may intimate to *him* (or *her)* by registered letter by its Clerk that, unless within thirty days *he* shall make known *his* willingness to submit to discipline (or, if the charge is denied, to discipline or trial), *he* will be suspended from privileges till such submission is made and disposed of, or till the Kirk Session is otherwise satisfied.

When an accused person has made known *his* willingness to submit to discipline, the Kirk Session may remit the case to the Moderator alone, or to the Moderator and one of the elders.

If a record be kept by the Kirk Session of all cases of discipline, it shall be in a book reserved for this purpose alone. The names, and all that might lead to the identification of the parties, shall be rendered illegible after five years. In such cases the Kirk Session shall not, unless requested by the person accused, be required to keep a Record Apart, but in the event of an appeal or dissent and complaint to any superior court other than the General Assembly, a Record Apart shall be kept by that superior court.

Kirk Sessions shall afford facilities for the transference of cases from one Kirk Session to another when this would be for the convenience of parties and Kirk Sessions.

III. Processes in which the Presbytery is the Court of First Instance

When a *fama* has arisen against an office-bearer (minister or probationer) who is subject to the jurisdiction of a Presbytery, it shall be the duty of the Presbytery to institute a preliminary inquiry, and if the offence is denied, and there still appears ground for investigation, the court shall, except in the case of a minister who demands that a libel be served on him, proceed to a formal inquiry or a trial by libel. In such cases a Record Apart is required.

Alike in the case of such a formal inquiry and of a trial by libel, there are certain principles to which it is desirable to give effect:—

(a) It is the right of the courts of the Church to adjudicate in all matters of discipline, and the court should not be both prosecutor and judge.

(b) The difficulties occasioned by the numerical size of Church courts ought to be recognised, and such procedure adopted as will ensure that findings on matters of probation will be reached only by those who have heard the whole of the case.

Accordingly there shall be a Committee on Cases against ministers (or probationers) appointed by the General Assembly, who shall advise with the Presbytery if it so desires as to the scope of a formal inquiry, and furnish prosecutors to conduct the inquiry; or in cases where a libel is instituted, who shall prepare the libel and prosecute it, after it has been submitted to and revised by the legal adviser of the Church.

There shall also be a Committee of Assessors appointed annually by the General Assembly, and when evidence has been appointed to be taken either in a formal inquiry, or in a trial by libel, the Presbytery shall commit the hearing of the evidence to a Committee of its own number, or to a panel consisting of, say, three or five of its own number and two Assessors, who may hear the whole case, and report to the Presbytery their findings on the extent of probation of the various charges, stating whether they are unanimous or with how many dissentients, and whether their findings are acquiesced in or appealed against by the accused.

It will be for the Presbytery to judge of the report, and to determine the degree of censure appropriate to the extent of the offence found to have been proved. In the event of an appeal to a higher court, this finding shall be transmitted with the other documents in the case.

[The above procedure has to be read, as far as Presbyteries are concerned, in conjunction with Act VII, 1935, which must prevail where there are differences; but it is the only extant law relating to discipline for Kirk Sessions. See Chapters IX & X.]

APPENDIX C

CERTAIN DECLARATORY AND UNITING ACTS REFERRED TO IN THE BASIS OF UNION

A. CHURCH OF SCOTLAND ACT ON THE FORMULA (XIII, 1910)

Edinburgh, 30th May 1910. *Sess. 7.*

WHEREAS it is expedient to amend the Formula of Subscription to the Confession of Faith required from ministers and preachers of this Church, and from persons appointed to Chairs of Theology in the Scottish Universities, and the Principal of Saint Mary's College, Saint Andrews, respectively, the General Assembly, with the consent of the majority of Presbyteries, declare and enact that in lieu of the present Formula of Subscription to the Confession of Faith, which is prescribed by Act XVII. of General Assembly 1889, the following shall be the Formula of Subscription by ministers at their ordination and by probationers when receiving licence, viz.:—

> I hereby subscribe the Confession of Faith, declaring that I accept it as the Confession of this Church, and that I believe the fundamental doctrines of the Christian faith contained therein.
>
> As likewise I own and acknowledge Presbyterian Church government, as now and for long time settled by law, to be the only government of this Church, and I will submit thereto and concur therewith, and never endeavour, directly or indirectly, the prejudice or subversion thereof. As also I will observe that uniformity of worship and of the administration of all public ordinances in this Church, as the same are at present performed and allowed, or shall be hereafter declared by the authority of the same.

And further, the General Assembly declare and enact that Subscription of the Confession of Faith, which has been made in terms of the Formula at present in use, or which may be so made prior to the 1st July after the passing of this Act, by ministers, preachers, or other persons above-named, shall be held to be equivalent to Subscription of the Formula herein enacted.

B. DECLARATORY ACT OF THE UNITED PRESBYTERIAN SYNOD

(Adopted May 1879)

Whereas the formula in which the Subordinate Standards of this Church are accepted requires assent to them as an exhibition of the sense in which the Scriptures are understood: Whereas these Standards, being of human composition, are necessarily imperfect, and the Church has already allowed exception to be taken to their teaching or supposed teaching on one important subject: And whereas there are other subjects in regard to which it has been found desirable to set forth more fully and clearly the view which the Synod takes of the teaching of Holy Scripture: Therefore, the Synod hereby declares as follows:—

1. That in regard to the doctrine of redemption as taught in the Standards, and in consistency therewith, the love of God to all mankind, His gift of His Son to be the propitiation for the sins of the whole world, and the free offer of salvation to men without distinction on the ground of Christ's perfect sacrifice, are matters which have been and continue to be regarded by this Church as vital in the system of Gospel truth, and to which due prominence ought ever to be given.
2. That the doctrine of the divine decrees, including the doctrine of election to eternal life, is held in connection and harmony with the truth that God is not willing that any should perish, but that all should come to repentance, and that He has provided a salvation sufficient for all, adapted to all, and offered to all in the Gospel; and also with the responsibility of every man for his dealing with the free and unrestricted offer of eternal life.
3. That the doctrine of man's total depravity, and of his loss of "all ability of will to any spiritual good accompanying salvation," is not held as implying such a condition of man's nature as would affect his responsibility under the law of God and the Gospel of Christ, or that he does not experience the strivings and restraining influences of the Spirit of God, or that he cannot perform actions in any sense good; although actions which do not spring from a renewed heart are not spiritually good or holy — such as accompany salvation.
4. That while none are saved except through the mediation of Christ, and by the grace of His Holy Spirit, who worketh when, and where, and how it pleaseth Him; while the duty of sending the Gospel to the heathen, who are sunk in ignorance, sin, and misery, is clear and imperative; and while the outward and ordinary means of salvation for those capable of being called by the Word are the ordinances of the Gospel: in accepting the Standards, it is not required to be held that any who die in infancy are lost, or that God may not extend His

grace to any who are without the pale of ordinary means, as it may seem good in His sight.

5. That in regard to the doctrine of the Civil Magistrate, and his authority and duty in the sphere of religion, as taught in the Standards, this Church holds that the Lord Jesus Christ is the only King and Head of the Church, and "Head over all things to the Church which is His body"; disapproves of all compulsory or persecuting and intolerant principles in religion; and declares, as hitherto, that she does not require approval of anything in her Standards that teaches, or may be supposed to teach, such principles.

6. That Christ has laid it as a permanent and universal obligation upon His Church, at once to maintain her own ordinances, and to "preach the Gospel to every creature"; and has ordained that His people provide by their free-will offerings for the fulfilment of this obligation.

7. That, in accordance with the practice hitherto observed in this Church, liberty of opinion is allowed on such points in the Standards, not entering into the substance of the faith, as the interpretation of the "six days" in the Mosaic account of the creation: the Church guarding against the abuse of this liberty to the injury of its unity and peace.

C. DECLARATORY ACT OF THE GENERAL ASSEMBLY OF THE FREE CHURCH, 1892 — ANENT THE CONFESSION OF FAITH.

Whereas it is expedient to remove difficulties and scruples which have been felt by some in reference to the declaration of belief required from persons who receive licence or are admitted to office in this Church, the General Assembly, with consent of Presbyteries, declare as follows:—

That, in holding and teaching, according to the Confession, the Divine purpose of grace towards those who are saved, and the execution of that purpose in time, this Church most earnestly proclaims, as standing in the forefront of the revelation of Grace, the love of God, Father, Son, and Holy Spirit, to sinners of mankind, manifested especially in the Father's gift of the Son to be the Saviour of the world, in the coming of the Son to offer Himself a propitiation for sin, and in the striving of the Holy Spirit with men to bring them to repentance.

That this Church also holds that all who hear the Gospel are warranted and required to believe to the saving of their souls; and that in the case of such as do not believe, but perish in their sins, the issue is due to their own rejection of the Gospel call. That this Church does not teach, and does not regard the Confession as teaching, the fore-ordination of men to death irrespective of their own sin.

That it is the duty of those who believe, and one end of their calling by God, to make known the Gospel to all men everywhere for the obedience of faith. And that while the Gospel is the ordinary means of salvation for those to whom it is made known, yet it does not follow, nor is the Confession to be held as teaching, that any who died in infancy are lost, or that God may not extend His mercy, for Christ's sake, and by His Holy Spirit, to those who are beyond the reach of these means, as it may seem good to Him, according to the riches of His grace.

That, in holding and teaching, according to the Confession of Faith, the corruption of man's whole nature as fallen, this Church also maintains that there remain tokens of his greatness as created in the image of God; that he possesses a knowledge of God and of duty; that he is responsible for compliance with the moral law and with the Gospel; and that, although unable without the aid of the Holy Spirit to return to God, he is yet capable of affections and actions which in themselves are virtuous and praiseworthy.

That this Church disclaims intolerant or persecuting principles, and does not consider her office-bearers, in subscribing the Confession, committed to any principles inconsistent with liberty of conscience and the right of private judgment.

That while diversity of opinion is recognised in this Church on such points in the Confession as do not enter into the substance of the Reformed Faith therein set forth, the Church retains full authority to determine, in any case which may arise, what points fall within this description, and thus to guard against any abuse of this liberty to the detriment of sound doctrine, or to the injury of her unity and peace.

D. FREE CHURCH ACT IX, 1894 — ANENT DECLARATORY ACT, 1892, ON CONFESSION OF FAITH

The General Assembly enact and declare as follows:—

Whereas the Declaratory Act, 1892, was passed to remove difficulties and scruples which had been felt by some in reference to the declaration of belief required from persons who receive licence, or are admitted to Office in this Church, the Assembly hereby declare that the statements of doctrine contained in the said Act are not thereby imposed upon any of the Church's office-bearers as part of the Standards of the Church; but that those who are licensed or ordained to office in this Church, in answering the questions and subscribing the Formula, are entitled to do so in view of the said Declaratory Act.

APPENDIX D

THE CHURCH OF SCOTLAND ACT, 1921

The operative clauses of the 1921 Act are as follows:

1. The Declaratory Articles are lawful articles, and the constitution of the Church of Scotland in matters spiritual is as therein set forth, and no limitation of the liberty, rights, and powers in matters spiritual therein set forth shall be derived from any statute or law affecting the Church of Scotland in matters spiritual at present in force, it being hereby declared that in all questions of construction the Declaratory Articles shall prevail, and that all such statutes and laws shall be construed in conformity therewith and in subordination thereto, and all such statutes and laws in so far as they are inconsistent with the Declaratory Articles are hereby repealed and declared to be of no effect.

2. Nothing contained in this Act or in any other Act affecting the Church of Scotland shall prejudice the recognition of any other Church in Scotland as a Christian Church protected by law in the exercise of its spiritual functions.

3. Subject to the recognition of the matters dealt with in the Declaratory Articles as matters spiritual, nothing in this Act contained shall affect or prejudice the jurisdiction of the civil courts in relation to any matter of a civil nature.

4. This Act may be cited as the Church of Scotland Act, 1921, and shall come into operation on such date as His Majesty may fix by Order in Council after the Declaratory Articles shall have been adopted by an Act of the General Assembly of the Church of Scotland with the consent of a majority of the Presbyteries of the Church.

[The Schedule to the Act contains the *Articles Declaratory of the Constitution of the Church of Scotland in Matters Spiritual* (see p. 159). These were duly adopted by the Assembly by Barrier Act procedure. The Church of Scotland Order in Council, 1926, fixed 28th June, 1926, as the date on which the 1921 Act would come into operation.]

APPENDIX E

ACT XIX, 1889, ON FORMS OF PROCEDURE IN TRIAL BY LIBEL AND IN CAUSES GENERALLY.

Edinburgh, May 28,1889. Sess. 7.

Whereas it is desirable to simplify certain forms and procedure now in use, the General Assembly, with consent of Presbyteries, hereby enact and ordain as follows:—

1. A libel may omit, and, if it omits, shall imply (1) that part which is known as its major premise setting forth the kind, criminality, and punishableness of the offence; (2) the conclusion presently in use beginning, "all which or any part thereof being found proven"; (3) the statement that the accused is "guilty, actor or art and part"; (4) the words "to the scandal of religion and disgrace of your profession"; (5) all expressions indicating the spirit or knowledge of the accused, such as "wilfully," "having reason to know," and the like; (6) all language taking latitude as to time, place, mode, words, &c., of the offence by alternative widening statements, except when the exact time, place, mode, or words, &c., is of the essence of the charge — provided that, as at present, the Court may, when exceptional occasion arises, decide whether too great latitude is taken.

2. It shall be sufficient that a libel sets forth facts which constitute a censurable offence, and this may be done after the manner shown in Schedule A hereto annexed. Charges shall not be stated alternatively, and any part of what is charged constituting in itself an offence may be separately found proven. Aggravations shall be called aggravations; and when an aggravation or a particular intent is libelled, the offence may be found proven apart therefrom. A document, or a part of one, need not be quoted, but may instead be designated; and when it is one of the productions, it may be referred to by its number in the list of productions. A person may be described by his name and ordinary address, such words as "now or lately residing" being implied. The warrant to cite, the citation and the execution thereof may be after the manner shown in Schedules B, C, and D.

3. A witness shall be sufficiently designated by his name and address, if he has resided there at some time within six months previous to the serving of the libel, such words as "now or lately residing" being always unnecessary. The inability of either party to find any of his own or of the other's witnesses, shall be no reason for delay, unless the Court shall, in the particular circumstances, see cause to determine otherwise.

4. In the inferior Courts, there shall in every case be an Inventory of Process, in which the Clerk shall enter and number all the documents. When any document is borrowed by a party, he shall write on the Inventory of Process a receipt and the date before which it shall be returned. The original libel, and the Inventory of Process, shall not be borrowed, and the Court may direct the Clerk as to what other documents may be borrowed, and for what period.

5. An appeal need not contain such words as, "for these and other reasons to be stated," &c., but this shall be implied; *and it shall not contain any crave, under penalty of being regarded as a petition, and dismissed as incompetent.* [The words in italics were deleted by Act III, 1981.] Appellants are hereby charged to state their reasons with the utmost brevity, and to state only such as they deem of real importance.

6. It is hereby declared to be the law of the Church

(1) that a Dissent and Complaint by a member of Court is, *mutatis mutandis,* subject to all the rules applicable to an appeal by a party, and to no other;

(2) that it is incompetent for any inferior Court to refuse or obstruct an appeal against any of its judgments whatsoever [*Note* 1.— This includes judgements even in matter which cannot themselves be competently dealt with by a superior court. In such a case the court appealed from may consider itself bound to proceed on the assumption that execution of its sentence is not sisted. Before this is done it should be very clear that there was nothing in the subject-matter, or the procedure, or the judgement which justified the appeal. Appeals that are evidently frivolous may be regarded after the same manner, the court bearing in mind that only the court of appeal can dispose of them, and accepting the risk of what that court may say. *Note* 2.— While the enactment includes all judgements, it does not commit itself to all kinds of appeals. Every court is entitled to protect itself from evident insolence and contumacy, and outside parties from unnecessary injury and may refuse to receive any document that involves such offences. (Cox, pp. 93-94, following Mair, p. 47)]

(3) that the protest for leave to appeal is for securing the privilege during ten days, in case of present unpreparedness to give in (what alone is valid) the appeal written with the reasons thereof and subscribed; (4) that appeals shall be to the next superior Court, not later than the first meeting thereof which is ten free days after the judgment in question; but if the appeal is to the Assembly, there is no such condition of time; and appeals which would have been to a meeting of Synod shall be to the Assembly if it meets earlier; (5) that in an appeal no document shall be read, or shall appear among the papers of the Court (printed or written), unless it was before the Court of first instance, or was offered to it and rejected, and has thence come up regularly; and no person shall be allowed at the bar unless he was at the bar of the Court of first instance, or applied to be so and was refused, and has thence come up regularly, or unless he is a member of the next inferior Court, complaining in the regular manner;

(6) that written answers to appeals are not required. [But written answers are competent, and are recommended.]

7. It shall not be necessary in any cause to take an appeal in any matter of incidental procedure, but an appeal on any part of the merits shall entitle any of the parties to bring up for review any prior relative deliverances given by the same Court; but such prior deliverances shall in other respects be brought up according to the ordinary rules, by an appeal in writing with the reasons, and given in within the ten days claimed for giving in the appeal on the merits to which they relate. [See Act VII, 1996 for clarification of this Section.]

8. In cases of discipline a Court appealed from may, *not later than seventeen days before the meeting of the Court appealed to (or, if less than seventeen days come between the date of the judgment in question and said meeting, then on the day on which said judgment is given)* [The words in italics have been replaced by provisions in the Standing Orders of the Assembly, and are omitted from the print on p. 96 of Cox.], resolve, either *ex proprio motu* or on the application of a party, to transmit the Record Apart, if any, to the Clerk of the Court appealed to, and parties shall be informed of such resolution. All productions shall in every case be so transmitted and also the Inventory of Process. The provisions of this section shall not interfere with the right of any party to obtain on timely application extracts of the record or of any of the productions in accordance with present practice. [*Note*— The first sentence deals with Records Apart. The provision removes the necessity of copying or extracting it, and is practicable because the record is not in the minute-book. The second sentence deals with productions, and requires that in all cases the originals will be transmitted. Both the Record Apart and the productions can be sent only from Clerk to Clerk. "Process" consists of all documents and articles lodged. It will be safe for an appellant craving extracts to crave the court or the Clerk to transmit the Process, and obtain satisfaction that this has been done, for it still rests with him (as laid down in the Kirkintilloch case, 1895, Sess. 8) to see that everything necessary is sent up. (Cox, p. 95, following Mair, p. 50.)]

9. [This Section dealt with cases coming from Synods.]

10. The word "Appeal" in this Act shall be held to include a Dissent and Complaint.

11. Proceedings under any libel served before the passing of this Act shall be conducted according to the present law and practice.

SCHEDULES REFERRED TO IN THE FOREGOING ACT.

SCHEDULE A.

Notes.— In a libel, the person indicted may be styled probationer or minister, as the case may be; and if he is the minister of a parish or charge, he may be designated accordingly, instead of by his address. When the libel is at the instance of individuals, their names and addresses shall be embodied in it. The attestation of the libel may be: Signed at......in name [, presence,] and by authority of the Presbytery of......this [*date*], by *[Moderator and Clerk]*.

The libel may be after the following forms:—

Name, &c., you are indicted at the instance of......, and the charge against you is (1) that you were in a state of intoxication on 20th December 1886, in a shop in George Street, Edinburgh, occupied by John Black, Bookseller; and (2) on 9th March 1887, on the public road which lies between the farmhouse of Loanend, in the parish of Lisburn, and the farmhouse of Fans, in the parish of Newton; and (3) on 3rd October 1887, at the village of Newton, Midlothian; and (4) that you are an habitual drunkard; and (5) that you were admonished for drunkenness by the Presbytery of Aberfour, on 6th April 1886, which is an aggravation.

......that on 11th April, and also in the month of May 1886, in the Manse of Camwell, you had carnal intercourse with Jane Sutherland, your domestic servant, whereof [*if such be the case*] a child was born by her on 7th February 1887, at Annfield, in the parish of Rodnam.

......that on 30th July 1887, in a wood near and to the north of the village of Bushby, in the parish of Balston, you used libidinous practices towards Helen Ford [*say what*].

......that (1) on 10th June 1887, at a meeting of the heritors of the parish of Eddle, you uttered falsehood respecting certain proceedings which occurred between you and William Wright, church officer of that parish, on the first day of that month, saying that [*state the falsehood*]; and (2) that in a letter dated 24th June 1887, and addressed to John Grant of Hilton Mains, Eddle, you uttered falsehood regarding the said William Wright, and slandered him, saying that [*state what*]; and (3) that on 12th and 20th August 1887, in the office of James Smart, Writer, Kelso, you used profane and scandalous language [*state the language*].

......that you are the author of the sermon on Hebrews x. 12, published in the volume entitled "Specimen Sermons," beginning on page 209, and containing unsound doctrine; and in particular in those passages which are numbered 3, 4, and 5 of the productions.

......that on 9th January 1887, in the Parish Church of Lawlace, in a sermon on 1 Corinthians xv. 20, you preached unsound doctrine; and in particular you said [*giving the erroneous statements, if the sermon or extracts cannot be produced as in last form*].

SCHEDULE B

Warrant To Cite

At [*place and date*], which day the Presbytery of......, being met and constituted, *inter alia* did, and hereby do, grant Warrant to the Presbytery Officer, and to all competent officers, to serve a copy of the foregoing libel and list of witnesses on Mr......, and to cite him to compear personally and answer thereto before this Presbytery at [*place, day, and hour*], and to give the said citation in writing, either personally or at his dwelling-house, at least ten free days before the day of compearance.

...........*Moderator.*
...............*Clerk.*

SCHEDULE C

The Citation

I, William Thomson, do hereby cite you, Mr......, to compear personally before the Presbytery of......[*place, day, and hour*], to answer the libel against you to which this citation is attached. This I do on [*date*], in presence of these witnesses [*names and addresses. The witnesses do not sign*].

WILLIAM THOMSON, *Presbytery Officer.*

SCHEDULE D

The Execution

On 10th April 1887, I, William Thomson, served on Mr......, in accordance with the Warrant granted me to that end, the foregoing libel and list of witnesses against him, with a citation thereto attached to appear before the Presbytery of......[*place, day, and hour*], which citation was subscribed by me, and bore the names of [*give names and addresses*], in whose presence as witnesses it was given, and who hereto subscribe with me.

WILLIAM THOMSON, *Presbytery Officer.*

JOHN SMITH, *Witness.*
MARY BROWN, *Witness.*
    [*Witnesses to be above fourteen*]

APPENDIX F

RECORDS

I. LOOSE-LEAF RECORDS (Reg. 4, 1964)

(1) *Communion Rolls*

That the type of Communion Roll in common use, that is, the permanently bound volume containing details of a member's joining and disjoining together with the record of attendances at Holy Communion, should continue to be available for such Kirk Sessions as wish to use it.

That there be no interference with the various types of loose-leaf Communion Rolls introduced by Kirk Sessions, in accordance with the opinion of the late Sir Randall Philip; and that Kirk Sessions might continue to use a loose-leaf system of Communion Roll, suitable for their own purposes, if so desired.

The Committee on Publications be authorised to make available for sale to Kirk Sessions the following:—

(a) A bound volume to contain the names of Communicants, together with a record of admission to full membership and disjoining;

(b) A loose-leaf volume as in (a) the pages of which shall be consecutively numbered, and ultimately bound into permanent book form;

(c) A type of loose-leaf Roll to be used along with (a) and (b) whereon to record the attendances of members at Holy Communion, with space for recording any other information deemed useful by the Kirk Session;

(d) A loose-leaf Roll combining (b) and (c).

(2) *Church Records*

Baptismal and Proclamation Registers — That no suggestions be made regarding any form of loose-leaf volumes for these Registers.

Minute Books and Finance Books —

(i) That each sheet as it comes into use shall be numbered consecutively from the page it succeeds;

(ii) That each page as it comes into use shall begin with the last word on the page that it succeeds;

(iii) That when minutes are approved, each page recording such minutes should be initialled by the Moderator who shall also, with the Clerk, sign at the end of the minutes;

(iv) That when sufficient pages have been completed to comprise a conveniently sized volume the Court concerned shall have such pages bound into permanent form.

II. REGULATIONS ANENT COMMUNION ROLLS ON COMPUTER
(Reg. I, 1996)

1. A Congregation's Communion Roll may be kept on computer provided that an up-to-date printout of the Roll as at 31 December is produced at the annual inspection of records.

2. The printout shall contain the names and addresses, with date and manner of admission, of all members as at 31 December of the year under inspection. It shall also contain an appendix recording the names and addresses of people who have been removed from the Roll during the year, along with the date, reason and means of removal. The form and style of the printout shall be approved by the Superintendence Committee, or other committee appointed by the Presbytery for this purpose, before it first comes into use, and the committee shall report such approval to the Presbytery.

3. Annual printouts shall be kept as historical records, and shall be preserved in a substantial looseleaf binder, or permanently bound at intervals not exceeding ten years.

4. It is advisable that whatever present manual system is in operation should continue to be kept up to date by the roll-keeper and attested by the Kirk Session. Where the computer system being used is personal to the minister it is important that there should be a roll-keeper, who should not normally be the minister.

5. Kirk Sessions proposing to store data in a computer must ensure before doing so that the requirements of the Data Protection Act will be satisfied, and to this end they should record their intent with the Presbytery Clerk.

APPENDIX G

DESIGNATIONS AND PROPER FORM

The use of the designation "**Reverend**" for a minister is of comparatively recent origin, and has been accepted by use and wont, tacitly adopted by the General Assembly rather than formally resolved. The older way of designating a minister was "Mr. John Smith, Minister at Such-and-such." The proper forms given here for "Reverend" are based on usage and on good grammar.

The abbreviation used by the General Assembly is "Rev." The forms "Rev'd" or "Revd." are sometimes found.

Normally the designation is preceded by the definite article, and this should be used in **addressing envelopes**, as e.g. "The Rev. John Smith", but on headed notepaper, and in lists, the form is usually "Rev. John Smith". (cf. Mr. John Smith" on an envelope, but "John Smith" on headed notepaper.)

"Reverend" should not be used, **in writing** or **in speech**, in the same way as a title like "doctor", for it is not a noun, but a gerundive, or verbal adjective, from the verb "revere", and literally meaning "requiring to be revered" (not personally, but in virtue of the office held). A minister should be referred to as "The Rev. John Smith", or simply "Mr. Smith", e.g. "I have pleasure in introducing The Rev. John Smith . . . and I now call on Mr. Smith to address us."

"Reverend" is grammatically similar in use to "honourable". It is wrong not to use the Christian name with it, addressing or referring to a minister as "Reverend Smith", just as it would be wrong to address anyone as "Honourable Smith" instead of "The Honourable John Smith".

A **letter** should begin, "Dear Mr. Smith", not "Dear Rev. Smith". A very formal letter should begin, "Reverend and dear Sir."

A **minister and his wife** should be designated "The Rev. John and Mrs. Smith", or possibly "The Rev. John and Mrs. Jean Smith", but not "The Rev. and Mrs. John Smith."

A **minister and her husband** might be designated "Mr. John and the Rev. Jean Smith", or "The Rev. Jean and Mr. Smith."

When a **husband and wife are both ministers**, "The Revs. John and Jean Smith" would be incorrect, because "reverend", being adjectival, does not have a plural form. "The Rev. John and Jean Smith" would be correct, but some might prefer "The Rev. John and The Rev. Jean Smith."

Although it appears to have been a common practice for some time to precede lists of names of ministers with "Revs.", this is clearly not grammatically correct.

The **Moderator** of the General Assembly is properly designated as "Moderator of the General Assembly of the Church of Scotland", not "Moderator of the Church of Scotland." The use of "**Right Reverend**" for the Moderator during the year of office has been tacitly recognised in use by the Church, and formally recognised by the State. The use of "**Very Reverend**" for former Moderators has been similarly recognised.

The designation "Very Reverend" is also given to the Dean of the Chapel Royal, the Dean of the Thistle, and the Principal of St. Mary's College, St. Andrews, the last during the term of office only.

In the Scottish Order of Precedence, the Moderator of the General Assembly, while in office, comes next after the Lord Chancellor of Great Britain, and before the Prime Minister.

A minister who receives a **knighthood** is not entitled to the title "Sir", nor his wife to that of "Lady". This follows the decision of King Edward VII to confer on a minister the insignia, without the accolade, on the grounds that the emblems of a knight were a sword, spurs and belt, which were unsuitable for an ordained man (Cox, p. 782; but there is reason to believe that this matter may be under review).

APPENDIX H

THE LORD HIGH COMMISSIONER

The Lord High Commissioner to the General Assembly of the Church of Scotland is the official representative of the Sovereign, who does not normally attend in person, but has done so, most recently in 1977. The office has over the years undergone some changes in title and functions. In times of tension between Church and State, after the Reformation, the Sovereign frequently attempted to exercise control over the Church by appointing a Commissioner, but it is now settled that the Lord High Commissioner has no authority of any kind over the Assembly.

It is an office of considerable importance to the Church, being symbolic both of the national recognition of religion, and of the Church's independence of the State. The throne gallery is outwith the Assembly, and the Lord High Commissioner does not, as such, enter the Assembly, although it is possible for a holder of the office also to be personally commissioned by a Presbytery.

The tenure of office of the Lord High Commissioner begins on the day before the opening of the Assembly, before the traditional Ceremony of the Keys, and ends when the Moderator closes the Assembly with the Benediction on the final day. During that time, he or she takes precedence in Scotland immediately after the Queen and the Duke of Edinburgh, is referred to as "His Grace" or "Her Grace", and addressed as "Your Grace". These forms were used when The Princess Royal was Lord High Commissioner, in 1996, because of the precedence of the office. It has been agreed that a woman appointed to the office may choose to be styled "Her Majesty's High Commissioner."

This is a unique office, whose holder, being the personal representative of the Sovereign, becomes in effect "royal" for a week, lives in the Palace of Holyroodhouse, and offers hospitality to a large number of guests at various functions, including a garden party to which all commissioners are invited. As well as attending the Assembly, the Lord High Commissioner carries out several other official engagements during the week.

Further information is contained in *The Office of Lord High Commissioner*, Stewart Mechie, The Saint Andrew Press, 1957.

The Commission

The text of the Commission in 1996 is given overleaf. The terms remain the same from year to year, with only the name and designation of the Commissioner changed.

COMMISSION in favour of THE PRINCESS ROYAL, ANNE ELIZABETH ALICE LOUISE, to be HER MAJESTY'S COMMISSIONER to the GENERAL ASSEMBLY

ELIZABETH THE SECOND by the Grace of God of the United Kingdom of Great Britain and Northern Ireland and of Our other Realms and Territories QUEEN, Head of the Commonwealth, Defender of the Faith, to all to whom these presents shall come, GREETING! WHEREAS We taking into Our Royal Consideration that the General Assembly of the Church of Scotland was appointed to meet on the eighteenth day of May next and seeing We by reason of Our other weighty affairs cannot in Person be present in the said Assembly And We being desirous that Our most dearly beloved Daughter, THE PRINCESS ROYAL, ANNE ELIZABETH ALICE LOUISE, Lady of Our most Noble Order of the Garter, Dame Grand Cross of Our Victorian Order, shall discharge the great trust of Our High Commissioner to the General Assembly: Do by these presents nominate constitute and appoint the said PRINCESS ROYAL to be Our High Commissioner to the said General Assembly of the Church of Scotland, GIVING AND GRANTING unto her full power commission and warrant to represent Our Sacred Person and Royal Authority and supply our Presence and hold Our place in the said ensuing General Assembly as Our Commissioner specially appointed for that effect, and to do all and everything belonging to the power and place of a Commissioner to a General Assembly as fully and freely in all respects as any other in that high station hath done or might have done in any time heretofore and as We Ourselves might do if Personally present, We hereby ratifying and approving all and whatsoever things the said PRINCESS ROYAL shall in the discharge of this Commission lawfully do or cause to be done: AND HEREBY requiring and commanding all the Ministers, Elders and Members of the Diaconate of the said Assembly and Church with all other Our good subjects in Scotland of whatsoever degree or quality to acknowledge reverence honour and obey the said PRINCESS ROYAL as Our High Commissioner to the effect and manner abovementioned, and We declare that this Commission shall commence and be in force from the Nineteenth day of May next and from thenceforward to continue during the ensuing session of the said General Assembly or until this Commission be by Us revoked and discharged: IN WITNESS WHEREOF We have ordered the Seal appointed by the Treaty of Union to be kept and made use of in place of the Great Seal of Scotland to be appended hereto. GIVEN at Our Court at Buckingham Palace the eighteenth day of October in the year One thousand nine hundred and ninety-five and in the forty-fourth year of Our Reign

Per Signaturam Manu Serenissimae Dominae
Nostrae Reginae Supra Scriptam

Written to the Seal and Registered and Sealed in Edinburgh

APPENDIX I

DEFINITIONS

Bar. The bar of a court is the place from which persons who are not members of the court address it. It is technically outwith the court. To be at the bar is therefore to be outwith the court and not able to participate in its deliberations or decisions. The principle of non-participation applies even if those placed at the bar are in fact physically within the hall or other room in which the court is meeting, without actually being in a place formally designated as the bar.

Canon Law. The code of law developed in the Roman Catholic Church from the sixth century, modelled on the *Corpus Iuris Civilis* (see Civil Law below) and becoming known as the *Corpus Iuris Canonici*, until it was replaced in 1918 by the *Codex Iuris Canonici*. In certain matters, such as marriage, it was one of the sources of Scots Law.

Civil Law. This term is used in a number of senses.

First, usually with capitals, Civil Law is the law contained in the *Corpus Iuris Civilis*, which was Justinian's codification of Roman Law in the sixth century. It eventually became, in Western Europe, the basis for national codes of law, in which particular laws were deduced from basic principles. This "Continental" system, in the Civil Law tradition, is to be distinguished from the English or "Anglo-Saxon" system, based on precedent. Scots law stands in the Civil Law tradition, but has been considerably influenced by English law.

Second, civil law is the secular law as contrasted with church law. Thus the Declaratory Articles refer to civil authority and the civil magistrate as distinct from church authority and church office-bearers. In this usage, civil law might be referred to as State law.

Third, within civil law in the second sense above, there is a distinction between criminal law and (other) civil law. Thus, for example, an action for damages will be a civil law action, not a criminal law one.

Conciliar. Made up of councils, corporate bodies. Presbyterian government is described as conciliar, the courts being councils, in which authority resides, rather than in individuals.

Contumacy. Contempt of court, failing to obey instructions of courts, breaking the law.

Episcopal. Adjective to denote a form of church government with bishops. As a generic term it applies not only to Churches with this term in their titles, such as the Scottish Episcopal Church, but also to the Church of England and the Roman Catholic Church. Some reformed Churches within the World Alliance of Reformed Churches include a modified form of episcopacy within their structures.

Heritors. Landowners who, as a legal burden on their heritable property, were obliged to maintain parish churches and pay ministers, through teinds and stipends. Under the system of patronage, they also had the right to present, and in effect to appoint ministers to charges, without the consent of the congregations. Patronage, having been restored in 1712, contrary to the Treaty of Union, became one of the issues leading to the Disruption. It was abolished in 1874. By the Church of Scotland (Property and Endowments) Act, 1925, ownership of church buildings was transferred from the heritors to the General Trustees, and special arrangements were made about teinds and stipends.

Homologate. Homologation is the retrospective endorsement or validation of an action. If, for example, in an emergency a Presbytery Clerk takes action in the name of the Presbytery without prior authorisation, the Presbytery may subsequently agree that the action should be treated as if it had been authorised, in which case it has homologated the action.

Interim Moderator. See Glossary.

Licentiate. A person who, having been a candidate for the ministry, and having satisfactorily completed the prescribed course of training, has been taken on trials for licence by a Presbytery, and subsequently licensed to preach the Gospel by the Presbytery. A licentiate is designated "Reverend", and may wear a clerical collar. Normally a licentiate then becomes known as a probationer through undertaking a probationary period under supervision. If that probationary period is sustained, he or she is eligible to be ordained to the ministry of word and sacraments, usually in connection with induction to a charge. When the probationary period has been sustained, and before ordination, he or she is again referred to as a licentiate, which status has in fact been continued through the probationary period. A licentiate who has been granted exemption from the probationary period is eligible for ordination. Changes in this area are proposed, and are due to be put to the 1997 Assembly.

Polity. Generic term for forms of church government, e.g. presbyterian polity, episcopal polity.

Patronage. See above under Heritors.

Probationer. See above under Licentiate.

Sist. To sist is to hold in abeyance the implementation of a judgment, or to bring proceedings to a temporary halt, pending some other action. Cox gives additionally a definition of "sist parties at the bar" as "to place and acknowledge each in his proper part there." This happens when parties are called, at the beginning of a case. It is different from "cite" which is to summon parties in advance. It would avoid confusion if the word "call" were always used instead of "sist" in this latter sense.

Timeous (time-ous, not tim-é-ous: derived from the English word "time", not from the Latin timeo or the Greek τιμη). This is a Scots legal term, used of adherence to prescribed times, as for example when an appeal is lodged within the ten days allowed after the protest for leave to appeal, when papers are submitted to the Clerks of Assembly by the dates required in Standing Orders, or when an objection to alleged procedural irregularity is made at the time of its occurrence.

Trials for Licence. The process whereby a Presbytery tests the suitability of a candidate to be licensed (see above under Licentiate, and see also Sections 51 and 52 of Act V, 1985).

APPENDIX J

GLOSSARY OF LATIN PHRASES

Ad hoc. For this purpose. An *ad hoc* committee is appointed to deal with a specified matter, and is discharged when it has performed the appointed task and made its report. The phrase is sometimes used of dealing with a matter on an *ad hoc* basis, with the meaning of treating it in a summary way as a one-off matter.

Apud acta. Of citations, during the proceedings, while the court is in session.

Ad vitam aut culpam. To, or up to, (the end of) life, or fault. Until comparatively recently, ministers were inducted to charges *ad vitam aut culpam*, meaning that their tenure could be terminated only by death or by their being found guilty of a censurable offence. Now that a compulsory retirement age has been introduced, ministers are not inducted *ad vitam*, but their tenure may still be terminated on the basis of *culpa*. Act III, 1972, stated that ministers were no longer to be inducted *ad vitam aut culpam*, but it is clear from the contents of the Act, and from the fact that it did not repeal any legislation dealing with censures, that it was only the *ad vitam* part of the phrase that would no longer apply. The current Act is IV, 1995.

Cuius regio, eius religio. Of each region its own religion. This refers to the time, following the Reformation, when countries were wholly Catholic or Protestant according to the dictates of their rulers.

Ecclesia reformata, semper reformanda. This Latin phrase was endorsed by the Assembly's decision to "reaffirm the Church's commitment to its continual reform— *ecclesia reformata sed semper reformanda*" (1986, Sess. 5). The use of *sed* (but) suggests that the Church needs to be reformed in spite of having been reformed, and *ergo* (therefore) might have been better, suggesting that commitment to continual reform is intrinsic to a reformed Church, which is also the significance of the comma as used here.

Ex officio. In virtue of office. This applies, for example, to those who, holding one office, have other positions as well: as when a trust deed states that the minister of a particular charge will be a trustee. Each succeeding minister of the charge automatically becomes a trustee. The plural is *ex officiis*, and the holders of certain offices in the Assembly are members of the Assembly *ex officiis*, in virtue of holding these offices.

Ex proprio motu. By its own motion, or will or decision. The normal usage is with reference to an action a court chooses to take, rather than being required or requested to take it.

Fama is defined by Cox (Glossary, p. 827) as a "scandalous report". It is an allegation of censurable conduct.

Fama clamosa is a an allegation of censurable conduct which is so public or notorious that the Presbytery is bound to take action in the interests of the Church, even if no formal report has been received.

In hunc effectum and ***Pro re nata***. Presbyteries may meet *in hunc effectum* (for this purpose) or *pro re nata* (for a thing which has arisen).

Inter alia. Among other things. For example, an extract minute, after showing that the court or committee was duly constituted, precedes the relevant extract with the words *inter alia*, to make clear that what follows was not the only matter dealt with at the meeting. It is also used more generally: the example given is itself *inter alia*.

Interim Act, Moderator. *Inter* means between, and *interim* could be literally translated "betweenly", if there were such a word. It refers to a period of time. In the case of an *Interim* Act, the time during which the Act is in force is that between one Assembly and the next. An *Interim Moderator* holds office for the period between the occurrence of a vacancy and the induction of a new minister. Interim is very similar to *pro tempore*, which means for the time being, temporary, but the latter usually involves a less definite period of time. An organist might be appointed *pro tempore*, for example, and still be in office many years later. Indeed, *pro tempore* can become *sine die* (see below)!

Ipso facto. By the deed itself, without need of further action. For example, by the act of induction to a charge, a minister becomes *ipso facto* the Moderator of the Kirk Session or Kirk Sessions of the charge.

Ius devolutum. A devolved right. The term is reserved in the Church for the right of a Presbytery to appoint a minister to a vacant charge if the congregation has not elected one within the time limit. In that case, the right which belonged to the congregation is devolved to the Presbytery.

Locum tenens. Holding the place. Usually abbreviated to "locum". In a vacancy, while the Interim Moderator is responsible to the Presbytery for everything for which the minister of the charge would be responsible, it is clear that an Interim Moderator, if a parish minister, cannot undertake duties which conflict with those in his or her parish, such as the conduct of Sunday worship, and much pastoral work. A *locum tenens* may therefore be appointed to perform these duties. A *locum tenens* should take no part, formally or informally, in discussion of readjustment, or in vacancy business.

Mutatis mutandis. With things changed that need to be changed. For example, if a Presbytery has no standing orders of its own, it should follow those of the Assembly, *mutatis mutandis*. This would mean that those standing orders which obviously apply only to the Assembly would not apply to the Presbytery, but those which can be applied should be applied.

Nobile Officium is a power peculiar to the Assembly in judicial matters, as far as the Church is concerned, though it belongs to supreme civil courts also. Cox states (p. 114) that it is a power "which would seem naturally and necessarily to belong to a supreme court, to determine and order such things as are necessary to be done in a pending case and for which there is no legal provision. It cannot overrule law, but only supply the want of it when necessary."

Oath, *de fideli*. *De fideli* is an abbreviation of *de fideli administratione officii*, literally, "concerning the faithful administration of the office." The form of the oath is: "I swear that I will be faithful to the duties of . . . ", naming the office concerned.

Per se. By itself, intrinsically, inherently.

Preses. The classical Latin form of this word is *praeses*, and the literal meaning is sitting before, hence president. In former United Presbyterian congregations, it is the title for the person who chairs the Committee of Management.

Pro tempore. See *interim*.

Prima facie. At first sight, on the face of it. *Prima facie* evidence is evidence which does not in itself amount to proof, but is of such a nature that it should be taken seriously, so justifying further investigation.

Primus inter pares. First among equals. This is traditionally used of a Moderator in relation to other ministers. A Moderator has no executive powers or episcopal authority. The parity of ministers is a presbyterian principle, meaning that all ministers have equal status, and there are no superior offices like that of bishop.

Quoad omnia, Quoad sacra. The Congregational Board had its origin in parishes *quoad sacra* (for ecclesiastical purposes), as distinct from the original parishes *quoad omnia* (for all purposes) in which the Kirk Session dealt with temporal as well as spiritual matters. Although in practice all parishes are now ecclesiastical, the term *quoad omnia* is still used to denote a parish in which there is no separate financial board, and temporal as well as spiritual matters are dealt with by a Kirk Session

Res noviter is an abbreviation of *res noviter veniens ad notitiam,* i.e. new matter coming to the notice of the court. If the new matter is sufficiently important, the court may be justified in reviewing its own judgement in the light of it.

Sine die. Without a day. This applies to a suspension imposed, or any arrangement made, with specification of a date on which it will end.

Status quo. This is an abbreviation of *status quo ante*, literally "the position before", i.e. the position before a change was proposed. Normally therefore it means the present position.

Ultra vires. "Beyond the powers". If a court takes an action which is *ultra vires*, it is acting without legal authority, and the action is null and void. For example, it is *ultra vires* of the Assembly to pass an Act which is inconsistent with the *Declaratory Articles*; and it is *ultra vires* of any church court to issue an instruction contrary to the law of the Church.

APPENDIX K

BIBLIOGRAPHY

Historic Works

The Scots Confession, 1560, Ed. G. D. Henderson, The Saint Andrew Press, 1960.

The First Book of Discipline, 1560, First printed edition 1621, Ed. James K. Cameron, The Saint Andrew Press, 1972.

The Second Book of Discipline, 1578, Ed. James Kirk, The Saint Andrew Press, 1980.

The Westminster Confession of Faith, 1647, William Blackwood & Sons, 1959

The Directory for the Public Worship of God, 1645, William Blackwood & Sons, 1959

The Form of Presbyterial Church Government, 1645; William Blackwood & Sons, 1959

The Form of Process, 1707, printed in Mair, Fourth Edition, pp. 549-573, William Blackwood & Sons, 1912

Church Law and Procedure

A Digest of Laws and Decisions relating to The Church of Scotland, William Mair, Fourth Edition, 1912.

Manual of Practice and Procedure in the United Free Church of Scotland, A Committee of the General Assembly, by authority of the General Assembly, 1905.

Practice and Procedure in The Church of Scotland, James T. Cox, Sixth Edition, William Blackwood & Sons, 1976.

Stipend in the Church of Scotland, A. J. H. Gibson, William Blackwood & Sons, 1961.

The Law and Practice of the Kirk: a Guide and Commentary, Andrew Herron, First Edition, Chapter House, 1995.

An Introduction to Practice and Procedure in the Church of Scotland, A Gordon McGillivray, 1995

The Laws of Scotland: Stair Memorial Encyclopedia, Ed. Sir Thomas Smith and Robert Black, The Law Society of Scotland, Butterworth & Co., 1981 *et seqq.*

Church History

A Church History of Scotland, J. H. S. Burleigh, Oxford University Press, 1960.

Kirk by Divine Right, Andrew Herron, The Saint Andrew Press, 1985.

The Scottish Ministers' Widows Fund, Ed. A. Ian Dunlop, The Saint Andrew Press, 1992.

Constitutional Questions

Of Presbyters and Kings, Francis Lyall, Aberdeen University Press, 1980.

British Justice: The Scottish Contribution, T. B.. Smith, Stevens & Sons, 1961.

Freedom to Reform, Douglas M. Murray, T. & T. Clark, 1993.

The Free Church of Scotland Appeals, 1903-4, Ed. Robert Low Orr, Macniven & Wallace, 1904.

> (Verbatim transcripts, containing *inter alia* the remark of Lord James of Hereford, in response to a learned argument from counsel about predestination, "I never knew how incapable I was of understanding these things until I heard your argument.")

Report of the Archbishops' Committee on Church and State, (Church of England), S.P.C.K. 1916.

> (Refers to the draft of the Declaratory Articles then available: "The breadth, completeness, and uncompromising nature of this Declaration make it one of the most remarkable expositions in modern times of the meaning of spiritual independence.")

Theology and Law

Institutes of the Christian Religion, John Calvin, Tr. Henry Beveridge, James Clarke & Co., 1957.

Juridical Law and Physical Law, T.F. Torrance, Scottish Academic Press, 1982.

The Westminster Confession in the Church Today, Ed. Alasdair I. C. Heron, The Saint Andrew Press, 1982.

Law and Order in the Church, article by D. W. D. Shaw, Liturgical Review, Vol. II, No 1, Scottish Academic Press, May 1972.

Worship

Ordinal and Service Book, Third Edition, Oxford University Press, 1962.
Common Order, The Saint Andrew Press, 1994.

Law in General

Institutions of the Law of Scotland, Earl of Stair, 1681.

The Scottish Legal System, David M. Walker, W. Green & Son, 1976.

Legal Values in Western Society, Peter Stein and John Shand, Edinburgh University Press, 1974.

APPENDIX L

LIST OF ACTS REFERRED TO IN TEXT

Acts of Assembly

Acts of Parliament

INDEX

Bold face type is used for Section headings of Chapters, and for the page numbers of these.
Section headings are also included, in plain type, under the names of the Chapters, which are in capitals.
Italics indicate Acts of Parliament, civil cases, books, and Latin phrases.
The remaining entries, in plain type, are words and subjects.
Plain type page numbers after an entry in bold face indicate pages on which the subject is referred to apart from the Section headings.